Katherine Tingley:

The Hijacking
of the
Theosophical Society in America

By
Ernest E. Pelletier

Published November 2024
Edmonton Theosophical Society
Cover - *New York Herald*, May 1896

Katherine Tingley:
The Hijacking of the Theosophical Society in America
by
Ernest E. Pelletier

All rights reserved. No part of this book may be reproduced, transmitted or stored in any form, or by any means, whether written, printed, electronic, or otherwise, without the prior written permission by the author, except in the case of brief quotations embodied in critical articles.

Library and Archives Canada Cataloguing in Publication

ISBN 978-0-9681602-5-1

Publication assistance by
PAGEMASTER PUBLISHING
PageMasterPublishing.ca

DEDICATION

This book is dedicated to the truth seekers:
To those who seek the truth wherever it may take them.

MADISON SQUARE GARDEN
AND TOWER

THE PLACE FOR THE CONVENTION.

[*New York Herald*, January 5, 1896]

Table of Contents

Foreword ix
    by Rogelle A. Pelletier

Preface xiii
    by Ernest E. Pelletier

Illustrations xix

Chapter One – "My First Meeting With William Q. Judge" 1
    Countess Cora di Brazza 3
    Dr. Jerome Anderson 10
    Meeting Judge 12
    Tingley Joins the Society 14
    Timing of Events – The Cloakmakers Strike & The Blizzard ... 19
    End of December 1894 22
    Judge's Deteriorating Health 23
    Mineral Wells 28
    Convention – April 1895 30

Chapter Two – Tingley's Strategic Maneuvers 33
    Events Following Judge's Death 36
    Enter Katherine Tingley 39
    And so it begins 45
    A Crusade to Save Humanity 49
    Who Visited Cheiro? 52
    Where's Flossie? 53
    The Enthusiastic Send-Off 54

  The Crusade Sets Sail... 55
  Events in India 58

Chapter Three – The Cascade of Realizations 61
  Dr. Franz Hartmann 64
  Countess di Brazza's Change of Heart..................... 66
  Katherine's Second Marriage and Her Adopted Son......... 69
  Countess di Brazza's Efforts 78
  The Theosophical Society in America 81
  Trouble in Paradise... 87
  Dr. Joseph Carter Hearne 89
  Katherine Tingley vs *Times-Mirror* Company............... 94
  Katherine Tingley vs Ernest W. Schmidt, et al 98
  The Neresheimers... 103

Chapter Four – Revelations 106
  John Morgan Pryse... 106
  Charles P. McCarthy.. 106
  Edward W. Parker... 107
  Dr. Henry Hugo Reuthling 109
  Seizing the Opportunity 110
  Taking Control 116
  A New Direction – Point Loma 119

Chapter Five – The International Brotherhood League 124

Chapter Six – Point Loma Homestead and Colony 133
  Dr. William Partridge... 133
  The "Black Magician" Period................................ 141
  James Morgan Pryse.. 143
  Robert Crosbie 143

    Must Have Absolute Control! 145
    Louis S. Fitch 148
    The Cuban Children & Commodore Gerry 150
    The Lischner Document 151

Chapter Seven – Conclusion 154
    Closing Words 160

Appendices
  A – The Cloakmakers Strike and The Blizzard 162
  B – The Lotus Circle 172
  C – Countess Cora Ann (Slocomb) di Brazza Savorgnan 174
  D – Clement Acton Griscom, Jr. 183
  E – Documented Horror Cases 192
  F – Richard Dean Arden Wade (Ingalese) 220
  G – Letter by Dr. Hyman Lischner 224
  H – Life in a Borrowed Body 227

Works Cited 239

FOREWORD

The Theosophical Society in America was flourishing under the guidance of William Q. Judge. There were approximately one hundred fifty active branches, and through quiet but steady promulgation of theosophic information, its philosophy was spreading across the land.

Ernest T. Hargrove had toured with Judge in the early 1890s but had returned to England for family reasons. In 1895 Judge was encouraged to inform Hargrove that he was needed in America. Hargrove was a lawyer from a very successful and respected family of lawyers but he gave up guaranteed financial security to pursue Theosophy. Hargrove was very close to Judge, with Judge insisting that Hargrove move in with him and Mrs. Judge upon their return from Aiken, SC. Judge instructed Hargrove, both theosophically and administratively, concerning T.S. in America.

Hargrove arrived in New York on August 30th, 1895 and seven months later, on March 21st, 1896, Judge died. Then Tingley made her move. She hijacked the Society within days of Judge's death. She landed her final thrust two years later, on February 18th, 1898 at the annual convention. Tingley maneuvered the takeover of T.S. in America and established the Universal Brotherhood, with every aspect of its operations solely under her absolute control.

This final step in Tingley's plans for her empire was complete. The momentum that had been perpetuated in the Theosophical Society in America, until Tingley's takeover, was crushed. Determined to continue to follow the original program as propounded by H.P. Blavatsky and W.Q. Judge, and with the name T.S. in America available, Clement A. Griscom, Jr. dedicated much energy to reestablishing the Theosophical Society in America. It eventually also resulted in Robert Crosbie establishing the United Lodge of Theosophists.

Using the legal structure of Universal Brotherhood, Tingley took all the assets of T.S. in America and moved the headquarters to Point Loma. She set up the 'homestead' for those of financial means and the 'colony' for those who could not pay for their stay and earned their way. In cult-like fashion inhabitants gave up their assets to the organization, which Tingley controlled completely.

Tingley attracted wealthy business people and received large donations of money and land, for which no accounting was presented. She also had a lot of influence with politicians and judges, which served her well in her numerous court cases.

During her years as Leader, Tingley did manage to accomplish many things; unfortunately it was, in large part, at the expense of focus on Theosophy itself. An extensive article appeared in the *Los Angeles Herald*, Sunday Illustrated Magazine in November 1901. The writer's impression:
> Of the philosophy of theosophy I learned very little. William Q. Judge, the successor of Madame H.P. Blavatsky, was preeminently a philosopher. Katherine Tingley, his successor, is pre-eminently an accomplisher. He might have tried to explain to me the theory of Karma; she showed me results. . . It has been said that "Lomaland," [is] the home of the humanitarian department of the Theosophists. . .

The focus on Theosophy took second place to her limitless grand plans. Tingley died July 11th, 1929. On July 29th her successor as Leader and Outer Head of the Esoteric Section, G. de Purucker, sent a General Letter to all members announcing the launch of the Point Loma version of *The Theosophical Forum: New Series*, "for a deeper study of the sacred teaching of Theosophy." During an interview with *The San Diego Union* on August 3rd, 1929,
> Dr. de Purucker made it clear that he feels the time has come for a slight change in the methods of administering the order. The expansion plans, which he hopes will bring many to the teachings of the Society, will make it almost necessary to organize branches at various places. Hitherto there has been no such thing as set meetings of Theosophists in the various cities and communities. [***The Theosophical Forum*, 1:1, Sep. 1929, p.13**]

In fact, under Tingley, branches had dwindled considerably—some withdrew, while she simply cancelled others for reasons of her own.

True to his intentions, de Purucker did lead the organization to focus once again on Theosophy and a more philosophical path, to become what The Theosophical Society International is today.

Tingley's attitude and ambitions, ironically under the banner of universal brotherhood, resulted in dissipation of a growing interest and acceptance of theosophical principles that had flourished under Judge's guidance, and that of those guiding him.

What follows is a side of the Tingley story that has so far remained mostly unexplored.

RAP

PREFACE

The Judge Case: A Conspiracy Which Ruined The Theosophical Cause (*TJC*) was published in 2004. Many people have since indicated they do not believe that the Cause was ruined, or at the very least, did not grasp the scope of what was meant by the subtitle. The information contained within the following pages should clarify what was implied.

In *TJC,* Part 2, Appendix G, it was intimated that there were pieces of the puzzle that did not fit the picture for true understanding of the history of the Theosophical Movement, especially the succession of William Q. Judge. It is hoped that a clearer picture will now emerge and be understood more fully.

The most comprehensive historical account available for many years was *The Theosophical Movement 1875 to 1925* published by the United Lodge of Theosophists. Since then numerous documents and letters have surfaced which provide further details about what really happened just prior to and after Judge's death on March 21st, 1896. One such document was written by Emil A. Neresheimer, titled "Some Reminiscences of William Q. Judge", published February 25th, 1932. Because Neresheimer was believed to be very close to Judge, over the years his document has been reprinted and heavily quoted, and his account accepted as truthful and accurate.

Careful examination and verification have proven his document to be quite faulty and inaccurate in some instances and very accurate in others. One must remember that most of Neresheimer's notes at the time they were recorded were heavily influenced by Katherine Tingley, and some were later written from memory. There should be at least some skepticism of a person's recollections some thirty-five years after the event. Another important factor to consider, which historians have mostly not investigated closely, was that Neresheimer and Hargrove became enemies. Neresheimer became very bitter towards Hargrove, his son-in-law. Hargrove eventually openly rejected Tingley's assumed successorship to Judge and her unilateral actions which followed. Neresheimer and Hargrove parted ways but not before considerable pain had been inflicted. Perhaps that story will someday be brought to light, which will explain the utter contempt Neresheimer held toward Hargrove.

Other important documents that surfaced in the 1930s were the letters written by W.Q. Judge to Ernest T. Hargrove. The first of these letters appeared in *The Theosophical Quarterly*, Vol. 28, April 1931. Clement A. Griscom Jr. was responsible for establishing and publishing the *T.Q.* Griscom stated upon its inception: "it is not designed to compete with, but to supplement *The Theosophical Forum*". Judge had started *The Theosophical Forum* in 1889. He took over editorship of it, with the addition of *New Series* to its title, after the formation of The Theosophical Society in America following the convention in Boston and so-called 'split' in 1895. Tingley discontinued it in 1897; Griscom restarted it in February 1898. The *T.Q.* first appeared in July 1903 and ran until October 1938.

Judge's last letter appeared in the January 1935 issue. Included with the letters are Hargrove's comments which present compelling details about what was going on during the years prior to Judge's death. His comments can be easily verified for accuracy. Because the *T.Q.* was not a magazine reported to have been read by members of other theosophical societies, its circulation was primarily among those associated with the original Theosophical Society in America (New York). This led to the magazine becoming quite scarce. These letters were basically ignored until republished in *The Judge Case*, Appendix D.

My wonder as to why Judge had been ignored by theosophists increased while at the European School of Theosophy in Camberley, Surrey, England in 1986. Attendees came from all over the world and yet no one seemed to care who William Q. Judge was or his contributions to the movement, in spite of the fact that he had written the Book of Rules for the Esoteric Section and was a co-founder of the Theosophical Society. It was hard to believe that hardly anyone knew of him, and those who did dismissed him as a fraud. I came to believe it was largely because of the strong influence emanating from Adyar, and the lack of defense by the Tingley lineage—the very people one would expect would be Judge's strongest supporters and inherent defenders.

To their credit, much of what Judge wrote was collected by Boris de Zirkoff, and compiled and published by Dara Eklund as the three-volume collection *Echoes of the Orient*.

Opportunities to get acquainted with theosophists from all continents have provided expansive perspectives on historical events. Edmonton T.S. has hosted many lecturers over the years; also, meeting theosophists in their own locales has been particularly interesting and enlightening.

The main lecturers at the European School were Geoffrey Farthing, Joy Mills, and Adam Warcup, who each granted permission for me to videotape their presentations. Adam's was of particular interest; he had come to Edmonton in 1985 and presented his three-part lecture series, "A Mind to Embrace the Universe". Leisure time at the School allowed numerous opportunities for discussions with international attendees.

Various perspectives were observed during a visit to southern California in 1988. My wife, Rogelle, and I first spent time with Emmett and Carmen Small at Point Loma, Richard Robb of Wizards Bookshelf in San Diego, Jerry and April Hejka-Ekins in Venice Beach, and the United Lodge of Theosophists in Los Angeles. We visited Dara Eklund and Nicholas Weeks of Studio City who brought us to Long Beach where we met Dr. Robert Bonnell and his group of theosophists. In Los Angeles we visited the Philosophical Research Society (PRS), received a guided tour with Librarian, Pearl Thomas, and also took in a lecture by Manly P. Hall, a sincere admirer of H.P. Blavatsky.

We then stayed at Deodars at the Theosophical Society, International, in Pasadena, as guests courtesy of Leader, Grace Knoche. We became acquainted with those present and visited the Library. In Ojai we visited Joy Mills in Krotona, the Krishnamurti Foundation, and Dennis Gottschalk, director of the Theosophical Book Association for the Blind. From there we attended a meeting at the United Theosophical Society in Santa Barbara, led by Nandini Iyer, wife of Professor Raghavan N. Iyer, its president and founder.

On our way home we met David and Nancy Reigle in Talent, Oregon and then in Vernon, British Columbia we visited Michael Freeman, who was then caretaker of The H.P.B. Library (started by Alice Cleather), and his wife Jean. We developed a trusting relationship with Michael and visited every year thereafter where he allowed us to borrow materials and eventually to bring a photocopier to duplicate files. The trust was much appreciated and it was a courtesy granted by few.

Following are impressions garnered while visiting the Library at the Theosophical Headquarters in Altadena/Pasadena. Rogelle and I were given the opportunity to look at and read parts of Judge's three (bound, 8.5"x11") notebooks. In my opinion they have been wrongly labeled diaries; some have even referred to them as occult diaries. The contents appeared to be mostly notes, occasional letters, and addresses to conventions (including the November 1895 address published in *TJC*, Appendix F). Judge was renowned for carrying pads for jotting things down or drawing sketches. James Morgan Pryse, who saw and read parts of these notebooks, insinuated that some of the material was simply not what he would have expected from Judge and that he would "like to have burned it".

The notebooks were brought out and shown to us by Kirby Van Mater, the archivist. A discovery that was upsetting to all present occurred while going through one of them. Rogelle noticed that some pages had been cut out close to the edge of the spine. When this was pointed out, Kirby grabbed the book and hurried out of the room saying "I know who did this." I have occasionally wondered if Kirby ever confronted that person.

In conversation with Kirby one afternoon he stated that Judge was not completely innocent of the accusations against him. That statement led me to do in-depth research about the controversy surrounding Judge and eventually to publish *The Judge Case: A Conspiracy Which Ruined the Theosophical Cause*. On the other hand, Kirby was visibly in awe of Katherine Tingley and left me with the impression of being very protective and committed to defending her. I was determined to learn why.

Kirby's brother John, on the other hand, was focused on the original teachings and was working on the *Index* for the *Secret Doctrine* at the time. John seemed more impartial and preferred to not talk about historical matters. Perhaps that is why Kirby was responsible for the Archives, to which not just anyone could have access, even under supervision.

Michael Freeman was a strong advocate for Alice Cleather and was somewhat accusatory toward Judge. My increasing familiarity with history led me to ask him questions regarding some of the ideas he maintained. Flaws became perceptible in his assessment from the Cleather standpoint, which only strengthened my resolve to delve deeper.

Two individuals who helped tremendously with my research were Dallas TenBroeck and John Cooper, my dear friend from Australia. Dallas TenBroeck of the United Lodge of Theosophists was a strong advocate for Judge. Dallas got me started on the chronology that eventually led to publishing *The Judge Case*, supplied some of the documents, and was always willing to help me find my own way.

John Cooper was not a member of any theosophical society and most organizations were open to him. He made arrangements for me to contact a number of people associated with what had become known as the New York Group, the original T.S. in America, sometimes also referred to as the Hargrove Group. Professor Raymond Tripp, one of the last surviving members, whom I spoke with many times, explained that their history was in the pages of *T.Q.* He never attempted to influence me; he simply assisted and eventually sent all he had regarding records and historical material. Past president of Edmonton T.S., Emory Wood, had collected the entire set of *Theosophical Quarterly*. Although aware of some of the contents I had not extensively perused these somewhat rare volumes.

It took fifteen years to research and complete *The Judge Case* and while doing so, a lot of information was found about other individuals involved at that time. One person of particular interest was Katherine A. Tingley, the so-called successor of William Q. Judge. It was eventually discovered that she was never the true successor but had simply taken over as Head of the Esoteric Section and also how, two years later, she formed the Universal Brotherhood with herself as absolute Leader.

What has been presented to date concerning Tingley is only what one can see above the water, and a bit of shadow underneath. Like an iceberg, most of Katherine A. Westcott/Tingley's life has been kept under the water line where few individuals have ventured to investigate. What was discovered is unsettling. It explains much of her actions, the secrecy about her past, why she was shunned by her eldest brother, and portrays a very different person than what has been accepted as historical truth. The standard narrative reads, 'look at all the wonderful things she accomplished'. However closer examination reminds one of the Jesuitical concept that "the ends justify the means". If one calls oneself a Theosophist, he or she should be cautious about "the *means*" to that end rather than "the end" itself.

A decision was made to not focus on her early years, and only minimally after she moved everything to Point Loma. The original intent was to establish when Katherine Tingley actually met Judge for the first time and how she took control of the Theosophical Society in America.

EEP

ILLUSTRATIONS

1896 sketch of Madison Square Garden and Tower	iv
To Help The Needy	8
General Register T.S.	15
General Register T.S. pp. 294 & 295	16
Boston Girl's Marriage (ceremony)	46
The Home of The Mahatma	47
The Residence of Katherine A. Tingley	48
The Court-Yard of the Hotel at Darjîling [Darjeeling]	60
The New Institution	68
"New Century Guard"	77
Vanity Fair - Photo of Tingley	79
Dr. Hearne's proposed Hospital (Architect's drawing)	90
Snapshot of Dr. J.C. Hearne's Sanitarium	90
New Century Guard Sentinels	115
Supreme Ruler of the Universal Brotherhood	123
I.B.L. and War Relief Corps Headquarters	124
Work Room at Headquarters	125
Photo of original "Point Loma House"	136
"Point Loma House" front view	137
Remodeling of the "Point Loma House" (Hotel)	138
East Entrance of the Raja Yoga Academy	139
An American Idyl (Countess di Brazza)	181
Judge Spares Mrs. Tingley	207

Chapter One

"My First Meeting With William Quan Judge"

Amidst the sense of great loss and confusion that reigned in the immediate aftermath of Judge's death on March 21st, 1896, his last instruction, "There should be calmness. Hold fast. Go slow," went totally unheeded. Katherine Tingley (July 6, 1847-July 11, 1929) quickly took control of the situation, hijacked the Theosophical Society in America and rebuilt it into her own empire, re-imagining her personal history as she proceeded. This chronicle begins by establishing when Tingley did in fact meet William Q. Judge.

Hard evidence has been gathered proving when, how, and where Judge and Tingley met for the first time. The commonly accepted date is incorrect. The details proved difficult to sift through because some of the historical records are sometimes incorrect and were written based on assumptions or rumors and not actual facts. Therefore many records and articles accepted as historical facts had to be checked and rechecked for accuracy.

Boris de Zirkoff (1902-1981) was compiling the writings of H.P. Blavatsky when he came across something of historical importance. For all we know he may have been sitting on various finds for years not knowing what to do with them. To this day most historians in the theosophical society rely on his excellent work for accurate information. Some of his discoveries did not belong in the *Blavatsky Collected Writings* so he reached out to friends to publish them.

In 1960 one of those finds appeared in *Eirenicon*, a quarterly publication out of Cheshire, England. *Eirenicon* was published by Peace Lodge of The Theosophical Society connected with the T.S. in Adyar, India. The Adyar society had always been at odds with the Tingley society, which Boris de Zirkoff was associated with. Upon Judge's death in 1896 both societies and their leaders vehemently opposed each other. Most of that animosity originated on accusations based on a pamphlet issued by Judge in November 1894 titled *By Master's Direction*. *Eirenicon*'s mission was to point out the existence of narrow partisan sectarianism in Adyar and other Theosophical societies. *Eirenicon* served as a liaison between factious organizations.

Boris wrote to Tom H. Redfern, the editor of *Eirenicon*. One can only speculate as to why Boris eventually reached out to this British magazine to publish his letter. It strongly suggests that his evidence supported Judge, that Judge was in communication with the Mahatmas and that *By Master's Direction* actually was at the direction of the Master. It would serve to quell rumors that Judge knew Tingley since 1893 and would also solidify the facts presented in *By Master's Direction* declaring "Annie Besant's headship in the E.S.T. at an end". **[*TJC*, Part 2, p.136]**

Boris wrote:
> Madame Tingley met Judge during a clockmakers' strike in New York (The Gods Await, Point Loma, 1926, Section III). The New York TIMES shows that this strike was of several months' duration, and the articles about it run from August 28, 1894, to February 22, 1895. To judge by the cold weather spoken of by Katherine Tingley, I would suggest that this [first] meeting took place rather late in the season, maybe late Fall, if not beginning of Winter. (Incidentally, this would dispose of Mrs. Cleather's statement -H.P. BLAVATSKY, HER LIFE AND WORK FOR HUMANITY, p.122 - that Judge's E.S. Paper BY MASTER'S DIRECTION, dated November 4, 1894, was dictated by Katherine Tingley, etc.) April 28, 1895, Judge 'seceded', at Boston Convention. Is it reasonable to suppose that Katherine Tingley would have produced such an impact on Judge within a matter of 3-4 months? Personally, I think it is a lot of 'bosh', but I do not expect everybody to agree with me. A lot of 'Theosophists' have been for years in the state of mind which is defined something like this: 'I have made up my mind, Sir; don't confuse me with the facts!' . . . **[Special Issue, Fall 1960, No.137, p.8]**

An error must be pointed out in Redfern's transcription of Boris' handwritten letter; he misread cloakmakers for clockmakers. When *The Judge Case* was published in 2004 this item was reproduced per Redfern's exact transcription, not with the correct "cloakmakers". The newspapers of the time were researched thoroughly for mention of any clockmakers strikes occurring during 1893 to 1895; no mention was found.

That Katherine Tingley dictated, or at the very least influenced the contents of *By Master's Direction*, has been accepted and repeated in order to protect the narrative that she met Judge much earlier. However, facts tell a different story.

We must now proceed to examine those "facts" or hard evidence to either substantiate or refute de Zirkoff's statement. His statement is based on the book *The Gods Await* by Katherine Tingley published in 1926.

Katherine Tingley's account as to when she first met William Q. Judge sounds very plausible. However, after over twenty years of researching the early years of her life, and with binders of documents, one can be assured that most of what she says is exaggeration at best. Her beneficent achievements are usually *over*stated and her psychic and mesmeric abilities *under*stated. Most of her early life has been kept secret and purposely skewed in order to prevent exposure of the real Katherine. The purpose of this article is not to delve deeply into those early years, other than some details relating to the time period in question:1893 to the early 1900s. To document her life prior to 1895 would require its own project. The contents of the chapter in *The Gods Await*, titled "My First Meeting with William Quan Judge" have been especially scrutinized and compared with documented historical facts.

Countess Cora di Brazza

One of Katherine's closest friends was Countess di Brazza, née Cora Ann Slocomb, born to Cuthbert Harrison Slocomb and Abby (née Day) Slocomb, in New Orleans.
> She married Count [Detalmo] di Brazza-Savorgnan, of Italy. The Count and Countess attended The World's Columbian Exposition, Chicago, [May - October]1893, together, where he represented his country, Italy, in the Agricultural Congress, and she was the only woman delegated to represent Italy, serving as President of the Committee of Italian Ladies Formed for the Exhibition of Italian Laces. [*The Slocombs of America and Their Alliances*, p.509]

She was also the only foreign woman invited to deliver an address at the opening of the World's Fair where she lectured on "Life of the Italian Women in the Country." [*Times-Picayune*, New Orleans, May 15, 1893] Count di Brazza was the Imperial Italian Commissioner to the Columbian Exposition. While staying at her mother's summer home in Groton, CT, Countess di Brazza was interviewed in New London. She stated that the entire profit from their exhibit was going "to the poor of Italy. . ." [*St. Paul Daily Globe*, St. Paul, MN, July 17, 1893]

The di Brazzas needed a home base to operate from so Cora asked her friend Katherine to find a residence in New York suitable for the next few years. Both had a keen interest in psychicism [the belief in or study of psychic phenomena – Collins Dictionary]; how they likely met will not be detailed here. There was a fifteen year difference in their age; Cora was born January 7th, 1862 and Katherine was born July 6th, 1847 [*Vital Records of Newbury*, **Mass. To the end of the year 1849, 1911**].

Tingley found a "Renaissance style" [*New York Herald*, **May 17, 1896**] corner house in the Upper West Side, a well-to-do neighborhood, at 373 West End Avenue between 78th and 77th street. Since the house was too large for the di Brazzas, Katherine, her husband Philo and Flossie, age twelve, who was in the care of the Tingleys at the time, also moved in. The building was a full four stories plus an attic. It is assumed that the di Brazzas kept the first two floors for themselves and the Tingleys occupied the other one or two stories. Count di Brazza and Philo Tingley were both amateur inventors; they likely got along quite well.

Thus far it has been determined that the di Brazzas and their five year old daughter Ida arrived in New York City on April 4th, 1893. In New York City the Countess, being an American, was in high demand to attend countless functions, including charity balls, concerts, receptions, operas, and meeting the rich and powerful of New York City and diplomats in Washington, DC. One of her passions was helping people in distress, feeding the poor and the homeless. She also tended to the desperate, for example she often visited prisoners who needed help. One such case was Maria Barberi. Father Ferretti of the Church of the Transfiguration invited Countess di Brazza to accompany him to visit

> the Italian girl convicted of murder in the first degree for the killing of Domenico Cataldo, and who is locked up in the Tombs awaiting sentence, after having borne the strain of the trial remarkably well, broke down on Tuesday night, when she appears to have realized for the first time that she would be sentenced to death. [**New York** *Times*, **July 18, 1895;** *Boston Herald*, **July 31, 1895**]

Tingley was invited to accompany the Countess on some of these occasions, which is where she got the idea to add this task to her resume of accomplishments. Michael Barbella (Barberi), Maria's father, and Countess di Brazza, who chaired a committee to secure the pardon of Maria, cooperated toward their mutual goal. Tingley was a co-worker on the pardon committee. [*Boston Globe*, **July 29, 30, 1895;** *Brooklyn Daily Eagle*, **July, 28, 1895.**]

> The child-woman had been condemned to be executed within a month, when the judicial machine might have shown clemency and given seven weeks. Seven weeks could have carried Maria beyond September 1, instead of forcing her to get an appeal granted within thirteen days, including two Sundays, that is to say, eleven working days before August 1. For the law stands that an appeal for a new trial, after such a verdict as that visited upon Maria, must be made before the first day of the month in which the execution is ordered. . . [*Brooklyn Daily Eagle*, **July 28, 1895**]

It is obvious that Countess di Brazza and her co-worker, Katherine Tingley, were under pressure, writing letters and gathering signatures for petitions to the court of Appeal before the allotted time. Tingley would not have had time to do anything for or with W.Q. Judge. (Maria was eventually acquitted.)

On examining the life of Countess di Brazza and her remarkable achievements there can be no doubt that she was a very influential person in Katherine Tingley's life. In fact Katherine was so enamored that she eventually adopted many of the Countess's ideas and accomplishments and made them her own. Feeding the poor, visiting prisoners, organizing and establishing schools (di Brazza started a school in lace making for young girls in Italy), the color purple (violet flowers especially), classical music and theater, and her charisma were all things that Katherine admired.

Before moving in with the di Brazzas the Tingleys kept moving from one apartment to another often leaving without paying their bills and rent—sometimes twice or more in one year. When she married Philo (April 26th, 1888), Katherine was living in a boarding house owned by Mrs. Caroline Weston, No. 215 West Twenty-third street where she had a large circle of friends and acquaintances. "Her gatherings there were of a spiritualistic character." Then they moved to a flat at No. 2,048 Seventh Avenue where she continued to hold spiritualistic gatherings. [*New York Herald*, **May 17, 1896**]

When contacted by the Countess, the Tingleys were living at 107 West 68th Street, next door to Dr. Henry Hugo Reuthling at 105 West 68th Street. It was at this time that Katherine's younger brother George came to see her, hoping she could cure him of his habitual use of cocaine. Reuthling explained:

> She was a magnetic healer and medium... Mrs. Tingley herself explained to me how she had cured people, for instance, how she had cured a sick brother, by treating him by magnetism, but he died very soon after he got in her house.
> [**Supreme Court of the State of California, Transcript on Appeal, Katherine Tingley vs Times-Mirror Company;** Filed August 13th, 1904 (Referred hereafter as **Tingley vs Times-Mirror**); paragraphs 1347, 1349, pp.337-338]

George W. Westcott died, at the age of 40, in Boston, May 28th, 1893, from a heart attack due to habitual misuse of morphine. [*Massachusetts Death records*]

Philo's extra money was usually spent on his latest invention and his travels, which kept him broke. According to the caretaker at a previous residence, in 1892 Kate, as she was known in her "faith cure business with clairvoyancy... and hypnotism" séance circles, provided enough to afford sustenance and occasionally be seen "under the influence of alcohol" but were "dis-possessed for non-payment of rent... and her apartment was in bad condition". [*The Sun* (NY), Nov. 8, 1902] Spiritualism never really made her any substantial money so that she might afford the luxuries of a higher social status, such as a permanent residence, fine clothes, a servant, and the finer things in life.

Reading and accepting Tingley's stories without hard evidence to substantiate her statements, one can come away thinking she was a true philanthropist at heart. In fact she had no money and barely survived let alone fed hundreds of people, as implied in *The Gods Await*. When she met Philo she was living in a Boarding house on 23rd Street. On her own she had no connections nor means to raise large sums of money. On the other hand Countess di Brazza, well known for her philanthropic work, had financial means and connections to fund-raise. Tingley does not mention having a close friend named Countess di Brazza and yet she owes most of her claimed achievements in New York City to this one person. Ernest Hargrove provided insight into Tingley's friendship with the Countess when he wrote the following about the Crusaders while in Italy:

> The journey to Venice had to be broken in any case, and a promise had been made by Mrs. Tingley to her friend the Countess di Brazza that if possible the members of the party would visit her at her old Frinlian castle, an hour's drive from the city of Udine. Two restful days were thus passed, Mrs. Tingley and Mrs. Wright staying at the castle, the men of the party sleeping at an hotel.... [*Theosophy*, 11:8, Nov. 1896, p.230]

The actual origin of the relief work lies with di Brazza. Near the end of the year 1893 and into 1894 a number of ladies gathered in the parlor at 373 West End Avenue, the above-mentioned official residence of the Count and Countess di Brazza and where the Tingleys also lived. The purpose of these meetings was to organize a "new relief scheme for the benefit of the poor, who are really destitute but shrink from going out to beg." [*The World*, **Jan. 5, 1894**] They organized the Women's Emergency Relief Association which "proposed to search out needy families on the east side and issue tickets to them for hot stews, soups, delicacies for the sick, clothing and other necessaries." [*The World*, **Jan. 5, 1894**] This is how Tingley later related it:

> I organized the Woman's Emergency Relief Association in my own home. It was in 1893, if I am not mistaken. This work I also did by similar direction [from a 'sacred source']. The object was to assist in relieving the terrible suffering then prevalent among the poor. It was on the same authority that I instituted the 'Do-Good Mission,' with the help of a few noble women, and, of course, none of us received any salary or compensation for our labors. [*New York Tribune*, **May 18, 1896**]

Tingley is taking full credit for something she could not possibly have initiated on her own and was only one of several participants in its implementation.

The Women's Emergency Relief Association opened on January 8th, 1894.

> [A] new organization . . . has opened rooms at No. 411 East [Fourteenth] Street. . . The officers of the association are Mrs Henry J. Newton, President; Mrs. P. B. Tingley, First Vice-President; Mrs. Milton Rathbun, Second Vice-President; Mrs. M. Gaden, Third Vice President; Miss M. J. Fitz-Maurice, Secretary; Miss A. B. Carmick, Treasurer; Mrs. N.A. Craig, Assistant Treasurer; Manager—Mrs. P. B. Tingley, Mrs. Carrie Weston. They have three rooms comfortably fitted up for the work, and are very thankful for the many donations of food, furniture, and clothing received. With this help they have been enabled to give nearly 1,500 meals each week. [*New York Times*, **Feb. 1, 1894**]

The World described the Association as

> . . . doing genuine good among the east side poor. It is an unsectarian organization of unsalaried women, whose sole aim is to assist the poor with food, clothing and work. [**Feb. 10, 1894**]

> **TO HELP THE NEEDY.**
>
> The Women's Emergency Relief Association, which has been but recently established at No.411 East Fourteenth strett, is doing genuine good among the east side poor. It is an unsectarian organization of unsalaried women, whose sole aim is to assist the poor with food, clothing and work.
>
> The President is Mrs. Henry J. Newton. Donations and clothing sent to the Society's rooms in East Fourteenth street, will be divided among those most in distress.

The cloakmakers strike started in August 1894. Later that year stories appeared about the suffering of the poverty-stricken on the East Side of New York as a result. Tingley wrote "These thoughts and feelings grew acute one bitter winter when the East Side was seriously affected by a strike of the cloak makers." [*The Gods Await*, p.62]

Tingley claimed a great deal of the credit for these compassionate achievements but reveals: "The rooms *we* had taken were on the first floor – the best *we* could get, though the house was old and ramshackle" [italics added] [*The Gods Await*, p.63]. It is obvious that she was not the only person involved in locating these rooms. Tingley also neglected to mention that all this could not have occurred without the help of her best friend and silent partner Countess di Brazza and the ladies from the Woman's Emergency Relief Association. Tingley referred to this charitable work as the "Do-Good Mission" but that name does not appear as such in newspapers except when she and her subsequent followers mention it, and for good reason. She called it *her* "Do-Good Mission" to avoid drawing attention to the fact that it was actually the Woman's Emergency Relief Association that organized it, and to mention the Countess would have diminished Tingley's claimed achievements. Tingley was one of the managers.

Tingley wrote:
> Day after day these people were holding out for what [the strikers] considered their rights, and the destitution had become terrible. They had no resources left and their children were on the point of starvation. One morning a baby died in its mother's arms at the door of the Do-Good Mission, an emergency relief society I had established . . . crowds used to come there daily for soup and bread and what else I could provide to help them. [*The Gods Await*, **p.62**]

Relating events of the day she first laid eyes on Judge:
> I remember that day well. Snow was falling when I started out in the morning to go down to the Mission to meet those discouraged persons in their poverty, an ordinary snowstorm that gave little warning of the tremendous blizzard that was to rage later in the day, the fury of which was beginning to be apparent when I arrived. In that fierce storm, now increasing momently, over six hundred women and children were waiting in the street for relief. They were but half-dressed—they had pawned most of their clothes—they were perishing with the cold; they were wailing out loud, many of them, and clamoring for help. [*The Gods Await*, **pp.62-63**]

It is evident that Tingley was the manager of the "Do-Good Mission" and had kitchen staff and attendants to help prepare and serve the food. It was the Countess who had the savoir-faire, the instant recognition, the contacts, and the ability to raise the funds that enabled the ladies to open and operate the 'so-called' "Do-Good Mission".

The landlord warned that the floor would collapse under the weight of so many people. She continues:
> There was nothing for it but for me to go out and talk to them, to keep them as well as I could in humor and patience while waiting. So I had a large grocery box placed on the sidewalk beside the door and, standing on it, told them why I could not ask them in and that the soup was not yet quite cooked and the bread not yet delivered from the baker's, but in a very short time both would be ready. All the while the crowd and the storm kept increasing, and with them my own distress, till I felt my heart almost at breaking-point to see so much keen misery and to know that all I could do was so wretchedly little, so ineffectual: to lift them out

of their present trouble and keep them secure against as bad or worse tomorrow or the next day. [*The Gods Await*, p.63]

Dr. Jerome Anderson

Tingley's story is most compassionate but when compared to a few years later with the children in her care at Point Loma, Dr. Jerome Anderson (1847-1903) in his testimony before the Supreme Court in the State of California had a different perspective. He testified that "... she desired to have them at first starved, because they could more quickly kill out the lower nature in those children." [Tingley vs Times-Mirror, 1258, p.315]

In an interview with the *San Francisco Call* Dr. Anderson stated:
> Mrs. Tingley is full of whims, oddities and uncertainties and resorts to things not exactly nice toward children. For instance, if a child disobeys, it is kept without food until it becomes obedient. She told me herself, that she starves them into submission. [*San Francisco Call*, Nov. 16, 1902]

Dr. Anderson was a highly respected physician, theosophist, lecturer and valued writer by Blavatsky and Judge. He was a remarkable child; he could read at the age of four. For questioning her methods of raising children Tingley "has been obliged to 'accept' the resignation of Dr. Jerome Anderson." [*The Sun* (NY), Mar. 30, 1902]

An article in the *New York Tribune* summarizing his testimony, includes examples of depriving children of food, and the following statement:
> Dr Anderson said that he left the Universal Brotherhood because Mrs. Tingley had substituted her will for the institution. As to writings, he had prepared for a publication managed by Mrs. Tingley, he said they were rejected by Mrs. Tingley because he would not acknowledge her as divine, as others did. [Dec. 24, 1902]

Tingley denied all these statements in court. She then sought to destroy his reputation; it caused him to become depressed and broken hearted. He died of cerebral edema on December 25th, 1903 at the age of fifty-six.

The *Los Angeles Times* wrote:
> Dr. Anderson had gained much publicity owing to his determined views and was especially drawn into prominence two years ago when through the medium of the press he attacked Mrs. K. A. Tingley and the United Brotherhood, of which sect she is

President. Mrs. Tingley sued General Otis of the Los Angeles "Times" for libel in reference to the Point Loma settlement and during the trial Dr. Anderson, though not called on the witness stand by the defense, made a strong advocate for General Otis by his attack on Mrs. Tingley in the papers.

Among other sensational accusations made by Dr. Anderson at that time was that Mrs. Tingley was not a Theosophist. He charged her with merely being a sharp, scheming, illiterate spirit medium, who had humbugged the public. He asserted that he had letters to show that she was a woman lacking even the first rudiments of a good education. He also accused her of forging mental messages supposed to come from the spirit world. Dr. Anderson's charges caused a profound sensation at that time. Mrs. Tingley replied, and as a result, several stormy letters were published containing the accusations of each side. **[Jan. 11, 1903]**

Shortly after leaving Point Loma, Anderson made a very emphatic statement in regard to Tingley:
> [H]er acts had disgusted the Theosophists to such an extent that numerous withdrawals have resulted; in fact, of the 140 societies which had amalgamated with the brotherhood a few years previously, only about 40 remained faithful. From 5000 members who were on the roll when the society was flourishing, the roll suddenly dropped to 500, and this the doctor alleged was due to the actions of Mrs. Tingley. [*San Francisco Call*, **Dec. 26, 1903**]

In the interview in *The Sun,* New York, March 30th, 1902, Anderson is quoted as saying that Tingley "usurped the place of leader of the theosophists" and that
> As an organization Theosophy has gone all to pieces under Mrs. Tingley. Of the 140 prosperous lodges organized by Judge not more than a dozen exist to-day, and the only work in the spreading of the truth has been by Col. Olcott and his loyal followers.

The *Tacoma Daily Ledger* quoted Dr. Anderson:
> More than $300,000 was poured into her lap by her followers in one year, and what did they receive for it? I have yet to know of a prominent member leaving the ranks who has not been accused of having done so from base and unworthy motives, and unmercifully slandered as to his private character. I have seen Theosophy travestied, cant substituted for philosophy, and a

world-wide organization degenerated into 125 people cooped up at Point Loma, with not a man, woman or child of them daring to oppose her slightest whim. . . .

She is a megalomaniac—suffers under the delusion that she is some exalted personality. The worst of it is that her followers are compelled to suffer, too. [Oct. 12, 1902; *Inter-Ocean* (Chicago), Oct. 5, 1902]

Albert E. S. Smythe who came to know Katherine Tingley very well had this to say after her death:

Her method was to take each of her counsellors apart and tell them what dreadful characters the others were . . . I was thus warned against Frank Pierce, Clark Thurston, E. A. Neresheimer, Herbert Coryn, H. A. Patterson, Dr. Anderson, D. N. Dunlop and many others of more or less importance, the object being to sow suspicion and distrust in all but herself.

Research indicates that Tingley continued to use this technique to her advantage over the years, as well as declare individuals to be 'black magicians' for "not being available tools for what she wanted to do." [*The Canadian Theosophist*, 10:6, Aug. 1929, p.182]

Meeting Judge

Tingley's narration about first spotting Judge in the crowd continues:

Suddenly my attention was caught by a pale face on the outskirts of the crowd—the face of a man standing under an umbrella, with his coat collar turned up and buttoned round his neck and his hat low down over his face—clearly not one of the strikers; a gentleman, I thought, suddenly reduced to destitution and ashamed to come forward with the rest and ask for the food he sorely needed. A face fine of features and strikingly noble of expression, with a look of grave sadness, too, and of sickness—caused by hunger no doubt. All this flashed through my mind in that one glance, and I turned to call one of our attendants to send her to him. But when I looked round again, he was gone.

Two days later he presented his card at my home: it was William Quan Judge, a leader of the Theosophical movement and H. P. Blavatsky's successor. He told me he had read of my work among the poor and had gone down there to see it for himself. [*The Gods Await*, p.64]

Here again Tingley overstates her status, claiming that plans for feeding the poor originated at *her* house yet all the evidence points to the fact that she was living in someone else's home, and not paying rent. The di Brazzas "did not exact any rent"—this was free lodging. [*New York Herald*, **Nov. 9, 1902**] Except for Tingley being mentioned in connection with establishing the Women's Emergency Relief Association in the New York *Times* in February 1894, no newspapers in New York City mention her name regarding feeding the poor. This recognition was minimal at best and there is no further mention of her regarding work among the needy as she claims. It appears unlikely that Judge read about her in any New York newspapers; Tingley's name does not appear until after WQJ's death.

In his February 25th, 1932 testimony sworn before a Notary Public, titled "Some Reminiscences of William Q. Judge", Emil August Neresheimer stated:

> Shortly after his return to New York City from the "Parliament of Religions" at the Chicago World's Fair in the Fall of 1893 Mr. Judge mentioned casually an invention made by an acquaintance of his, Mr. Philo B. Tingley. He said he would like me to look into it, and, if agreeable, he would introduce me to Mr. Tingley. Accordingly we called at Mr. Tingley's home in 95th Street, where I was introduced to both Mr. and Mrs. Tingley. I decided not to engage in Mr. Tingley's proposed enterprise, wrote him to that effect, and dismissed the matter from my mind.

Neresheimer's version contradicts Tingley's as to when she first met Judge. She ties it to the blizzard and cloakmakers' strike of 1894-1895 whereas he dates it circa the World's Fair of 1893. Neresheimer provided his sworn statement in February 1932, nearly forty years after the so-called event was said to have occurred. He relied on his memory for details whereas the timing of the blizzard and strike can be corroborated. Interestingly, Neresheimer mentions Tingley's home as 95th Street which is the address she used on her application form when she joined the Theosophical Society, but not where she was living at the time.

The more likely version of what happened is that Neresheimer met Count di Brazza or Philo Tingley or both at the World's Fair or possibly on a train back from Chicago in 1893 and was invited to visit them at their residence on West End Avenue. Neresheimer was told about the inventions that they were working on so he quickly took up the invitation. He became very interested with the work that 'Kate' had been doing as a medium and psychic. From that first visit Neresheimer was hooked on her ability and consulted with her on numerous occasions. In his "Reminiscences" he describes private sessions of psychic training; they became extremely close friends.

Tingley Joins the Society

In a letter to Mrs. H. Beane, dated October 1st, 1894, Judge wrote:
> I have been requested by Mrs. Kate A. Tingley to send you some elementary documents on Theosophy and a form of application for membership in the T.S., so I presume that you have had some conference with her upon the subject. [**The Judge Case**, Part 1, p.301; *Theosophical Forum* (Point Loma), 7:2, Oct. 1935, p.26]

Apparently Judge had some contact with Tingley but, according to her own account, they had not met in person at this point.

Katherine Tingley joined the Theosophical Society on October 13th, 1894. Two endorsers were required on all application forms to join. [ETS has hundreds of those early original application forms in its archives.] Research indicates that Emil August Neresheimer was one of two endorsers who signed her application form. The records at Adyar state that Tingley joined as an unattached member, that is, not affiliated with any theosophical Branch. This is rather odd when considering that one of the most dynamic Branches in New York City was only two miles away, in Harlem. Repeated exchanges of letters over these many years with the Archivist(s) at Adyar indicate that they have either misplaced or destroyed Tingley's application form; the details of her endorsers may never be proven. [**Adyar Library Research Centre, General Register I, 17 Novr 1875 to 8 Octr 1896, p.295**]

[See photos]

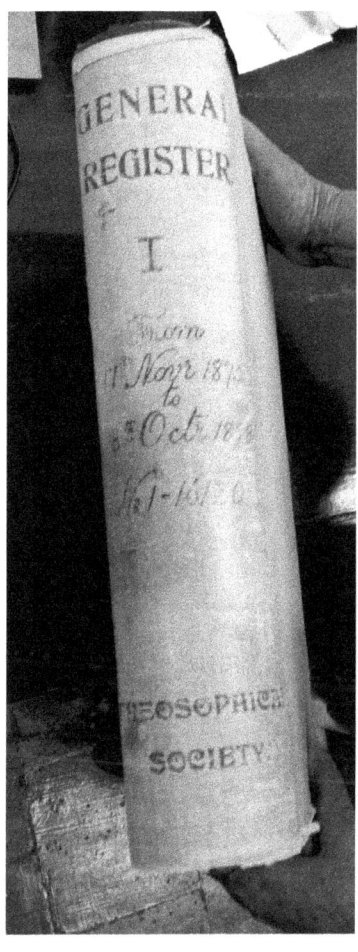

In a biographical sketch of Katherine Tingley, written by Grace F. Knoche which appeared in a Special Issue of *Sunrise*, April-May 1998, she wrote that after joining the Theosophical Society "a fortnight later Judge accepted her into the Esoteric Section. She worked closely with him." [p.101] No evidence was provided to substantiate these claims and no corroboration found for this statement. There is no evidence that Judge knew Tingley personally at this time and therefore could not have accepted Tingley into the Esoteric Section nor could she have worked closely with him. In fact there is no evidence Tingley ever joined the Esoteric Section until she took it over as Outer Head after Judge's death.

Neresheimer was a close friend of Anna Miller Stabler who established a theosophical Center in Harlem, New York, on March 20th, 1891 where Judge agreed to speak for the occasion. It is well known that Neresheimer, a fine baritone, loved to sing and Stabler was a vocal teacher. Neresheimer was a contributor in starting the Center. [*Theosophical News*, **2:2, June 28, 1897, p.5**] It became known as the H.P.B. Branch. Their application for a charter was completed on May 8th, 1891—the day Blavatsky died. The Branch was located in Miss Stabler's Studio at 142 West, 125 street only two miles from where Tingley lived.

On her application form Tingley gave her address as 164 West 95th street, a real estate holding purchased by the di Brazzas. It was not where the Tingleys resided at the time, but it was the address where Philo was working as a clerk. [*1895-96 New York Directory*] Why Tingley gave this address is anyone's guess; considering her history of payment evasion, perhaps it was to avoid collectors or other agencies from showing up at the house, or she

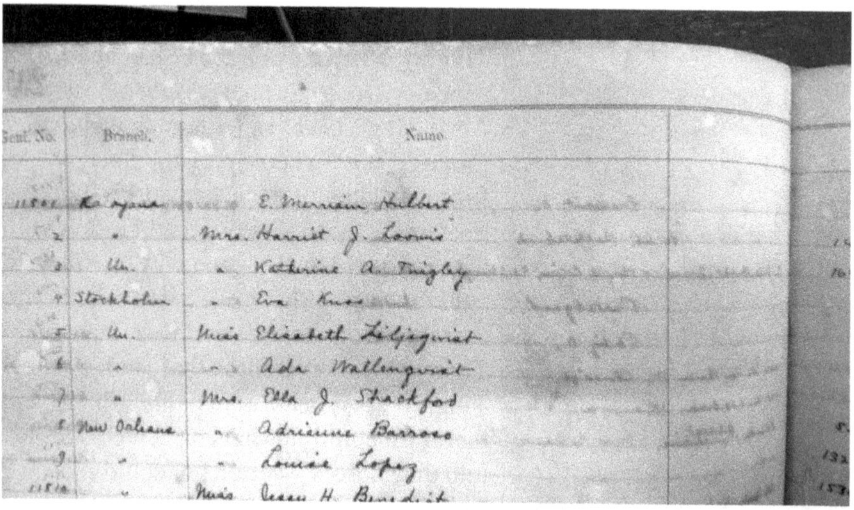

[Third line from top]

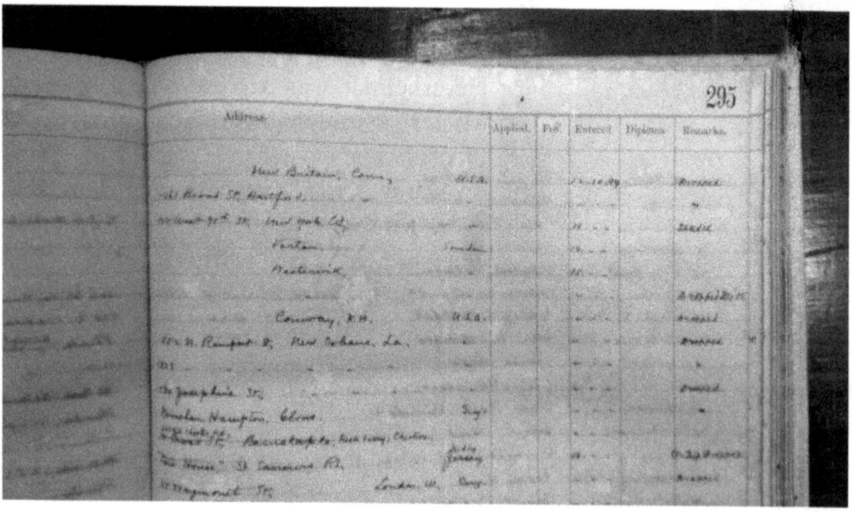

did not want to be contacted by the Society. Whatever it was, she likely had a good reason.

The address Tingley gave was only two miles south of the H.P.B. Branch but in fact she was actually living one mile further south. Even though this was the closest and the easiest Branch to get to from Tingley's actual residence, it was also one of the strongest in devotion and unity and one of the most attended. There is no evidence of Tingley ever attending any theosophical meetings before she met Judge. All overseas lecturers spoke at this Branch when visiting, including Alice Cleather who made her maiden speech before this Branch on April 21st, 1895. [*New York Tribune*, Apr. 21, 1895; *Theosophical News*, 2:2, June 28, 1897, p.5; *The Path*, 10:3, June 1895, p.104]

An article praising the H.P.B. (Harlem, N.Y.) T.S. in *Theosophical News* states:

> Much of its success is also due to the help received from the Aryan Branch. Mr. Judge used to call the H.P.B. the 'Baby' Branch and the 'Feeder to the Aryan,' and was kind to the 'Baby,' and in return the 'Baby' made it a point to advise all inquirers who resided nearer to the Aryan quarters than the H.P.B. to join the Aryan; for the H.P.B. has had the peculiar good fortune of getting more notice in the newspapers than the Aryan, the result of having two reporters as members. [**2:2, June 28, 1897, p.5**]

The Aryan Branch kept records of those who attended. They held meetings twice a week, Sunday and Tuesday evenings. Earlier in the year it had "been decided to recommence the method of admitting visitors by ticket, and of associateship... Mr. Harry Steele Budd has been appointed doorkeeper and he has a small staff of assistants." [*The Path*, 10:6, Sep. 1895, p.194]

The other endorser to Tingley's application more than likely was Joseph Hall Fussell. Fussell was mesmerized, literally, by Tingley's abilities; so much so that around 1894, perhaps sooner, he too moved into the di Brazzas' house at 373 West End Avenue. According to the 1893 New York Directory Fussell's address was 144 Madison Avenue, headquarters of the Aryan T.S., but then he started spending more and more time at the Tingleys' so he moved in. In an article in the New York *Sun* [**Nov. 2, 1896**] Fussell is quoted as saying "I live there now, you know". He too became an extremely close friend. Fussell was one of the first to speak out about how great Tingley was. He was perhaps the most influential person to forward Tingley as the "great unknown" and "secret" successor of Judge. He wrote:

> [I]nstead of being deserted, [TS in America] would, on the contrary, ... still have in its ranks a high adept, "one who all these years had purposely kept himself in the background." [***The Sun* (NY), Apr. 3, 1896**]

Fussell purposely used "himself" to confuse the media. Either Fussell was being deceitful or he had already been bamboozled into thinking that Judge had known Tingley for much longer. It really served the purpose of those who wanted Tingley as the successor, to make sure people believed that Judge had known her for a long period of time when in fact he hardly knew her.

On April 11th, 1897, shortly after the return of the Crusaders from their world tour, an article appeared in the *New York Daily Tribune* titled "Katherine A. Tingley: A Leader of the Theosophical Movement Throughout the World" and sub-titled "Interesting Biographical Sketch of a New-England Woman—Things That She Can See That Others Cannot." This article is also quoted in "Katherine Tingley: A Biographical Sketch" by Grace F. Knoche in *Sunrise*, April/May 1998. **[p.99, fn. #2]**

At first glance it appears to have been contributed by one of the *Tribune*'s reporters. However, analysis of the writing style and its contents, when compared with verifiable historical facts, proves that there are many errors in this article. Aside from obvious incorrect statements regarding her youth, there are numerous insinuations in line with a narrative to promote Tingley. One particular statement which is clearly meant to influence the reader is "Mrs. Tingley was intuitively a Theosophist in doctrine and sympathy long before she became an actual member of the society . . ." Evidence shows that she had neither of these traits. This article has a very similar style to one written by Joseph H. Fussell found in a very rare edition of *The Theosophical Path* where he presents her in a most positive light and attributes traits that are clearly false. He wrote:

> Few knew how close was her relationship to H.P. Blavatsky, or how true she was to the original program of the Theosophical Society inaugurated by H.P. Blavatsky as the Messenger and Servant of the Great Teachers who stand back of this Movement. **[36:9, Sep. 1929, p.401]**

Evidence proves otherwise.

Timing of Events — The Cloakmakers Strike & The Blizzard

The timing of two events is critical in order to substantiate Tingley's story: the dates of the cloakmakers strike, and the blizzard in the New York region. She wrote that she saw Judge for the first time when a storm was brewing, "an ordinary snowstorm that gave little warning of the tremendous blizzard . . . ." New York newspapers for 1893 and 1894 were checked to find a storm that would fit Tingley's story; it also had to tie in with the cloakmakers' strike she refers to.

Articles about trouble stirring at the Central Labor Union involving the cloakmakers started appearing by mid-August 1894. Strife arose between two unions.
> The Socialists succeeded in organizing a cloakmakers' union on Socialistic principles, in opposition to the old Cloakmakers' Union, No.1. . . . [*New York Times*, Aug. 13, 1894]

This set the stage for the beginning of a bitter strike to follow between the owners and the workers which lasted into spring of 1895.

By late August the cloakmakers and the clothing cutters went on strike seeking "for an advance of $2 a week."[*New York Times*, Aug. 28, 1894] Others in the clothing trades also wanted an advance of wages. The general perspective was that
> This is the beginning of what will probably be the largest strike in the clothing trades that has taken place in New-York, as it will include, besides the finishers, the tailors, basters, cloakmakers, and suitmakers. . . . New York is one of the largest clothing manufacturing centres in this country and more clothes are made here than in London or any other large city in Europe. [*New York Times*, Sep. 3, 1894]

A few days later the Knights of Labor tailors decided to strike as well which added about 4,000 more men to the already 8,000 out of work. "The Knights of Labor say they have 15,000 men on strike." [*New York Times*, Sep.7 & 8, 1894]

This strike was a heavy burden on all who lived on the East side of New York City and there was much suffering. One of the men explained that their situation was not well understood.
> The men employed in those shops realize that the times promise to be good; that there is work to be done; that it must be done right now and that, if the men who are going to do it want to get their

wretched circumstances improved, they must ask for that improvement now. [*New York Times*, Sep. 13, 1894.]

In spite of various efforts to help them and their families, there were thousands of starving cloakmakers in New York City. [*The Evening World*, Nov. 24, 1894] Many of them were utterly destitute. [*The Evening World*, Dec. 22, 24, 1894]

Then on Wednesday December 26th a severe storm hit New York City. This is the only storm that fits the criteria Tingley presented when she claimed to have first seen Judge standing outside the perimeter of the crowd that was waiting for food at the soup kitchen she was managing. The next day *The New York Times* reported:

> [T]he first real snowstorm of this season visited this section yesterday afternoon. The snow swirled in and out among the high buildings where the drafts of air were the strongest and beat down upon the unfortunate passers with cutting and chilling effect.
>
> Beginning, as it did, at a little before 6 P.M., the storm increased in intensity and volume until at midnight but few conveyances were running, and it was with the utmost difficulty that pedestrians were enabled to keep upon their feet. [**Dec. 27, 1894**]

The Evening World reported:

> The severe storm which has been raging since last night along the Atlantic coast from Maine to Florida will be followed by a cold wave, which Signal-Service Officer Dunn believes will cause a drop of 20 degrees in the temperature within the next twenty-four hours. . . . The storm is central over this immediate vicinity, and covers a radius of from 500 to 600 miles. . . .
>
> When the snow began to cover the town last night with a fine white powder every one confidently believed it was going to be a decent self-respecting sort of arrangement of flakes. There was a difference this morning, and the snow worked itself in easy stages first to hail, and then to a cold, miserable beating rain, which drenched everything in sight. . . .
>
> And here is where the snow did a very bad thing. It blocked up the sewers; it formed itself into basins and troughs to hold the fickle rain, and the slush . . . .

> As for umbrellas, the City Hall Park at 8 o'clock was a perfect Bay of Biscay of them, and there was a dado of them on the Broadway side of the Post-Office, with their ribs stripped and shorn of the covering and with their handles broken by the wind. An umbrella this morning was not the good thing it is usually supposed to be. [Dec. 27, 1894]

Tingley stated that Judge was using an umbrella at the time she saw him, one can only imagine what happened to it.

The storm created much havoc.
> New York was the first big city it struck, and here it lingered. During its stay it left a nine-inch enamel of snow, and then further discouraged the Street-Cleaning Department by wetting that layer with a half-inch rainfall. . . . In this city the wind attained a velocity of 35 miles per hour in some places, about 100 miles an hour in others, especially around street corners. [*New York Times*, Dec. 28, 1894]

People were dying in the streets and across NY State places like Troy, Kingston, and Syracuse up to two feet of snow had fallen, snow drifts delayed railroads, and street car lines and highways were blocked. [*New York Tribune*, Dec. 28, 1894] Snow and wind were reported in Albany, Poughkeepsie and Newburg, NY. Surrounding States were also severely affected. Risks of fire and loss of life were reported in Camden, NJ due to issues with the electrical plant. Snow five inches deep accumulated in four hours in Red Bank, NJ. [*New York Times*, Dec. 28, 1894]

In New York City,
> Traffic was everywhere impeded, and to walk for a distance without getting the feet wet was practically impossible. The surface cars had such hard work in the morning in making their trips on time that many of their usual customers patronized the elevated railway, ... [*The Evening World*, Dec. 28, 1894]

The storm compounded the misery of the strikers. On January 1st, 1895, *The Evening World* headline read: "Twelve Thousand Idle Men: Cheerless Outlook for Cloakmakers and Their Families. No Prospect for Work Until March at the Very Earliest." [Jan. 1, 1895]

End of December 1894

There is no doubt about the timing of the cloakmakers strike and the blizzard. Returning to Tingley's account, according to her, Judge presented himself at her residence two days after the storm. This would bring it to Saturday afternoon, December 29th, 1894 as the most probable date Judge first met Katherine Tingley. If that is the case Judge would have invited her to attend the public entertainment that the Aryan T.S. was hosting the next day. This time line coincides with John Pryse's testimony under direct examination during the Tingley vs Times-Mirror court case where he stated "I knew her when she attended Theosophical meetings at 144 Madison Avenue in the year 1894 or 1895." **[Tingley vs Times-Mirror, 1433, p.359]** and with the following statement by Claude Falls Wright, after the meetings held between March 24th and 27th, 1896 where the individuals chosen by Tingley were informed who this "Chela" apparently was.

> I met this Chela—"Promise"—several times in 1894 and 1895. Mr. Judge introduced me at a meeting of the Aryan T. S. in 1894, saying to me beforehand: "Here is some one I want you to look at closely; it is a particular person." He afterwards told me that 'Promise' frequently was in touch with the Lodge. Later he sent me to a house where 'Promise' was staying, and there this chela went into a trance and told me much of the future . . ." **[To the Members of the EST, April 3, 1896, 19 pp.;** *The Theosophical Movement 1875 -1925,* **p.666]**

"Promise" was what Tingley insisted on being known as for one year after she took over; it was not a reference Judge ever made.

In *The Theosophical Movement 1875-1925,* the author(s) state:
> If it were Mr. Judge who sent him later to see Mrs. Tingley, and if, as Mr. Wright says, she "went into a *trance,*" it only shows Mrs. Tingley to have been a medium, or "sensitive," *not a chela.* "Mediumship," wrote H.P.B. in "Isis Unveiled" (Volume 2, p.588) "is the *opposite* of adeptship." **[p.668]**

The full statement in *Isis* continues:
> the medium is the passive instrument of foreign influences, the adept actively controls himself and all inferior potencies.

At the Sunday afternoon, December 30th, 1894 event
> The Aryan T.S. had a public entertainment by the Lotus Circle . . . [with] vocal and instrumental music, a "Wisdom Play" was given by the children, ten characters being represented, and a

special feature was a Rainbow Scene, seven very young children representing the different colors of the spectrum. There was a very full audience and no little appreciation.

In the evening Judge was scheduled to give a talk on "Theosophy". [*The Path*, 9:11, Feb. 1895, p.406]

The following evening,
>On New Year's Eve a "Watch Meeting" was held at the Aryan Headquarters. After a cordial social . . . Judge read some selections from the *Bhagavad-Gita* and *The Voice of the Silence*, made some practical remarks on the topic selected, and suggested a few moments of silence, during the passage of which the New Year was ushered in. [*The Path*, 9:11, Feb. 1895, p.406]

On this special occasion the League of Theosophical Workers had raised sufficient funds to hang a framed life-size photo of W.Q. Judge in the Lodge Headquarters room. A silver plate was incorporated into the frame with an inscription of all the Branches that donated. [*The Path*, 9:12, Mar. 1895, p.435]

Judge's Deteriorating Health

The first letter that Judge wrote to Tingley, a few days after first meeting her in person, is the January 5th, 1895 letter that he wrote while on the train to Forth Wayne, IN. Judge addressed it to "Purple", a sobriquet for Katherine Tingley. [*TJC*, Part 2, p.396; *OE Library Critic*, 22:3, Oct. 1932] Historically purple, because of its bold hues, was a colour reserved for royalty and often forbidden for commoners to wear, at times under penalty of death. Countess di Brazza had a special fondness for this colour and embraced its usage whenever she could. Tingley adopted 'Purple' as her moniker and eventually wore purple clothing as well.

Judge returned to New York from his mid-western trip on January 17th, 1895. On January 18th he wrote to E.T. Hargrove,
>I am so sick just now that I cannot send any letters. Take it all for granted. My Chicago trip was all right and useful, but this is my ordinary death year, and hence I am just waiting until the Rubicon is passed. [*TJC*, Part 2, p.261; *TQ*, 30, July 1932, p.31]

Judge kept in frequent contact with Hargrove and wrote him another letter on January 21st.

Again Judge's health had utterly broken down; he "left New York on the [Feb.]13th, for a month's rest and treatment." [*The Path*, **9:12, Mar. 1895, p.439**] This is when Judge would have left for Mineral Wells, TX.

During this time Judge was also dealing with the ongoing accusations of "forging Mahatma letters" brought against him by Annie Besant. On February 23rd, 1895 Judge wrote to the General Secretary of the European Section, G.R.S. Mead, regarding the evidence against him which Besant had promised:

> ... instead of pursuing the impartial course as required by your office, you have taken the position of prosecutor, attorney and pleader against me, making a long argumentative reply, full of assertions and conclusions of your own, and signed officially, so that you might print it, as you say with my letter, in *The Vahan*.
> [*TJC*, Part 1, p.153; *The Vahan*, 4:9, Apr. 1895, p.1]

Judge was unable to have the much needed rest. The weight of those accusations tormented him and his health handcuffed him. The matter had supposedly been considered closed at the Judicial Committee in London in July 1894 but Besant and her followers refused to let it go. Their objective was for Annie Besant and Col. Olcott to rid themselves of Judge and ensure he would not become President of the T.S. after Olcott retired.

Hargrove explains quite clearly the situation that Judge was facing.
> On this plane, Judge was the Guardian of the whole Society, and felt deeply responsible for all its parts. He had inherited that responsibility directly from H.P.B., and it had become greater with his own continued inner growth. It was, therefore, both his duty and desire to avoid what we then referred to colloquially as "a split", so long as there was a ray of hope for his enemies. That they were his enemies, as well as enemies of the Society, complicated his task. If they had attacked and persecuted some other member of the Society, instead of himself, he could and would have acted against them, drastically, from the beginning. As it was, the initiative, under occult law, could not come from him. He *had* to be "ordered"—one might almost say "pushed"—by other members of the Great Lodge before consenting to cut off the gangrened membership. Further, "orders" received by him directly, had to be confirmed by similar "orders", from the same source, sent to him through others. None of this has been understood or taken into account by those who have attempted to criticize his procedure at that time. They have revealed nothing

except their own ignorance,—including their ignorance of the truth that to be bound by occult law is equivalent to being bound by the finer shades of honour.

Judge's friends were not bound as he was. Their duty was entirely different. Those among them who had any real insight knew well that *Judge was the Society*, just as H.P.B. had been the Society during her lifetime; they knew that to save him would save the Society, and that it could not be saved in any other way.

Some people find this principle difficult to understand. I have heard Christians say: "Christ is Christianity", and other Christians object on the ground that this ignored the Church. A student of Theosophy ought to know that it takes only one real Christian to make a Church, and that, in the same way, it takes only one real Theosophist (which implies a great deal) to make a Theosophical Society,—and that without the reality, the organism is a danger and a snare.

It followed that several of Judge's friends had advocated a "split", long before he was willing to entertain the idea. His letter of March 10th, which follows, was the first intimation we, in London, received, that he had consented finally to an "operation" on the body entrusted to his care. [*TJC*, **Part 2, p.262;** *TQ*, **30, July 1932, pp.32-33**]

On March 10th, 1895, Judge wrote a letter to his friends in England: A.K. [Archibald Keightley], J.C.K. [Julia C. Keightley], E.T.H. [Ernest T. Hargrove] (and others).

> I have changed my plans because of information and instructions from △ [designates " Mahatma"] in regard to an American split; and that information is being confirmed not only by reflection but also by facts. The fact J.C.K. gives about the insane proposition of Sturdy and Co. confirms. They are all mixed up and incapable of leading, and to remain tied to them means years of strife and bitterness. A.B. [Mrs. Annie Besant] is determined to destroy me, and hence we must get apart, for U.S. is the real T.S., and their rot and rioting over there under A.B. is something we must separate from. So, I am now in the split party, though I have not as yet said so openly. I have told a few only. Previously I was against talk of split, proposing that April Convention should stand for unity, after passing certain resolutions, and then see what the other two [Sections of the T.S.] would do.

This is what ∴ says: Write London and tell them to write to, or see, the different parts, and ask what steps they (such places or Lodges) are prepared to take in reference to the U.S. April Convention, not only on the question of separation and affiliation, but as well on sending delegate or delegates to America. Give them directions if they do not know.

Well, I don't think you need instructions. The more resolutions you can bring with you, the stronger we shall be. If Europe will not delegate you—and of course you would not accept if determined to go a way it [the European Section] would not sanction—you can get some Lodge or Lodges or centres to delegate you specially to represent them. Ireland of course; Sweden and others I of course do not know about, but you will know. I suppose the form of resolution on the special point can only be that if U.S. splits, they will affiliate. But you are competent to draw that up.

The chief reason some will have for "no split" is sentimental,—a desire not to split the T.S. But it is already split, and the Sturdy thing shows what it will come to for certain. So you must meet that the best way you can. If you meet one or two *safe* persons who say that J. [Judge] was against it, you can say you have reason to believe I changed my mind.

As ever,
William ♃

[*TJC*, Part 2, p.263; *TQ*, 30, July 1932, pp.33-34]

The Masters gave Judge their guidance regarding the troubled membership within the Theosophical Society—no matter what happened a split would always be there and at some point an amputation had to occur because the minds of the membership had been poisoned. On the matter of using the sign Jupiter, Hargrove stated: "When writing informally and intimately, as in this letter . . . Judge often used the sign Jupiter to represent the Q. and J. of his initials." [*TQ*, 28, Apr. 1931, fn.p.326] Judge was using this symbol in 1893 well before he met Tingley. At other times Judge would simply use "J".

To backtrack a bit, on July 30th, 1894, Judge and Dr. Buck returned from London after attending the Judicial Committee or "Trial", in reality the persecution of W.Q. Judge. His already ill state of health was deteriorating under the strain of this oppression as well as concerns surrounding the upcoming April convention and potential split. Neresheimer wrote where Judge went for rest and treatment, attempting to recuperate.

The agitation quickly began again so that it became clear that nothing short of the utter destruction of Mr. Judge's influence would ever satisfy the conspirators against his Theosophical reputation. Mr. Judge's health, by this time, was greatly broken down. Something had to be done to secure rest and relaxation from the terrific strain of the continual pressure of events besides the heavy burden of his daily work. Mrs. Tingley proposed to me that Mr. Judge be induced to go to Mineral Wells, near San Antonio, Texas, where she offered to go, and, if possible, nurse him back to health. This was early in 1895 when it was becoming every day more apparent that some decisive action would be necessary at the forthcoming Convention of the American Section, to be held the last Sunday in April at Boston. Arrangements were made accordingly, Mr. Judge going by way of Cincinnati for a short visit to Dr. Buck, one of his staunchest supporters, who was to receive and forward all mail to Mr. Judge, whose real destination was kept secret in order to secure the needed privacy. Mrs. Tingley went direct to Mineral Wells in order to make the necessary arrangements before Mr. Judge arrived. She rented a small, poorly-furnished house from a German woman. Mrs. Tingley rendered invaluable service, both by her devoted care of Mr. Judge and by acting as his amanuensis when he was too ill to write himself. Occasional long typewritten letters were sent by Mr. Judge himself to me, containing instructions and suggestions in elucidation of the various matters alluded to in Mrs. Tingley's letters, which were in her own handwriting.

Preparations for the coming American Convention were hampered by the absence of Mr. Judge from New York City, so that a committee, consisting of C.A. Griscom, Jr., A.E. Spencer and myself met daily to deal with such matters as Mr. Judge entrusted to us. Mr. Judge was confined to his bed most of the time, and towards the end of his absence, the committee was enlarged by adding other well-known Theosophists from New York, Brooklyn, Boston, Buffalo and Chicago, whom Mr. Judge named in his letters to me. He was away, in all, about two and a half months, and when he returned to New York City in March, 1895, he was still very weak but sufficiently improved in health to be able to direct with comparative vigor the strenuous work requiring his immediate attention. So far as I am aware, none but Dr. Buck and myself knew of Mr. Judge's whereabouts during his absence from

New York City, though notice that he was away was published in his magazine *The Path*. **[Reminiscences]**

Mineral Wells

In some instances it has been found that Neresheimer's writings are inaccurate in details and at times possibly fabricated. Whenever possible his writings have to be verified. Assuming that the above narration is mostly accurate, when Judge did return to New York in March 1895 as noted by Neresheimer himself (and mentioned in *The Path*) he would have been away about thirty days; he had left for Mineral Wells on February 13th. One could be left with the impression from Neresheimer's words that Judge was in Mineral Wells for two and a half months. Some believe that Judge was under Tingley's influence; this has led many into thinking that such an extended period of time had an effect on him. Similarly, Neresheimer stated in his "Reminiscences" that Judge knew Katherine and Philo Tingley in the fall of 1893 and wanted to introduce him to them, implying Judge already knew Katherine. This statement is implausible because the facts contradict this testimony but this too has created much confusion. Tingley herself refutes this when she claims to have seen Judge for the first time during the blizzard of 1894-1895.

When Judge returned from his stay in Mineral Wells his health had perhaps improved a little but his voice had deteriorated. What is of particular importance, as has been interpreted by many, is whether Judge did fall under the influence of Katherine Tingley or if he was simply noting his experiments, testing her as he had done with many other psychics before, for example Laura Holloway. The 'evidence' appears to be damning and historians have been divided. Many have concluded that Judge fell under Tingley's influence based on their own interpretation of details and their biases. What the evidence does support is that Judge chastised Tingley for her action at the American Convention in Boston in April 1895, which basically ended their relationship.

James Morgan Pryse had this to say about Judge's diary and his trip to Mineral Wells.

> The *C.T.* is in error when it states that "no one ever saw the alleged 'Diary' except Mr. Hargrove, Mr. J. H. Fussell and Mrs. Tingley herself". For Mr. Hargrove loaned me the Diary without my asking for it (and I wish to add, incidentally, that I regard Mr.

Hargrove as a sincere and honourable Theosophist, though I cannot say that of the two other persons mentioned); and that Diary was not an "alleged" one, for it was all in Judge's handwriting. But though the writing was clear and legible I didn't read much of it. I've read a great deal in English, Latin, Greek, Sanskrit, French and Spanish, but that Diary belonged to a class of literature that I don't care to read in any language. It was too sentimental, mushy and, spiritualistic for me to wade through it. Among other matters, it covered the period when Mr. Judge and Mrs. Tingley, his favourite spirit-medium, went into seclusion together at Mineral Wells, and in it there was much fulsome praise of her, while the estimable Mrs. Judge, who had been left in Brooklyn, whenever referred to was nick-named "Kali"—after the most hideous Goddess in the Hindu pantheon. In sorrow for Judge I gave the Diary back to Hargrove mostly unread. I'd like to have burned it. Whoever has it now should consign it to the flames without delay. Even the Tingleyites have not dared to besmirch Judge's memory by publishing it. [*TJC*, **Part 2, p.395;** *CT*, **13:4, June 1932, p.125]**

There are many questions that need to be resolved concerning Judge's trip to Texas. It seems very strange that Judge would be living with Tingley, a stranger, at Mineral Wells and not have brought his wife along. What about Flossie, the girl who was then in her care? When her father, Katherine's first husband, Richard Cook found out how Tingley was treating his daughter he took her back. He wrote: "Florence remained with her until November, 1895. When I learned how she was being treated I took her away." [*California Utopia: Point Loma: 1897-1942*, **p.59.**] It had been reported in newspapers that Tingley did not send Flossie to school and treated her as her personal maid, cleaning, washing dishes, and running errands. Flossie's actual name was Florence M. Cook (born January 7th, 1881). Richard's second wife, his children's mother, ended up in a mental hospital and he could not take care of them. In a letter to Edward Parker, Cook explained:

> She [Katherine Tingley] assured me that she was married to Geo. Parent and was living respected by everyone. . . She begged me to let her have the two children to live with her, as she had an elegant home and I was only able to work part of the time. I let her have them, but would not let her adopt them. The boy proved too much care for her and I sent him to school in Connecticut for a while and afterwards to my brothers, where Florence is now and where he has remained.

The real story of the marriage of Richard Cook and Katherine Westcott has never been fully exposed. Emmett A. Greenwalt only presented carefully selected details in his book but stayed away with dealing with what Cook himself described as scandalous facts about their relationship.[R.H. Cook to Edward Parker, Nov. 9, 1899, Exhibit D in *Cuban Children Case*, Proceedings of the U.S. Board of Special Inquiry at Ellis Island, Nov. 1, 5, 7, 1902]

Convention — April 1895

On April 23rd, 1895, Archibald and Julia Keightley, Alice Cleather and Fred Dick arrived in New York City on the *SS Trave*. [Ancestry]

On April 25th, 1895 Judge wrote to Hargrove stating that he was leaving for Boston the next day with Archibald and Julia Keightley and "so will not be able to write". [*TJC*, Part 2, p.264; *TQ*, 30, July 1932, p.35] Included with his letter was a memo dictated mentally by the Masters to Judge, but also meant for Hargrove, explaining the situation in the Theosophical Movement. Hargrove explains:

> The memorandum dated April 1st, 1895, was enclosed with a letter addressed either to Dr. A. Keightley or to me: I do not remember which. In any case, I have the original, which is in Judge's handwriting, though with occasional modifications.

The Memo was as follows:

> April 1st, 1895 — ∆ For letter to —.
> Tell him that you have watched events, have waited, have given the persecutors, the destroyers of Theosophy every chance, and now the hour has come when it is no longer possible for you to remain with them. To what are you pledged? For what through centuries have you worked? For the Theosophical Movement, or, the spiritualizing of the race. That movement is now endangered by the state of the T.S., which cannot be cured by any further temporizing. The only part of the T.S. that has any theosophical vitality is the group of American Branches. It is their duty to cut themselves off, or like good apples in a barrel with rotten ones, they will be rotted. Remember the picture of the T.S. as a tree torn by the roots and cast upon an arid plain. Quite true you may keep alive this organization for some three years, but it would be a period full of bitterness and strife, ending in the ruin of the Theosophical Movement. Even now, as you know, they are trying to undermine you in your own place. By striking at you, the centre, they are striking at Theosophy. This the Dark ones know,

and are pushing that poor woman [Mrs. Besant] on, while she and her friends are working for their own self-righteous ends as they suppose. The Dark ones know that such as they cannot head nor carry on a real movement. Waste no more thoughts on them; devote all your helpful thoughts to those brave souls who have stood, who have worked for Theosophy and not for themselves, who have seen through those illusions, who have not mistaken hypocrisy for truth. The others will have to be left to learn the lessons of their experience so that those may profit them in other lives under similar temptations. [*TJC*, **Part 2, pp.263-264;** *TQ*, **30, July 1932, p.34**]

The Ninth Annual Convention of the American Section T.S. and First Convention of the Theosophical Society in America was held at Boston, April 28-29, 1895. The delegates assembled at the New England Theosophical Headquarters, 24 Mt. Vernon street, Boston, some time before 10 a.m. Dr. Keightley read thirteen greetings from European societies and a long, interesting and witty letter from Dr. Hartmann, which "was listened to with attention". A little dispute arose here, it being proposed to print the letter in the Proceedings. On this there were speeches, but on request of Judge, it was ordered not to be printed. [**Report of Proceedings, p.6;** *The Path*, **10:2, May 1895, p.65**] One of the short speeches was by Tingley. "Judge glared at her with deep displeasure while she spoke and after she resumed her seat; and that at the end of the session he called her to him and rebuked her so severely that she wept. . . ." [*TJC*, **Part 2, p.259,** *TQ*, **30, July 1932, p.29**] Hartmann's letter probably included personal information regarding Judge while they were both at Adyar in 1884, which would have been of great interest for this audience. Judge did not want it published for personal reasons. Tingley perhaps felt compelled to add her own personal anecdotes about Judge, which clearly irritated him.

The Convention was followed by a summary of events regarding the charges against Judge.

> After the Convention had adjourned, the delegates and members again assembled (April 29th, at 3.30 p.m.) 'to listen to a written explanation of the charges against William Q. Judge of forging "Mahatma messages". Judge said his health would not permit him to read the paper himself, but that Dr. Keightley would do it for him, adding that the explanation had been purposely kept back until the final action of the Convention should be known. Dr. Keightley then read the paper, which occupied one hour and a

half, to an audience which paid the deepest attention. The six charges made by Mrs. Besant were given in full and answered *seriatim*. At the conclusion of the reading there was long and loud applause, after which it was moved and carried:
That the meeting considered the explanation perfectly satisfactory, but that, so far as those present were concerned, it was entirely unnecessary. [*TJC,* **Part 2, p.259,** *TQ,* **30, July 1932, p.29]**

There are two possible explanations for Judge's behavior from the time he first met Tingley up to the end of the Boston Convention a few months later. Some say Judge was keeping notes regarding Tingley's psychic abilities while others say that Judge was under her spell. What is known is that his behavior prior to meeting Tingley and his behavior following the American Convention in Boston is consistent. It can be surmised that during his stay at Mineral Wells Judge quickly deduced that Tingley was simply a medium and knew nothing about theosophical teachings, which Neresheimer corroborated in his "Reminiscences" where he wrote:
I think it proper to say that my impressions of Katherine Tingley's genuineness as an Occultist were not always completely convincing to me—indeed I already had my misgivings in this respect even at a much earlier date. I soon discovered that she had never studied Theosophy, in fact she never claimed at any time to have done so.

Chapter Two

Tingley's Strategic Maneuvers

Judge knew the depth of Hargrove's knowledge and understanding of Theosophy, having been on a lecture tour in California with him a few years prior. Hargrove lived in England and Judge was being encouraged to contact him to come as quickly as possible if he could, to help spread the teachings of theosophy to the American Branches, and to prepare him for a leading role in the society in the event of Judge's death. Judge had alluded in his letter of January 17th that 1895 was his "ordinary death year". One important fact to keep in mind is that Hargrove was only twenty-five years old at the time.

Numerous instances can be found indicating that Judge was most impressed with Hargrove's knowledge and understanding of the esoteric teachings. Hargrove had proven himself with his article "Some Modern Failings" written under the pen name Chew-Yew-Tsang, which appeared in *Lucifer*, October [pp.97-100] and December [pp.321-327] 1893. In fact the editors of *Lucifer*, Annie Besant and G.R.S. Mead, [*BCW* 13, p. 393] were convinced that this had been written by some unknown adept. When the identity of the author was discovered it created much resentment toward Hargrove and also toward Judge. Besant and Mead insisted that it was a planned deception.

Judge's actions seemed to indicate that he considered Hargrove the most suitable individual to head T.S. in America and the Esoteric Section and was apparently training him. Judge was aware of Hargrove's esoteric knowledge and his wisdom on matters relating to the theosophical teachings. He occasionally tested Hargrove by sending him private letters he had received asking him for his impressions. Judge made reference to the following in *The Path*, and in a memo found among his papers he had written:

> There is a peculiar and definite odor which comes with all genuine objective messages from the masters which cannot be imitated by any chemist, but which when once identified cannot be mistaken.

[Reminiscences]

After the Boston convention Judge left with his wife for Cincinnati to stay with Dr. Buck. On May 20th, 1895 Judge wrote to Hargrove from Cincinnati,

Dear Bro. —— I am away from home for my health [which is] much hurt by others' hate" * * * I wish we could all ignore Mrs B. [Besant] once and for all. She lives by fighting or flattery now. But what blasphemy to say that, even be I guilty, the Master would stoop so low as to bid her hound me over the world trying to murder my character. . . [*TJC*, Part I, pp.180, 418; *Letters that Have Helped Me*, p.185]

On June 14th, 1895 from Cincinnati, Judge wrote to Hargrove:
There was no need for me to write you because we communicate other ways [obviously meaning mind to mind]. But —— wrote me now and then as if I should tell you one way or the other if you should come here. At least it read that way to me. No such responsibility should be put on me as that I must tell you to come, or be the active compeller, so to say. Each must decide such a thing for himself. And I think you know that as well as I do. I do not assume, mind you, that you have any such idea, but write about it because of what was said.

Then, regarding his situation, Judge added:
Claude [Wright] is now running the T.S. office in my absence, as it appears I shall have to stay away a considerable time. I am on the move like a pilgrim. But I am better a little each day. Been with Dr. Buck for a month. Don't give away the address. Address will remain 144 Madison Avenue for all. [*TJC*, Part 1, pp.188, 418, Part 2, p.266; *TQ*, 30, July 1932, pp.37-38]

Upon receiving Judge's letter of April 25th, 1895 and the enclosed Memorandum of April 1st, 1895 Hargrove had quickly taken action and told his father (a well known Solicitor in London who had hoped that Ernest would follow in his footsteps) that he must leave for New York as soon as feasible as he was needed there and that this was his duty. Hargrove was described in a newspaper article as
6 ft. 3 in. tall, Britisher by birth, and a barrister of Middle Temple, London, who is said to have renounced his father's proferred $25,000 a year to become an American citizen and a theosophist.
[*The Lewiston Daily Sun*, Lewiston, ME, Aug. 17, 1896]
The approximate equivalent of $25,000 currently is $865,000. Hargrove was obviously very devoted to theosophical ideals. In an interview with *The World* (NY), he described how he found Theosophy:
Walking down the street one day at an English seaside resort . . . I saw a big sign . . . "Theosophy". I read the word. I didn't know

what it was. I'd not heard it. But when I read it . . . that word became alive to me. It affected me curiously. . . I have to find out what Theosophy is. . . . I read and read, and became a Theosophist. **[May 19, 1896]**

Hargrove joined the Theosophical Society as a member-at-large in late summer of 1891, a few months before his twenty-first birthday (b. Dec. 17th, 1870). He met Judge at the Convention of the European Section in July 1892 and had been very deeply impressed. [*TJC*, Part 2, p.219; *TQ*, 28, Apr. 1931, p.317]

Three months after Judge's April letter and Memorandum:

On July 20th I had written Judge that I had taken the plunge, had arranged matters with my parents, and was sailing for New York at an early date. [*TJC*, Part 2, p.267; *TQ*, 30, July 1932, p.37]

Hargrove left London on August 24th, 1895, arrived in New York on the 30th, and found a letter from Judge awaiting him. [*TJC*, Part 2, p.268; *TQ*, 30, Oct. 1932, p.122]

Judge's letter was dated August 23rd, 1895:

Dear Boy,
When you get this, I shall probably be in Cincinnati with Buck. That will alter the tone of former letter. For if you wish you can arrange to see me there—unless I go to New York. So, better find out by wire or otherwise first. It is not far. Have no hurry.
Best love,
♃.

[*TJC*, Part 2, p.268; *TQ*, 30, Oct. 1932, p.122]

On September 2nd Judge wrote "There is no telling where I may go, at this critical point." Hargrove noted that this was in reference to "Judge's physical condition," that Judge's health had greatly deteriorated.

The letter from Judge to Hargrove, September 2nd, 1895 continues:

You had better do as I said first—don't alter my original plans—that is, work around Aryan [T.S. Branch], H.P.B., Brooklyn, Newark, Yonkers, etc., which will use up a couple of weeks or so. In the meantime, we shall have heard from each other. [*TJC*, Part 2, p.268; *TQ*, 30, Oct. 1932, p.122]

Judge told Hargrove to stay with the Griscoms, who lived in Flushing, Long Island, until about September 15th or 25th. He told him to familiarize himself with all the theosophists in the New York area, and instructed him to be careful what he said, who he could trust and who to be on his guard against. He also told him that when the time was right they would meet again and spend time together but that in the meantime they could communicate in ways other than writing. [*Fohat*, 7:2, Summer 2003, p.33]

Events Following Judge's Death

Severely ill, Judge continued to pursue rest and recuperation, yet working until the end.

> In October 1895, Mr. Judge left New York for Ashville, S.C., but finding the climate there too cold, he had gone further south to Aiken. Finding no relief, he left there January 9th, 1896, and on his way back to New York stayed two weeks with Dr. J.D. Buck in Cincinnati, and one week with Dr. Buchman in Fort Wayne. He reached New York on Feb. 3rd, much weaker than when he had left it. After a brief stay at the Lincoln Hotel on Broadway, he was moved to an apartment on the third floor of 325 West 56th Street. In spite of his alarming condition, he continued to dictate letters and make notes for future work. He would have liked to write another book on Occultism, a plan which was never realized.
>
> On March 21, 1896, W.Q. Judge passed away, sitting upright on the sofa, at about nine o'clock in the morning, in the presence of Mrs. Judge, E.T. Hargrove and an attending nurse. 'There should be calmness. Hold fast. Go slow,' were some of his last words. A brief memorial service was held at 144 Madison Avenue, New York, on the following Monday, March 23rd, at noon, and the remains were cremated the same afternoon at the Fresh Pond Crematory on Long Island. [**WQJ: *Theosophical Pioneer*, p.34; *TJC*, Part 2, p.360, 362, 365**]

During Judge's final months Hargrove, Ella (Mrs. Judge), and a nurse were the ones who looked after his every need. Visitors were few and Katherine Tingley was not among them. After the Annual Convention in Boston at the end of April 1895 Tingley was not seen nor heard from. In a letter to Albert Smythe Neresheimer stated: ". . . during Mr. Judge's *last illness* Mrs. Tingley did not, as far as I am aware, even visit Mr. Judge." [*CT*, 15:9, Jan 1934, p.311] In his "Reminiscences" he wrote "indeed I frequently wondered at her apparent indifference to his condition."

Hargrove had spent about two weeks lecturing and meeting theosophists in all the New York area Branches and at no time did he ever meet Katherine Tingley. On May 18th, 1896, in an interview with the New York *Sun* Hargrove admitted that he "had never met Mrs. Tingley before the death of Mr. Judge" and that he met her for the very first time "five or six days after his death." **[May 18, 1896]**

After being introduced to Katherine Tingley, by those who had already been influenced by her, Hargrove then gives his opinion of her qualifications for the position of Outer Head of the esoteric section.

> She is a woman of indomitable courage, of utter fearlessness; and, once believing that a thing is right she would not budge an inch if the whole country was howling at her heels. She is a woman of immense resources, with a high forehead and big brain. Furthermore I have received the most absolute proof of her occult attainment. *[The Sun* **(NY), May 18, 1896]**

Hargrove had not realized that Tingley was trained and very proficient in the use of hypnotism, which she applied to bring him on board [see Chapter 4]. Hargrove's disposition at the time: he was very naive—he only saw the good in people. This tendency at times served him well, kept him out of trouble, but it proved disastrous in his personal life. Hargrove was interested in Neresheimer's daughter Aimee (they married in January 1899), which likely compromised his clarity and made him vulnerable to influence. In late 1908 Hargrove moved back to New York City, after his divorce from Aimee, who then married Milton Smith, Neresheimer's partner in the dam project in Colorado.

Hargrove re-immersed himself more fervently into the day to day workings of The Theosophical Society ("in America" was dropped in April 1908) under the leadership of Clement A. Griscom Jr. By this time Hargrove had overcome his naiveté and realized that not everyone was always truthful. His motto in life was "He who thinks the truth spreads the truth." **[*TQ*, 7, July 1909, p.95]** (To document Hargrove's life experiences would require a project of its own.)

Another theosophist who was a member of the personnel at headquarters, 144 Madison Avenue, was John M. Pryse. Under oath in court at the Tingley vs Times-Mirror case, he stated that he "was personally associated with all the leading members" in the Theosophical Society and that he got to meet

Tingley in "1894 or 1895". "Previous to Mr. Judge's death, I simply saw her as a visitor, a member of the society." And after Judge's death, "She then obtained control of the theosophical society by that announcement which I now believe to be fraudulent." By "that announcement" he meant the announcement that Tingley was Judge's occult successor,

> That Mr. Judge had left ample papers, papers in every way appointing her as his occult successor. And that such papers would be within the year produced to the satisfaction of all members; that they were asked to accept her on that statement for a year. No such papers were ever produced. . . . and I made diligent inquiries as to her papers . . . and found no one who had ever seen them. [**Tingley vs Times-Mirror, 1438-1439, p.360**]

> . . . . the only ground for her claiming to be the successor of Mr. Judge was her own statements while in a state of trance, claiming to be the spokesman, while in trance of Mr. Judge and of Madam Blavatsky. I have frequently seen her in a trance. [1444, p.361]

> . . . . I know of my own knowledge, that Mrs. Tingley is a spiritualist in belief, and is given to going into trances as a medium. I have seen her in a trance giving forth prophecies that never come true and in every other way. She uses, or claims to use, clairvoyance in all her dealings in the Theosophical society. I am speaking from personal conversation. [1453, p.364]

When asked about Tingley's reputation among theosophists, Pryse responded:

> At the time she became Mr. Judge's successor, or claimed to be such, she was unknown to the members of the society; previous to that having been a spiritualist. . . . But of late years those who have claimed to know her intimately consider and claim her to be a fraud and in every way a bad woman. [1447-1449, pp.362-363]

Enter Katherine Tingley

First, we have to realize that Katherine Tingley was a gifted hypnotist. Of all her abilities this was her true genius. The main people who supported Tingley, and who were under her spell, were Cora Slocomb (Countess di Brazza), Emil A. Neresheimer, Joseph H. Fussell, Henry T. Patterson, Claude Falls Wright, Frank M. Pierce, and later, Clark Thurston and others. After Judge's death Ernest T. Hargrove also came under her hypnotic influence.

One thing that must be clear is that Judge never appointed Katherine Tingley to replace him in *any* capacity. It should also be clear that Ernest T. Hargrove was elected with unanimous approval to replace Judge as President of the American T.S. at the Convention in April 1896. **[Report of Proceedings, 1896, pp.18-19]** Anyone familiar with the details surrounding the last few months of Judge's life will realize the numerous indications that Judge wanted Hargrove to be the next president. But Judge, like Blavatsky, would not appoint a successor, leaving the future in the hands of those left behind. Judge's last message was delivered directly to Hargrove who had sat by the sofa watching Judge as he dozed. Hargrove explained that "the 'Rajah' suddenly came to the fore, and with his unmistakable force said, among other things: 'There should be calmness. Hold fast. Go slow'." It is quite likely that those closely involved were aware of Judge's esteem for Hargrove in regard to leadership positions.
[see Appendix H: "Life In a Borrowed Body" for details re 'the Rajah'; https://www.theosophycanada.com/files/the-judge-case-volume-ii.pdf pp.487-493]

Neresheimer, knowing that there was no evidence that Judge had appointed anyone to replace him as the Outer Head of the Esoteric Section, was instrumental in swaying the trusting members into accepting that Tingley was the chosen one.

Decisions evolved as events unfolded in the first few days following Judge's death—under the control of Tingley. Neresheimer's recollections cannot be relied upon for total accuracy, having been written many years later. However, he relates in "Some Reminiscences of William Q. Judge", that on the evening of March 24th while sorting papers and Judge's various notes in the office at 144 Madison Avenue with Hargrove and Griscom, whose assistance he had requested, he recognized the sign Judge supposedly used to designate Tingley, adding that this sign "bore in no way upon the question of leadership or successorship." He decided to bring the "memorandum book" to Tingley that evening, even though it was past nine o'clock, stating he would be back as soon as he could. Frank M. Pierce, who was living in the same house, sat in on the meeting. Neresheimer wrote that this is where Tingley "displayed the first signs of her intention to step into Mr. Judge's shoes as his 'successor'[and] assumed an air of authority which she maintained thereafter."

He returned to the office at 11:00 pm but, "having been warned by Tingley not to give any definite information" he informed Hargrove and Griscom that "I would tell them what they desired to know at a meeting, that would be called as soon as the 'Chela' had selected those who should be present."

The following morning, March 25th, he and Tingley discussed who should attend this meeting. He wrote:
> It developed that she had a decided aversion to including Mr. Hargrove and Claude Falls Wright. I insisted on the desirability of having at least Mr. Hargrove present, to which she finally consented. C.A. Griscom Jr., H.T. Patterson, Joseph H. Fussell, and James M. Pryse were added to the list.

The next day, March 26th, they all met "in a private room at the Hardware Club for luncheon. . . . I told the party that Mr. Judge had left no special instructions for the future, either by word of mouth or in his will. . . . [but] that Mr. Judge had been closely connected . . . with one who was apparently a 'Chela' of the Masters . . ." Neresheimer then invited them to a meeting at Tingley's at 8:30 that evening.

However, with the evidence presented so far (and aside from those with biases against him), it becomes clear that Hargrove was the individual closest to Judge, and that "Chela" alluded to in Judge's notes was in fact Hargrove.

In 1934 in a reply to Cyrus "Willard's Statement" that Judge never appointed Tingley, published in *The Canadian Theosophist*, Neresheimer wrote to the editor (Albert Smythe) to clarify his position.
> It is true that Mr. Judge did not appoint Mrs. Tingley as his successor, but those who did elect her as the new head were Messrs. Griscom, Hargrove, James Pryse, Fussell, Patterson and Neresheimer. **[15:10, Dec. 1934, p.311]**

At the March 27th meeting Tingley proposed a "Council of Guardians" and "to choose the personnel. . . to consist of fifty-two members chosen from among the general membership of the Society." Genevieve Griscom and Claude Falls Wright were subsequently added to said "Council". It was also at this meeting that "Tingley had insisted that her identity must remain unknown for a year to all except the 'Council of Guardians'. To all others she wished to be known only by the name of "Promise". [Reminiscences]

Neresheimer continues, wanting to correct Mr. Willard's statement that Neresheimer had hired "Mrs. Tingley to nurse Mr. Judge".
> I will ask you to kindly publish the above in your next issue, for I feel that, in common justice, such a statement [by Willard] should be retracted, so as to prevent its circulation, and, as is so often the case, further enlarged upon.

From the decisive process Tingley put into place within days of Judge's death, one can assume that she already had plans in mind to build an empire, with herself in complete control. And that is indeed what ensued.

It is also conceivable, and probable, that her plan to also become 'Leader' of the Theosophical Society in America took shape shortly after the Boston Convention in April 1895 where Judge reprimanded her. After years of studying her behaviors, especially against those she deemed to have wronged her (and the list is long), it became obvious that anyone questioning her authority in particular, suffered greatly for doing so. In the transcript of de Purucker's comments at a meeting in 1930, he mentioned that "If you didn't do just what she wanted in a certain thing, she would have her own reactions." [*Eclectic Theosophist*, **July/Aug. 1985, p.6**]

Tingley claimed to have received messages from Judge the day he died where he gave her "his wishes and intentions" and she proceeded to supposedly channel the spirit of Judge at subsequent meetings of the Committee. It was then "declared that Mr. Judge had left 'directions' for the future management of the E[soteric] S[ection], including the designation of a new 'Outer Head' . . . [as well as] the formation of a Council and an Advisory Council" whose members were responsible for the abrupt and drastic changes that followed. [***Theosophical Movement* 1875-1950; p.265**]

Neresheimer indicated in his "Reminiscences" that after March 24th and "assuming an air of authority which she maintained thereafter," at the meeting held on the 27th, at her home once again, Tingley "almost peremptorily assumed . . . direction of the Esoteric Section" but refused the Presidency.

Tingley had years of experience doing hypnotism and séances; it was just a matter of convincing the remaining members of the Committee. The extent of the secrecy is stressed by Greenwalt when writing about Neresheimer's letter to Alice Cleather:

> The secrecy surrounding the meetings where this was accomplished is emphasized in the letter by the use of a symbol ≠ to designate Katherine Tingley, although he occasionally referred to her as Purple, because of her fondness for the color. [*California Utopia: Point Loma: 1897-1942*, p.16]

This is how Neresheimer described events in his March 31st, 1896 letter to Cleather:

> The day after he [Judge] died he sent for me through ≠ with whom he made me acquainted in 1894. . . . Next day early I called, could not connect with him, all I could get through ≠ was 'to go slow, immensely slow.' He had something to say before the incineration. He came again at 12 m[idnight] next day but said nothing of any account. ≠ was not conscious.
>
> Two days afterward I was sent for in the evening. We (Griscom, E.T.H. [Ernest T. Hargrove] and myself) had been engaged all along night after night sorting papers and things; I went, made notes of what he wished me to say to the others, which was mostly retailing my entire connection, introduction by him to ≠, all that transpired about the arrangement for the Convention in 1895, program of which was furnished me by ≠ and which was carried out. This I did to the (skeptical) audience consisting of E.T.H., Patterson, James Pryse, Griscom, Fussell (who were all designated to hear it) and I also transmitted the appointment for all of us to meet at Purple's [Mrs Tingley] same evening at 7:45 p.m.
>
> The Rajah [Judge] commenced to talk almost immediately through ≠, suggesting to select the Outer-Head and the Council. First change of feeling occurred at recognition of the Rajah. Skepticism was carried to the winds, doubts vanished, and spontaneity prevailed. . . . I tell you the thing was most wonderful

and impressive. [**For more information see** *TJC*, **Part 2, p.401;** *California Utopia: Point Loma: 1897-1942*, **pp.16-17.**]

This was not a meeting; it was a séance. It occurred on March 27th, 1896 at Countess di Brazza's residence where Tingley also resided, mere days after Judge's death. Any student of the original theosophical teaching knows, as emphasized by Blavatsky and Judge, that summoning the true spirit of a deceased person, such as Judge, is complete nonsense. All messages supposedly received by Tingley from Judge were bogus. Nevertheless, men who should have known better were swayed, seemingly unquestioningly.

It is important to point out that in his article "A Stone of the Foundation" Henry Bedinger Mitchell detailed how Judge spent weeks at a time at the residence of Clement and Genevieve Griscom in Flushing, Long Island, and that "the preliminary arrangements for the convention in Boston in April 1895 where 'the split' occurred were made at the Griscom home." [*TQ*, **17, July 1919, pp.3-21**] Tingley's claim of having been instrumental in the outcome of the Convention of 1895 is a claim without credible evidence.

A plausible explanation for the acquiescence of those present at the March 27th meeting is if they were under the influence of hypnotism. It also explains the bizarre incidents that happened and continued to happen long after Tingley took over. One incident in particular played a defining role in Tingley's takeover. At this meeting, in Tingley's home, while discussing the positions of president and outer head, Hargrove, who had been sitting at Tingley's right, suddenly could not speak, grew rigid, and then in "stentorian tones" said "Make up your minds, and go through with it." [**Reminiscences**] This incident demonstrated her ability as a hypnotist and for years coloured Hargrove's actions and those of the others in attendance.

At a meeting of the Aryan T.S. in October 1892, John M. Pryse and W.Q. Judge presented a talk about the astral body. Judge explained what happens to it under hypnosis.

> When the person is hypnotized the astral body is temporarily disconnected from the physical one, but this is done without the consent of the inner man, and he himself is not acquainted with his own powers, the astral body is, as it were, drunk, and therefore is unable to impress the physical one with the facts occurring and cannot resist suggestion. [*Brooklyn Times Union*, **Oct. 8, 1892**]

Tingley was an accomplished hypnotist; Judge's words explain Hargrove's experience, and the passive acquiescence of the others. For some the hypnotic effect was lost over time as one by one they eventually realized how they had been taken in.

A year or so later, on September 13th, 1897, Hargrove resigned as President of T.S. in America. On January 20th, 1898, E.A. Neresheimer, Joseph H. Fussell, H.T. Patterson and James M. Pryse swore an Affidavit in the presence of a Notary Public in New York pertaining to possible influence the above incident had in the selection of Tingley as Outer Head:

> We, the undersigned, who were present at the first Council Meeting held after Mr. Judge's death, on March 27th, 7.45 p.m., at Mrs. Tingley's house, 373 West End Avenue, hereby declare that we did not depend upon Mr. Hargrove's statements or actions in our acceptance of Mrs. Tingley as Outer Head of the E.S.T., but that the position taken by each of us, was due to the direct personal knowledge of each irrespective of all he—Mr. Hargrove—said or did. [*The Search Light*, Vol.1, p.30, Apr. 1898; *O.E. Library Critic*, Vol.22, Oct. 1922, p.4]

It is a well known fact that Judge hated ambiguity, therefore

> It should be self-evident that if Mr. Judge had had anything to do with selecting his alleged successor, he would not have left the students dependent upon "messages," either before or after his death, which they would have no means of verifying, nor upon the verbal say-so of any, but would have left clear, indisputable evidence, in his own physical handwriting of his own opinion and advice." [*TJC*, Part 2, p.386; *The Theosophical Movement 1875-1925*, pp.667-668)]

In 1906 a reporter for *The Washington Post* rather sarcastically summarized Tingley's takeover:

> From spiritualism Mrs. Tingley turned to theosophy, which was then attracting much attention. She made the acquaintance of William Q. Judge, who was the boss of the theosophists, and she succeeded in impressing him with her powers as a hypnotist. When he died several fragmentary references to her were found among his writings. She pieced them together, and upon them

based the claim that she was the reincarnation of Mme. Blavatsky, and had been chosen the successor of Mr. Judge. **[July 6, 1906]**

An article titled "An Interview With Mrs. Alice L. Cleather" in *The Lamp*, quotes the following:
> "Have you any evidence that Mr. Judge appointed a successor?"
> "No. I never saw any of the documents said to exist."
> "You accepted the 'Leader' then, simply on faith?"
> "Entirely, and was utterly disappointed in the result. So far as I have been able to observe from pretty close association she showed no real knowledge of the esoteric philosophy, and constantly violated the occult teaching." **[*The Lamp*, 3:12 (36), Feb. 1900, p.208]**

When asked "Did you hear the 'Leader' depreciate H.P.B?" Cleather responded "Yes, repeatedly." **[p.208]**

And so it begins . . . .

The month of May was truly a whirlwind of activities in the Theosophical Society. One event, that can only be classified as bizarre, was the strange performance where Claude Falls Wright and Catherine Leoline Leonard were married May 3rd, 1896 in a mystic rite by the "Great Unknown", as Tingley was referred to in newspapers.

The *New York Herald* wrote about the ceremony:
> On the platform, sat the fourteen persons of the inner council of the 'Blank.' 'Blank' stands for the occult organization within the Theosophical Society, the name of which is known only to the few. It is never spoken above a whisper. These persons, resplendent in regalia of purple, ornamented with a silver check, were arranged in a semicircle. The front of the stage was held by the adept in occultism, otherwise known as 'He-Who-Must-Be-Obeyed.' The readers of the *Herald* will remember that when the Theosophical Convention met here in the latter part of last month it was officially declared that William Q. Judge had, before his death, named his occult successor, who was not to be known to the world until a year thereafter.

This adept was on the platform, yet he was so closely veiled that no one was able to distinguish his features. He wore a long purple robe, which reached to his feet. A full view of him was cut off by a paper maché stump, covered with Grand street artificial leaves. It was symbolical of the tree of life. On the right of 'He-Who-Must-Be-Obeyed' sat Ernest T. Hargrove, president of the society, and on the left the impetuous bridegroom, Mr. White [Wright] was becomingly attired in a black suit and a patient smile.

Behind the inner circle were thirty persons who are not so proficient in mysticism as the inner circle. They were called the Outer Guard. Besides these there were 150 invited guests sitting on the benches. They were all Theosophists. **[May 4, 1896]**

[See Appendix F: Richard Dean Arden Wade (Ingalese)]

There had been much speculation as to who this "Great Unknown" was. Some reporters even considered Nikola Tesla. After the ceremony a reporter from the *New York Herald* followed the "Great Unknown" to her residence and discovered:

> The identity of the mysterious Mahatma whose every word and wish are henceforth, to dominate the Theosophical Society of America, that hitherto invisible personage who has simply figured as "He-Who-Must-Be-Obeyed," is revealed by the HERALD this morning.
>
> The veil of obscurity pulled aside, and behold the conical cap of Thibet wool such as Mahatmas are usually supposed to wear—being true adepts in occultism—is found to be fitted to a woman's head. It is no longer "He" that is to be obeyed, but, like unto the everyday life in things earthy, the Theosophist's word of command and law will fall from a woman's lips. A "She" will reign in the kingdom of the mysteries.
>
> The Mahatma of the American Society is not from Asia, as has been conjectured, but from Massachusetts. **[May 17, 1896]**

THE HOME OF THE MAHATMA.

THE RESIDENCE OF KATHERINE A. TINGLEY.

[*The New Century*, 1:19, 20, February 18, 1898, pp.2, 6]

[The editor, Katherine Tingley stated: "It may further interest our readers to know that at this house Mr. Judge did some of his most important work for the Movement during the last few years of his life, and also, that here the Council first met with his Successor after his death." The is no corroborating evidence to support her statements.

This photograph is actually of the di Brazza residence. The Tingleys, Pierce and Fussell also lived there and did not pay rent, thanks to the generosity of the Countess. However, Tingley never mentioned Countess di Brazza's name.]

[Riverside Drive and the Hudson River are in the background.]

That the identity of the "Great Unknown" was to be kept secret for a year was Tingley's idea, but it was justified by asserting a different reason. Greenwalt wrote:
> The anonymity of the Outer Head was explained as a stratagem to shield that person from 'the inevitable slander and persecution' which had fallen upon previous holders of the office, Madame Blavatsky and Judge. [*California Utopia: Point Loma: 1897-1942*, **p.17**]

Tingley had a questionable reputation and did not want her history uncovered; it was actually a strategy to cover her past.

Judge died on March 21st, 1896. The following day the *Boston Daily Globe* wrote that
> The American headquarters of the society are at Aryan hall, 144 Madison Av.... The present secretary of the society, Claude Falls Wright, will probably act as its chief until the annual convention, to be held in Chicago next month. **[Mar. 22, 1896]**

However, a few weeks before her identity was revealed and within days of the event, "She-Who-Must-Be-Obeyed" moved the location for the Convention from Chicago to New York. On April 19th, 1896 the *Boston Daily Globe* carried the headline:
> Ordered by an Unknown.
> Theosophical Society Will Meet in New York.
> Place Was Changed at the Behest of Mysterious Adept.

The article which followed mentioned that the principal session would be held at Madison Square Gardens and after the convention "a reception will be given in the evening at 144 Madison av. where the society has a $50,000 headquarters."

A Crusade to Save Humanity

While still "the great unknown" Tingley arbitrarily concocted plans for a world tour—a Crusade, supposedly "directed by the Master" for which "the members were to supply the material necessary in order to complete the plan." Then within weeks of the convention (held April 26-27, 1896), and a few days prior to her identity being revealed to the public by the *Herald* on the 17th, on May 14th a "strictly private and confidential" circular titled "An Urgent Appeal" was sent to E.S.T. members asking for money to finance the

Crusade. It included a message from Tingley asking for funding, dated May 12th, signed P_____, Outer Head of the E.S.T.:

> Today the needs of humanity are embodied in one great *call:* "O God, my God, is there no help for us?" All people should heed the call of the Master and help to belt the world within the compass of the "cable tow" of the crusaders, for in their force is a quality of the "golden promise"—the Light of the Lodge. It will radiate throughout the world, and with the aid of the widow's mite will make perfect the Master's plan. **[pp.1, 3]**

"Promise" (P_____) was the name "the great unknown" wanted as her secret identity until she was to be revealed one year later.

On May 17th a seven-page circular glorifying Tingley titled "An Occultist's Life", issued under Hargrove's name, greatly influenced financial support for the Crusade. The author(s) of *The Theosophical Movement 1875-1925* described it as a "gem of inanity from the new 'Outer Head'":

> In prefacing this remarkable contribution Mr. Hargrove assured the members that it was sent out "unknown to the O[uter] H[ead]," and that the members "should use great discrimination in giving out the facts it contains." Those "facts" are unaccompanied by names, dates, verifiable references of any kind, and from first to last are such as could only have emanated from "Promise" herself. **[pp.672, 673]**

Great discrimination was indeed required—to keep the fabrications in the circular under wraps and not brought to the awareness of those who could counter the so-called "facts". A quick examination of a few examples is in order. One concerns Tingley's second husband, George W. Parent:

> She was at last allowed by the Master to separate herself from her husband and to return to her father's home. Three months later her husband died in the house of his mistress. **[p.4]**

George and Katherine married in 1871, and at the time, she was still married to her first husband, Richard Cook. The Parents separated officially in 1887 but not because of another woman; she married Philo Tingley in April 1888. The supposed 'mistress' was actually the landlady of the building where George lived. [See the section titled **Katherine's Second Marriage and Her Adopted Son** for details]

A second example: "Mr. Judge . . . told me at Aiken in 1895 . . . ." **[p.6]** Actually, Hargrove was with Judge in Aiken for two weeks in late 1895 **[*Theosophy*, 11:2, May 1896, p.34]** and he makes no mention of Tingley having been there. In fact Hargrove states that the first time he met Tingley was five or six days after Judge's death. It becomes questionable whether Hargrove even wrote this article; it is highly unlikely that he would have been familiar with the 'facts', embellished as most of them were presented.

It was also claimed that:
> "Promise" has suffered as very few have suffered. . . . "Promise" reached Theosophy by degrees, and in the process of reaching it underwent a training and preparation even more rigid and comprehensive than that experienced by either H.P.B. or W.Q.J. Always guided by the Master, every event in her life had a meaning and a purpose . . . . **[pp.6-7]**

Tingley's biography does not lend itself to this grandiose evaluation.

"An Occultist's Life" ends with the following words:
> Let us all bear this warning in mind: "Do not let us in any way throw the slightest obstacle in the path of our chosen leader. If we do, we shall regret it. **[p.7]**

Those words proved both foreboding and accurate.

The Crusade was not mentioned in the Report of the Second Annual Convention T.S.A. held in New York, April 26-27, 1896, yet "An Urgent Appeal" to the general membership was included in the April 1896 issue of *The Theosophical Forum: New Series*:
> The members in America now have the opportunity to show their loyalty to the Cause, and to the Masters, by carrying out the wishes of the Rajah and H.P.B. . . . Those of us who cannot take a direct part in the crusade have most vital work to do in providing the necessary funds to carry it on. A most urgent appeal is therefore sent out for help to defray the expenses of this trip to Europe and other parts of the world. The crusade will last till March, 1897. A very large amount of money will therefore be needed. **[1:12, p.191]**

An interview in New York on May 31st, 1896, appeared in the *Boston Daily Globe*. Excerpts include:

> The Theosophical crusade which is to arouse the whole world to the consciousness of the existence of the "Lost Mysteries of Antiquity," and aid in their restoration, is to start from Boston. . . . "[W]e will hold a big public meeting in that city on the evening of Sunday, June 7 in some large hall in that city. . . . This will be the only meeting outside of New York, where we shall hold one June 12, and the next day we shall embark for Europe." [*Boston Daily Globe*, **June 1, 1896**]

The Crusaders sailed from New York, June 13th, 1896, arrived back on U.S. soil in San Francisco on February 11th, 1897, made their way through the United States and Canada, and returned to point of departure, New York, on April 4th, 1897.

Who Visited Cheiro?

An interesting but baffling story that also occurred in May 1896 is the supposed visit to Cheiro, the famous palmist, living at 422, 5th Ave., New York City at the time. According to his account William Q. Judge and Katherine A. Tingley visited him one afternoon. Cheiro had consulted Blavatsky in March 1889 and Annie Besant in July 1894. According to his account Judge and Tingley visited him on May 30th, 1896 and she left him her dated and signed hand impression. How could a visit by Judge be possible when he had died two months earlier, on March 21st, 1896? This is an example of another questionable account.

Cheiro described him as "the heavily built man", which Judge was not; he was frail and thin. Also after returning to New York City on February 3rd, 1896 Judge never went anywhere. Assuming, the date on the hand impression is correct, who was the man impersonating Judge during this visit? [*Mysteries and Romances of the World's Greatest Occultists*, **pp.185-187**] Assuming the year to be incorrect, this visit could not have happened May 30th, 1895 either because Judge went to stay with Dr. Buck in Cincinnati on May 20th and was there for well over a month. Cheiro's story appears to be totally bogus. Even more troubling, if this account is partly true, is that Tingley could have brought an imposter with her to see Cheiro.

Where's Flossie?

Another topic of interest to the newspapers at that time was the confusion surrounding the whereabouts of Flossie, the young girl who had been in Tingley's care. Mystery and suspicion surrounding the disappearance of Flossie continued to plague Tingley and became a possible obstacle to the June 13th, 1896 departure of the Crusaders on their world tour.

Katherine was married to her second husband, George W. Parent, when she "begged" Richard Cook, her first husband, to have his children live with her. He agreed to her taking them but did not consent to adoption. Florence (Flossie) remained in Tingley's care until her father took her back in November 1895 upon learning that she was not going to school and was basically treated as a maid in the Tingley household. The *Chicago Daily Tribune* later had a field day with this story.

> Theosophists, who are supposed to communicate with each other by means of their astral bodies, are unable to locate Flossie Tingley, the adopted daughter of Joseph and Katherine A. Tingley, the latter of whom is the "great unknown," who succeeded William Q. Judge as leader of the Theosophical Society at his death. Mystery surrounds the vanishing of Flossie last May, and to skeptics it is more mysterious that communication in the astral way has not been had with her and her father by adoption long ago. Equally strange is the fact that $10 reward has been offered for information that would lead to her discovery. But this information is lacking. The Mahatmas are all puzzled and don't know what to do. **[Nov. 3, 1896]**

It turned out that the reward had been posted by Annie Besant. Tingley would not explain what happened with Flossie. There was speculation that Flossie had been placed in a convent or a mental institution, and claims that Tingley experimented with hypnosis on Flossie which had made her anxious.

The night before the Crusaders left New York City, President Hargrove let it be known at a public meeting in Madison Square Garden Theatre "that there were in New York six persons who were sworn enemies of the society" and that these persons would bring charges against them.

> They will attempt to have warrants served . . . on the crusaders directly after the meeting this evening, in order to detain them as long as possible. . . . But we are fully prepared for them . . . If this child's play of fake arrests is attempted we will take out warrants on the charge of perjury and attempt to blackmail. We do not want revenge, but rather than pay five cents of blackmail we will stay and fight it out if it takes all summer. [*New York Herald*, **June 12, 1896;** *New York Times*, **June 12, 1896**]

Was this public declaration of an attempt "to prevent the departure of the crusaders for Europe" merely a ploy to divert attention from an attempt to serve Tingley with a warrant to prevent *her* from leaving the country? Any other individual could have simply stayed home. The New York Society for the Prevention of Cruelty to Children, sometimes called the Gerry Society after a co-founder, may have been investigating the supposed mysterious disappearance of Flossie. The article continues:

> What the nature of the charges would be Mr. Hargrove was unable to say, as no member of the cult could possibly be charged with having committed any wrong. [*New York Herald*, **June 12, 1896**]

Hargrove claimed that the threat came from "personal enemies of prominent members." [*New York Tribune* **June 12, 1896**] The most prominent was Katherine Tingley. 'Enemies' was a perpetual theme with Tingley. Research indicates that the supposed warrant, which could have been for any number of reasons, was never served. There seems to be more to this story.

The Enthusiastic Send-Off

The following morning, Saturday June 13th, members and friends gathered at the dock to see the Crusaders off. It was reported in *Theosophy* that:

> The gathering of friends of the party at the dock was very large and the "send-off" extremely enthusiastic. Just as the steamer was about to start, the well-wishers of the Crusade came together in a compact square on the platform at the end of the dock, and as the ship backed out there was loud cheering and great waving of handkerchiefs, to which of course the Crusaders responded. [**11:5, Aug. 1896, p.130**]

Among those gathered was Dr. Alfred A. Walton (1853-1920), a respected surgeon in New York City. He attended the Second Annual Convention held

April 26-27, 1896 where the request was launched for donations toward the projected construction costs of $15,000 to $20,000 for the School for Revival of Lost Mysteries. When the list of donors was announced, Dr. Walton, who was introduced as "a new member of the Society," had subscribed $1000, the largest amount. **[Report of Proceedings, p.34]**

In addition to his medical career, Dr. Walton was proprietor of the Oxygen Gas Works (which produced oxygen and nitrogen gas) [*The Evening World*, **Mar. 27, 1889**], was reasonably wealthy, and separated from his wife. Some of his early years were spent in Newburyport; he was aware of Tingley's past. An incident that happened the morning of the Crusaders' departure was recounted by Edward Parker, who had investigated Tingley sometime after meeting her in 1897.

> He had learned from Dr. Walton of New York City that the doctor's belief in Mrs. Tingley had been shattered in the ecstasy of an affectionate farewell at the wharf when Mrs. Tingley and her party were starting on a tour of the world. **[*Omaha Daily Bee*, July 15, 1906]**

Dr. Walton was mentioned in an article in the *New York Tribune* as having attended a lecture by Annie Besant at Chickering Hall on April 4th, 1897. **[Apr. 5, 1897]** It seems that he was interested in Theosophy but not in being associated with Tingley. Dr. Walton joined Griscom and Hargrove in the regenerated Theosophical Society in America.

The Crusade Sets Sail

The Crusaders sailed from New York on the American Line *S.S. Paris* at 10 o'clock Saturday morning, June 13th, 1896. They arrived in San Francisco from their eight-month journey on February 11th, 1897 on board the steamer *S.S. Alameda*. [*New York Times*, **Feb. 12, 1897**]

The Crusaders who boarded ship for the world tour consisted of:
- Katherine Tingley, the new Outer Head of the Esoteric School.
- Ernest T. Hargrove, duly elected President of The Theosophical Society in America, Europe, Ireland and Australia; lecturer.
- Claude Falls Wright, President of the Aryan T.S. He was Secretary to the late H.P. Blavatsky and W.Q. Judge. He loved to work and "he has had a most varied experience of the work in the movement, both in the office

and in the lecture-field". *[Theosophy,* **11:8, Nov. 1896, p.228]** He authored reports and wrote letters as "Secretary to K.A. Tingley."
- Leoline Leonard Wright, recently married to Claude; invented the "Brotherhood suppers" in Boston; invaluable assistant to Tingley, basically her maid.
- Henry Turner Patterson, devoted theosophist and rich industrialist; President of the Brooklyn Theosophical Society. His task was shepherding the trunks and hand-baggage.
- Philo B. Tingley, husband of Katherine, a non-member of the TS, said that "he doesn't believe in theosophy himself". *[Independence Daily Reporter,* **KS, June 20, 1896.]** He just wanted to see England and France and returned to New York August 25th, 1896, on the *S.S. New York.* **[Customs List of Passengers, Ancestry]**
- Frank M. Pierce, close friend of Katherine; non-member of the T.S.; acting as the representative of the School for the Revival of the Lost Mysteries of Antiquity; tagged along for a free trip.

A few others joined along the way and paid their own expenses:
- Alice Leighton Cleather, experienced lecturer from England; joined the Crusade September 20th, 1896 in Rome.
- Rev. Walter Williams, of the British Army; joined the Crusade in Cairo.
    - Cleather and Williams were appointed European Delegates on the Crusade at the Convention of The T.S. in Europe, held August 2-3, 1896 in Dublin, Ireland. *[Theosophy,* **11:6, Sep. 1896, p.167]**

Others joined them briefly:
- Emil August Neresheimer and his son Fred, Joseph H. Fussell, Dr. Walton, Dr. Lorin Wood and Mrs. Wood of Rhode Island, met the Crusaders on July 31st, 1896 in Dublin, Ireland. *[Theosophy,* **11:6, Sep. 1896, p.167]**
    - Neresheimer and Fussell spent time with the Crusaders before returning to New York. While there Neresheimer claims he was surprised to hear Tingley refer to herself as "Leader." **[Reminiscences]** By August it was reported that she held "the position of corresponding secretary, which was once the post occupied by Mme. Blavatsky, and which is one of the most important in the society." *[The San Francisco Call,* **Aug. 30, 1896;** *Theosophy,* **11:6, Sep. 1896, p.192]**
    - Dr. & Mrs. Wood travelled with the Crusaders to Paris on August 13th then sailed on the *S.S. New York* from Southampton, England and arrived in New York on August 25th, 1896, along with Philo Tingley.

[Customs List of Passengers, Ancestry] Dr. Wood met the Crusaders when they sailed into San Francisco on February 11th, 1897 and joined them for the remainder of the tour.

- Myron H. Phelps, a New York lawyer, member of the Aryan Branch since 1890, travelled with the Crusaders as far as London. At the time of "The Judge Case" Phelps gave his written legal opinion, supporting W.Q.J.'s, that the President and Vice-President "could only be tried as such by such Committee for official misconduct." [*Neutrality of the T.S. An Enquiry*, 1894, p.9] Phelps did not follow Tingley; he joined the re-formed T.S. in America, the Griscom/Hargrove group, in 1898.

Among the passengers on the *SS Paris* en route to Europe was a journalist with the New York *World*. Her article, "Miss Gilder's Trip", included the following observations of the theosophists on board:

> The lady crusaders wear a uniform of dark blue silk, when they do not wear their bath robes. The men are distinguished by the large signet rings they wear on the forefingers of their right hands. Mr. Hargrove, the President, seems to be the youngest of the party. He is thin, smooth-shaven face, and stands some six feet three inches in his steamer shoes. The other men are bearded or mustached, or both, as the case may be. [July 5, 1896]

The Crusaders arrived in Southampton on June 21st and were welcomed by Dr. Archibald Keightley who travelled with them to London. The report dated July 4th, 1896 in *Theosophy* presented glowing accounts of events at their various stops in England. Included is an item by Herbert Crooke who wrote that the meeting in Liverpool "at once stamps the undertaking as one of a noble and philanthropic purpose." [*Theosophy*, 11:5, Aug. 1896, pp.131-134] However *Pall Mall Gazette*'s assessment of the July 3rd meeting in London reported: "When all was over, the *raison d'être* of the crusade, and indeed of Theosophy itself, was still obscure." [July 4, 1896] The New York *Sun* reported:

> The first London meeting, July 3, at the Queen's Hall last night was a dull affair, and the attendance was small. Not one of the speakers developed a spark of enthusiasm, and somehow the impression prevailed that the group of so-call Propagandists have started on a pleasure trip round the world, of course at their own expense, with theosophy as a convenient *raison d'être*. [July 5, 1896]

Events in India

The Crusaders progressed through various countries in Europe and left Italy for Bombay on October 18th, 1896, arriving on October 25th. They were in India until early December.

Tingley claimed that she received "an invitation to meet a great teacher" while "on my first tour through Egypt and India." It is in late November 1896 that an excursion to Darjeeling is claimed to have occurred. Tingley wrote that early one morning before sunrise she "had a call from the teacher's chela, who brought four servants and a special escort with their open palanquin" and carried her up a mountain where she reached the teacher, who was "leaning against a tree with an English jackknife in his hand" whittling a piece of wood. [*The Gods Await*, 1992 ed., p.123; *Sunrise*, April/May 1998, p.126]

In her "Preliminary Report" which appeared in *The Grail* and then reprinted in two issues of *Theosophy*, Tingley wrote:
> Before leaving Calcutta some members of the Crusade went on a tour of inspection, and for other reasons, to Darjeeling, a small town on the borders of Bhutan and Sikkhim. [11:12, Mar. 1897, p.381; 12:7, Oct. 1897, p.371]

At the time, Darjeeling was actually described as a small, scattered village.

In his report in "Screen of Time" in the February 1897 issue of *Theosophy* Ernest Hargrove wrote that the last meeting held in Benares was on November 23rd, then
> On the 25th those members of the party who had not gone on to Calcutta ahead, started on their way there. They held a meeting on the night of their arrival ... another on Sunday the 29th, conducted by those members of the party who did not go with Mrs. Tingley to Darjeeling—a small town not far from Kinchinjunga, one of the Himalayan peaks.

> On the afternoon of the 30th the Crusaders left Calcutta on board the British India S.S. "Golconda" for Madras .... [11:11, Feb. 1897, p.324]

It's interesting to note that Tingley only published her account of "My First Meeting with H.P. Blavatsky's Teacher" thirty years later, in 1926 in her book *The Gods Await*. Most of the individuals who had accompanied her on the Crusade had predeceased her; their version of events could neither confirm nor contradict her story. Reaching Darjeeling was challenging and would have involved a multiple days' journey.

The September 1929 issue of *The Theosophical Path* includes a photo with the statement "Katherine Tingley . . . in the court-yard of the hotel at Darjiling, India" and was republished in the April/May 1998 issue of *Sunrise* as "Katherine Tingley in Darjeeling, India, 1896." The scene is in front of a structure with multiple, large stone pillars. Research to establish which building is depicted in the photograph resulted in finding that none with this type of construction can be found in Darjeeling, then or now. Buildings in the region are made of wood. The oldest hotel, now regarded as a heritage building, was erected in 1887 as a manor house, and was remodelled as a hotel in 1965. It does not include stone pillars. [*Theosophical Path*, 36:9, Sep.1929, p.403; *Sunrise*, p.126] Monasteries in the region of Darjeeling were also researched; they are built of wood. The most famous is the Gelukpa sect monastery a few kilometers away in Ghum (Ghoom), constructed in 1850, which houses a fifteen-foot statue of Maitreya Buddha.

An interview with Alice Cleather that appeared in *The Lamp* in 1900 included the following response to "What about India? Did you meet any Chelas there?"

> At Benares, a 'little' Hindu appeared. He was, I believe, a high caste Brahmin. The 'Leader' told us he was a chela who had come to arrange for her and another to see M____ at Darjeeling. I do not remember her referring to him again until this last autumn in Sweden, when she said that both she and the 'other' had discovered him to be a fraud. [*The Lamp*, 3:12 (36), Feb. 1900, p.207]

Cleather added that the general conduct of the Crusade made her want to resign then but that she was "prevailed upon to remain." She claimed that "During the recent 'American Crusade' I was subjected to a mental and moral inquisition of the worst kind." [p.206]

It seems doubtful that "My First Meeting with H.P. Blavatsky's Teacher" ever happened. However, an additional caption under the photo in *The Theosophical Path* states:

> Many of Katherine Tingley's friends and followers have often heard her describe with illuminating wealth of detail the very interesting interview that occurred during this meeting in 1896. **[p.403]**

KATHERINE TINGLEY, THE THEOSOPHICAL LEADER AND TEACHER, IN THE COURT-YARD OF THE HOTEL AT DARJILING, INDIA, JUST BEFORE LEAVING IN THE EARLY MORNING FOR A MEETING WITH ONE OF THE GREAT TEACHERS WHO FOUNDED THE THEOSOPHICAL MOVEMENT IN MODERN TIMES

[*The Theosophical Path*, 36:9, September 1929, p.403]

Chapter Three

The Cascade of Realizations

Experiences and observations of certain events during the world tour altered the perception of some Crusaders about Katherine Tingley. Departures from the ranks soon after their return evidenced that something had changed.

The Crusaders sailed into San Francisco on February 11th, 1897 and arrived back in New York on April 4th. Their return to New York was a major event in the media. *The New York Tribune* issue of Monday April 5th featured a lengthy article detailing the celebration.

RETURN OF THE CRUSADE
HEARTY WELCOME FOR THE THEOSOPHISTS.
PUBLIC RECEPTION FOR MEMBERS OF MRS. TINGLEY'S PARTY —
THEY TELL OF THEIR SUCCESS IN THE MANY COUNTRIES WHICH
THEY HAVE VISITED IN THE LAST TEN MONTHS.

> The Theosophical crusaders, who for nearly ten months have been on a tour of the earth, carrying into many countries the principles of Theosophy, returned to New York last night. On June 13 last they departed from the Madison Square Garden Concert Hall upon their mission, and last night in the same place the end of their journeyings was marked by an enthusiastic public reception. Altogether, the crusaders have travelled over forty thousand miles, and have visited Great Britain, Holland, France, Germany, Austria, Italy, Switzerland, Greece, Egypt, India, Australia, New-Zealand, Samoa and Canada. . . . [*New York Tribune*, **Apr. 5, 1897**]

The Crusaders who arrived in America were: Ernest T. Hargrove, President; Mr. & Mrs. Claude Falls Wright, Mrs. Alice M.[L.] Cleather, of England; Henry Turner Patterson, president of the Brooklyn Theosophical Society; Rev. W. Williams, of the British Army; Frank M. Pierce, of New York, and Dr. Lorin F. Woods, of Providence, R.I. [*New York Tribune*, **Apr. 5, 1897**] Also on board was Osmar Falls Wright, born at sea on January 26th, 1897, not far from the Island of Samoa.

The Crusaders were greeted in Albany by Mr. & Mrs. E.A. Neresheimer, Mr. & Mrs. A.H. Spencer, Dr. & Mrs. J.D. Buck of Cincinnati, Charles & Vera Johnston, Basil Crump of London, Herbert Crooke, vice-president of the European T.S., Joseph H. Fussell, Constance Hargrove (Ernest's sister), Mrs. E.C. Mayer, president of the Lotus Circle, and Philo B. Tingley. They took a train to New York and arrived at Grand Central Station where they were greeted by another fifty or so theosophists. They all proceeded to Madison Square Garden Concert Hall where the public celebration was held.

The *Tribune* article continued:
> In addition to the crusaders . . . there were also on the platform Archibald Keightley, president of the Theosophical Society in England, and Mrs. Keightley, Countess di Brazza, George D. Ayers, president of the Boston branch; Robert Crosbie, Barcham Harding, Clark Thurston, president of the Providence branch, and M.S. Wadham, secretary of the New-Haven branch. As the crusaders were escorted to their seats they were received with a prolonged outburst of applause.[**Apr. 5, 1897**]

Mrs. Tingley was to give an address but was unable to speak "in consequence of the demands that have been made" on her voice recently and "Mr. and Mrs. Claude Falls Wright were absent through indisposition. . . . Dr. J.D. Buck, whose name is prominently known in theosophical circles all over the country, presided." [*New York Tribune*, **Apr. 5, 1897**] Clement A. Griscom, Jr., who was a member of the Crusade Committee T.S.A., and Genevieve Griscom were also absent.

Countess Cora di Brazza may have wondered why Claude Falls Wright, an integral member of the T.S. in New York and frequent visitor at the Tingley's, was absent from the stage and did not participate in the celebrated return of the Crusaders. She likely arranged for him to visit at her residence, 373 West End Avenue. Wright must have informed her he was going to resign all his offices and that he wanted nothing more to do with Tingley; that he realized he had been badly influenced by her, and come to the conclusion that she was a fraud. Wright's story apparently resonated with di Brazza because she too immediately withdrew her support for Tingley.

Although she had never joined the theosophical society she was a sincere believer and was also now extremely concerned about the leadership it was under. The reason circulating at the time was that Wright was dissatisfied with the conduct of the affairs of the T.S. in America headed by Katherine A. Tingley. However there was more to the story, details which led him to resign shortly after his return from the world tour and before the April 25-26, 1897 convention.

The Crusaders were in Madras from November 30th to December 6th, 1896. It was there that Claude Falls Wright witnessed an incident that led to his complete dissociation from Tingley. Newspaper articles one year later, while noting the resignations of Archibald Keightley, "president of the society in Great Britain" and Ernest Hargrove, president of the society in America, included details of what had led to Wright's sudden disappearance upon the return of the Crusaders from the world tour.

> One of the Tingley lost mysteries . . . is the once ubiquitous and devoted Claude Falls Wright . . . He has, it is said, disappeared utterly . . . It was a spurious chela in India that filled Mr. Wright's soul with pangs and impelled him to remove and occlude himself. He told a friend of his awful experience when he returned from the great crusade which Mrs. Tingley led around the world. It was at a séance given for the benefit of anxious novices in the top story of a hotel at Madras. Mrs. Tingley . . . had announced that a message would be received from one of the mahatmas. A door opened and there materialized a chela (disciple or messenger of a mahatma) and he, or it, tendered a note to Mrs. Tingley. Unfortunately for his peace of mind, which he has ever guarded carefully, Mr. Wright recognized in the chela a scissors grinder he had seen turning his wheel on the street in the afternoon. When Mrs. Tingley asked Mr. Wright to read the mahatma's message which the chela had brought, he declined to do so. Mr. Hargrove offered to read it and Mrs. Tingley handed it to him. Mr. Wright then . . . looked over Mr. Hargrove's shoulder and recognized in the message the handwriting of Mr. Hargrove. This was too much for C.F.W., veteran as he was and faithful Ganymede as he had been to Blavatsky and Judge. He determined to quit. . . . **[*The Sun* (NY), Dec. 28, 1897; *The Evening Journal*, Wilmington, DE; *Trenton Evening Times*, (NJ), Dec. 29, 1897]**

On numerous occasions during the world tour some individuals, which usually included Wright, were sent on various excursions to other locations, either in advance to make arrangements or to represent the Crusaders at an event. Neresheimer wrote in his "Reminiscences" that Tingley had a noted aversion to Wright and refused to include him in her group of selected individuals following Judge's death. It seems she did not want him present at the initial stages of her taking over the society. Distancing him during the Crusade may have had a two-fold result, one that led Wright to be less subservient to Tingley's control.

Tingley was quite ill and isolated herself during the journey to Ceylon, December 6th to 9th. Stories emerged of tense arguments during the remainder of the tour.

Upon the Crusaders' arrival to San Francisco, Wright left immediately for New York. He was scheduled to speak at the laying of the cornerstone ceremony at Point Loma; he was replaced by Alice Cleather at the last minute.

Dr. Franz Hartmann

Dr. Franz Hartmann arrived in New York on April 17th, 1897 from Austria; he stayed with the di Brazzas. [*New York Tribune*, **Apr.18, 1897**] The Countess explained her situation and told him about Claude F. Wright's position. It is not clear if Wright was present. She gave Hartmann the reasons why she was not going to attend the American Convention although she had been present for the Crusaders' reception on Sunday April 4th.

Hartmann did attend the Third Annual Convention of the T.S. in America held in Madison Square Garden, Concert Hall, April 25-26, 1897. He was introduced as the President of the T.S. in Germany but spoke very little and mostly observed. The New York *Sun* wrote that he praised Mrs. Tingley as being "recognized as the head of theosophy all over the world." [**Apr. 26, 1897**] What Hartmann had learned was that Claude Falls Wright, one of the important and influential persons in Judge's surroundings, had suddenly resigned from the Aryan T.S., the New York branch of the Theosophical Society in America of which he was then president, and also as a member of the executive committee of the general society. Without any fanfare, at the convention, Wright's position was immediately "filled by Mr. A. E.

Neresheimer—being practically a matter of course, this preliminary work only took a few moments." [*Theosophical News*, 1:46, May 3, 1897, p.1]

After the Convention Hartmann "set out on a rather extensive lecture tour through the Central States, in company with Cyrus F. Willard, a prominent Mason and active in the T.S." [*BCW*, 8, p.452] Hartmann was touring to promote his latest books *Magic White and Black*, and *Buried Alive*. While in Chicago Hartmann was interviewed by the *Inter Ocean*. Of note is that he never spoke of Katherine Tingley, unlike one year earlier in Germany when he wrote:

> During an hour of private conversation which followed, I was often struck with the great resemblance between this occasion and the olden times, when I used to sit alone with H. P. Blavatsky. More than once it seemed to me as if the aura of H.P.B. were surrounding Mrs. Tingley and penetrating her person; in fact I often felt as if I were talking with H.P.B. herself in a rejuvenated state. [*Theosophy*, 11:7, Oct. 1896, p.222]

Interestingly, a few weeks prior to the Crusaders' departure a reporter for the *Boston Daily Globe* wrote about Tingley's speech:

> These words had been uttered by Mrs. Tingley with a fiery earnestness which was almost enough to convince the most skeptical of doubting Thomases, while her big black eyes glowed and shimmered, and her face seemed to take on a resemblance to Mme Blavatsky, whom she is said to represent. [**June 1, 1896**]

It appears as though Hartmann may have fallen for Tingley's charm and hypnotic spell in 1896, but if so, he recovered and moved on after the April 1897 Convention.

In the interview, concerning the so-called "split" in the Theosophical Society in 1895, Hartmann said:

> I do not consider that any split has occurred. All that I have seen is that certain people who are incapable of grasping the idea of universal brotherhood, which is the basis of the Theosophical Society in America, have left the society and are in search of other objects. [*The Inter Ocean*, Chicago, IL, May 19, 1897]

Hartmann simply indicated his developing perspective without going into details. His association with Tingley quickly came to an end although he still kept communication open with the Society. Shortly after returning to

Germany he "disbanded the newly-formed group" which had been founded by Tingley during the world tour, and to which he had been elected President on August 30th, 1896. He then "founded in Munich on September 3, 1897, a body known as the *International Theosophische VerBrüderung*, on lines which he considered to be closer to those indicated by H.P.B. in the early days." [*BCW*, 8, p.452]

Countess di Brazza's Change of Heart

Shortly after di Brazza's talk with Claude Falls Wright following the celebration at Madison Square Garden, a heated conversation likely followed with Katherine Tingley at their home, 373 West End Avenue, at which time di Brazza directed Tingley to move out of her residence immediately. Their long relationship had come to an end. Although there are no records of what actually happened, di Brazza's demeanor took a drastic 180 degree turn. She came to realize that she had made a mistake supporting Tingley for all those years and took action to try and rectify it. One major problem facing di Brazza was reporters showing up at the door requesting an audience with Katherine Tingley, the new Mahatma of the Theosophical Society. Countess di Brazza utilized her large home to help various charitable organizations, for example to establish a local branch of the Greek Red Cross, etc., so having reporters coming around asking questions about the new Mahatma, and since she had completely lost faith in Tingley, she could no longer have her stay there without compromising her own integrity and reputation.

After being expelled from di Brazza's residence in the spring of 1897, the Tingleys appear to have moved to the "Lotus Bud Home" in Pleasant Valley, NJ, near Fort Lee. It was described as a three-story brick building, partly plastered outside and included about twelve acres of land. It housed "twenty-five homeless tots" from the East Side of New York. "The Home For Destitute Children, which was established at the suggestion of Mrs. Tingley a few weeks ago, was formally dedicated" in July 1897. The attendees included theosophists and dignitaries.

> They considered that the Lotus Home was the beginning of a new era in the regeneration of society. They prophesied that it would expand until it became one of the great institutions of the age. [*Los Angeles Express*, **July 31, 1897**]

It was situated about five minutes' walk from the One Hundred and Twenty-fifth Street Ferry." Anna Stabler, "a well-known humanitarian worker of Harlem" was Superintendent of the home. [*New York Times,* **July 4, 1897**]

It was at this time that Tingley contacted Elbridge T. Gerry, then president of the Society for the Prevention of Cruelty to Children. She asked Gerry if there would be objection to her starting a school in New York; he informed her to not attempt it. [*New York Tribune,* **Nov. 2, 1902**] She then appealed to Vernon Davis, who had replaced Gerry (until elected judge on the Supreme Court in November 1902) to endorse her scheme.

> He investigated and replied that, far from indorsing her, he might find himself under the painful necessity of prosecuting her if she continued her operations in New York. She didn't; she went to California. [*The Brooklyn Eagle,* **Nov.30, 1902**]

Background explanation is needed here: At the Convention of the Theosophical Society in America in April 1896, following the announcement that some time in the future a school for the revival of the ancient mysteries would be established by the society, a building fund was started; "an architect offered to draw up the plans and specifications and superintend the work of construction." [*New York Tribune,* **Apr.28, 1897**] The *Wilkes-Barr Semi-Weekly Record* carried the subheading: "It Will Shortly Be Established Somewhere on the Atlantic Coast" and ascribed the following to "Treasurer Neresheimer who has outlined the plans of the society as follows:"

> Within the next week or so negotiations for about three hundred acres of ground near New York on a site overlooking the ocean, will be concluded. On this ground there will be erected a temporary building of Egyptian design, and of considerable size, to serve as the headquarters of the society until such time as the needs of the work demand more room. . . .
>
> The ceremonies in connection with the laying of the corner stone of the first building to be erected in America, will take place early in February. The corner stone itself, in accordance with the international idea that permeates the whole plan of the institution, will be formed of four triangular sections, which fitted together, will form an exact square. Each section will be brought from a country that is considered to be a representative one. The United

States, Ireland, Scotland, and Egypt have been chosen as the countries that are to have the honor of furnishing the foundation sections, but after the laying of the corner stone, America the country where the idea of the school first took root, will be honored by having the entire foundations built of stones quarried within her borders. Each of the states will furnish an equal quantity of material, so that the foundation of the building will be built of forty-four different kinds of stone. The remainder of the building will be built from stone contributed by Norway, Sweden, Holland, Greece, India and Australia.

In the centre of the colony as it is designed to appear when completed, there will be a main schoolhouse and several halls for minor purposes. Plans for the first building have been drawn by Architects Pickering and L'Homedeau, of New York, and have been approved by the directors of the institution. **[Feb. 2, 1897]**

A cornerstone was laid at Point Loma on February 23rd, 1897. However, wherever it was intended to be built, whether in New York or Point Loma, the stone building was never constructed.

THE NEW INSTITUTION

In the centre of the colony as it is designed to appear when completed, there will be a main schoolhouse and several halls for minor purposes. Plans for the first building have been drawn by Architects Pickering and L'Homedeau, of New York, and have been approved by the directors of the institution.

[*The Record of the Times*, Wilkes-Barre, Pennsylvania, February 2, 1897]

Katherine's Second Marriage and Her Adopted Son

An interesting and important event occurred in August 1897, shortly after the Tingleys' stay in New Jersey. Missing the conveniences of the West End avenue location, they rented a place at 474 West End avenue which was just a few minutes north of the di Brazza home. This is when her adopted son, Henry, returned home after having been away for about seven years.

According to Ancestry records Katherine Augusta Westcott married her second husband, George W. Parent, in 1871 in Newburyport, Mass. During their marriage Florence (Flossie) Cook and her brother Dick Cook, lived with them. Their father, Richard, as explained elsewhere, did not consent to adoption. Sometime in 1880 Henry Baron (b. Aug. 1876) was adopted from an institution in Harlem supposedly at three years of age; he does not yet appear as a member of their household in the June 7th, 1880 US Census. This Census is also the last known record of Lulu Parent, where George and Katherine are listed as parents of a daughter born in 1872.

Few details have emerged about George and Katherine's marriage other than that they had come to an amicable arrangement of separation in November 1887, which included transferring a major portion of his estate to her.

George Parent died February 23rd, 1888. An article that appeared in the *New York Times* on February 28th, 1888, claimed that he had been ailing and "feeling himself dying, Parent sent for his wife, but on arriving at the rooms she was refused admittance."

At the time of his death, Parent was the chief of detectives at the secret service bureau at No. 71 Broadway for the Elevated Railroad System and was residing at 1001 Sixth avenue.

> As there had been some intimation that a dispute might arise over the possession of the dead man's effects, Colonel Hain, of the elevated roads, shortly after Mr. Parent's death, sent two men to the flat to take charge of his personal estate and attend to the funeral arrangements. Shortly before the hour set for the funeral yesterday, a man apparently about twenty-five years of age entered the parlor where the coffin rested, and saying that he was Mr. Parent's son and had come there to secure his property, sat down in a corner near the window and declared that he would not leave

until the property was turned over to him. Notwithstanding this awkward incident, the funeral arrangements were proceeded with, and the mourners left with the remains, which were interred in Cypress Hill cemetery. The guards from the elevated road remained and remonstrated with the young man, telling him that he would have to go, and that he would not be allowed to touch any of Mr. Parent's effects. Two young women were the other occupants of the apartment, and they made frequent threats to eject the obstinate youth, which, however, they did not carry into effect. [*The Hutchinson News*, **Mar. 2, 1888**]

Further to the "intimation that a dispute . . . might arise . . .", *The New York Times* reported that:

Mrs. Kate A. Parent yesterday [February 27th, 1888] instituted replevin proceedings against Mrs. Leech to recover possession of some furniture. Mrs. Leech is landlady of the furnished rooms at 1,001 Sixth avenue, in one of which George W. Parent, husband of the plaintiff, died last Thursday. A young woman with whom he lived claimed the furniture in question, but the Marshal removed the property to a store-house, there to abide the trial of ownership, . . . in the Eighth Civil District Court March 6. [**Feb. 28, 1888**]

Henry Baron, Tingley's adopted son, was about twelve years old at the time and would not fit the description of a twenty-five year old man. The only young man who may have had an interest in Parent's personal effects and who fits the age mentioned was George Westcott. If so, he was not Parent's son but Kate's brother who was living with them at the time of the 1880 census and likely for some time after. It would appear that Kate made her brother go to the house to secure what she deemed her property. George Westcott then contacted their father in Newburyport to come immediately to see what he could do. Baron explained in his November 16th, 1902 interview in the *San Francisco Examiner*:

Then her father, a man named Westcott, who kept a saloon in Newburyport, Mass., came to New York and together they went to the house at 1001 Sixth avenue to take a last look at George W. Parent, but neither of them went to the funeral. [**Nov. 17, 1902**]

It is unlikely that Katherine personally contacted her father because he had been shamed by her years ago and had wanted nothing to do with her, although there does appear to have been some reconciliation by 1896. [*Boston Daily Globe*, **May 19, 1896**]

Evidence indicates that the two young women at Parent's apartment were James Neale Plumb's daughters, Marie Jeanette, and her younger sister Sarah Lineta Plumb, twenty-one and eighteen years of age. James Neale Plumb was a well-respected lawyer but was being stalked relentlessly by someone determined to ruin him and to drive his children away from him. It's a complicated story that need not be covered here, but it is very bizarre. In order to help his friend, George Parent agreed to be the General Guardian for the younger under-aged daughter's wealth which had been left to her by her deceased mother. [**Will and Probate Records for George W. Parent.**]

The *Hutchinson News* article continues:
> Detective Lawless had meanwhile called at No. 1001 Sixth avenue and seen the young woman in charge of Mr. Parent's apartments. She refused to give her name, but said he had lived there as her lodger for some time and that she had nursed him in his recent sickness, in return for which he had given her some jewelry. She also said that she had never heard Mr. Parent speak of having either a wife or son alive, and that she did not believe the young man's statement. [**Mar. 2, 1888**]

George W. Parent was interred (February 26th, 1888) in the Cypress Hills Cemetery with his father Daniel (d.1872) and his older brother Daniel Jr. (d.1879). George's funeral was attended by the members of The Hancock Post of the Grand Army of the Republic [G.A.R.] [*The Hutchinson News*, **Mar. 2, 1888**] After the 1880 census there are no records or mention of Lulu Parent's whereabouts. It is presumed that she died before her father; Cypress Hills Cemetery has confirmed that Lulu was not interred there. [**Cypress Hills Cemetery, Nov. 18, 2022**] One is left to speculate as to why, if Lulu had in fact died, they were not interred at the same cemetery.

Misinformation about George Parent is found repeated in numerous articles. It is often stated that he was a detective who afterwards became a saloon keeper. Evidence proves that he was a saloon keeper on Center Street in New York City and then was a detective for the Elevated Rail Road, which is recorded as his occupation in the 1880 US Federal Census. George apparently met Kate in the late 1860s or early 1870s during which time she was bringing women from Boston to New York for better paying customers. Kate was about twenty-three years old at the time. The Center street bars were known as the hub for deviant activities and "a hotbed of vice and crime". [New York Saloons, https://historicaleye.com/ma-work/new-york-saloon]

A long article appeared in *The Sun* (NY) November 8th, 1902, reporting on the immigration hearing for the Cuban children Tingley had brought into the country with the intention of bringing them to Point Loma, and which the Society for the Prevention of Cruelty to Children wanted to prevent (see Chapter 5). It included details from Edward Parker's testimony:

> At Newburyport, Mass., Mrs. Tingley's native place, Mr. Parker said he learned that she had broken up at least one family. He was there informed also that she brought young girls to New York on visits, who, after their return, told of entertainments in the nature of carousals.

The Merriam-Webster Dictionary defines carousal as "a wild, drunken party or celebration".

In the *New York Herald* article of May 17th, 1896, Parent is correctly mentioned as "a detective employed by the Manhattan "L" Company. Previous to that occupation Parent was a bartender in a Centre street saloon." This was repeated in the *Boston Daily Globe*, May 18th, 1896. Shortly thereafter the sequence of his occupations was reversed. This incorrect information was still being repeated ten years later, for example, in *The Washington Post,* July 9th, 1906 and *The Pittsburgh Press*, August 5th, 1906. Considering Tingley's early history, this reversal played in her favor—she married the detective, not the saloon keeper on Center street. Another interesting shift at about the same time was altering her name from "Kate" to "Katherine".

Her first husband, Richard Cook, explained that two months following their marriage he "found out that she was visiting a Boston woman who was in Savannah, and whom I knew was a woman of evil reputation. I told her that she must either leave her alone or leave me. The result was we separated." He also admitted they had been sexually active at twelve years of age. [*The New York Press*, Nov. 8, 1902; *New York Herald*, Nov. 8, 1902]

George would have been aware of Kate's reputation but it is unknown when he discovered the full extent of her being a liar, bigamist, as well as manipulative and secretive. He had been supporting her, the children she brought into the household, and her younger brother for a number of years. In the June 1880 census, Lulu was eight years old, healthy, not going to school and living with her parents. No other record of her can be found.

Court documents indicate a very different version about George Parent's estate than what Tingley told Henry Baron when he discovered in 1897 that he had been left an inheritance. Search and inquiry by the administrators of the estate determined that when George died some of his possessions were held "in the Safe Deposit Vault of the Central Safe Deposit Company in 14th street in the City of New York." The administrators were demanding access to the vault, through the Surrogate Court, because the Company could not allow it "on the ground that the said vault stands in the joint names of the deceased George W. Parent and one calling herself Mrs. Kate A. Parent now known as Mrs. Kate A. Tingley, who appeared in this proceeding by Cromwell G. Macy, her attorney." Tingley was refusing to grant access and made it difficult to settle the estate of George Parent. **[Petition in N.Y. Surrogate's Court, County of New York, In the Matter of the Estate of George W. Parent, dec'd, filed December 21, 1888]**

Tingley apparently always sloughed off Henry Baron's questions about his origins, and her responses were sometimes contradictory. On November 16th, 1902 Baron "ran away" from the Point Loma "Homestead" for the second time. In a lengthy interview with a reporter from the *San Francisco Examiner*, published the next day, Baron gave historical background:

> Mrs Tingley had two adopted children, Flossie Cook and Dick Cook. Flossie was in an insane asylum for a time. We all lived at first at 152 West Twenty-second street, in New York. I have been told that Flossie and Dick were Mrs. Tingley's children.
>
> After that (the death of George Parent) we went to West Bergen, N.J. to the house of Philo P. Tingley, who at that time was a clerk or something of that kind at Bowling Green for the White Star line of steamships. Then we lived in a flat at the Graylock, 2048 Seventh avenue, and here my adopted mother developed as a trance medium and afterwards became a theosophist.
>
> When I was fourteen years old I was shipped by Mrs Tingley in the navy. . . I didn't see her again for seven years. I served as an

> ordinary seaman on board the Minnesota and afterward on the various ships on the European station.
>
> I came home in August, 1897, and one day while I was looking through a lot of papers in a desk in my room at 474 West End avenue, in New York, where Mrs Tingley lived, I found a clipping from one of the local papers saying that when George W. Parent died he left Harry George Parent $1,500 and a gold watch worth $1,000. I asked Mrs Tingley what had become of this money, and she said that woman got it all, meaning that he had given it to the woman for whom he had deserted my mother. Then I asked her for papers relating to my parentage, but she put me off by saying that they were in the bottom of a trunk and she did not want to bother hunting for them. She has never said anything to me since about the matter and I have not dared to ask any questions. [*San Francisco Examiner*, **Nov. 17, 1902**]

A correction is required regarding Baron's statement, "that he had given it to the woman for whom he had deserted my mother." It is understandable for Henry to repeat this statement because this is what Katherine told him. Henry may have been ten or twelve years old when George and Katherine separated. Evidence indicates that George was the one who terminated his relationship with his wife, Kate, and *not* because of another woman.

Continuing Baron's story:
> I enlisted in the Spanish war. Mrs Tingley wanted me to enlist in the army, but I was afraid that she wanted me to be shot and went in the navy... When she came to Point Loma I accompanied her. I have been working in the garden and the stables over there ever since except for a short time about a year ago, when I ran away as I am running away now.
>
> I left Point Loma because I am discouraged and broken-hearted. I am disheartened by the way the poor are treated there. I don't believe some of them get enough to eat. Those who are not rich enough to pay their way must work for the others. There are members over there who are not allowed to see their children. Mrs Tingley says that mother love breeds selfishness. So they keep the children by themselves. Nobody except the 'Cabinet of the Purple

Mother' are allowed to converse with these children or have anything to do with them. I do know, however, that there are two divisions—one at the colony and one at the homestead. The homestead is where the better class of children live. These are fed on the best the market can produce—the students, as they are called, who live at the colony are stinted. In the morning they get what is called an ideal breakfast, consisting of an apple, seven nuts, two eggs, three slices of bread and a cup of coffee. This they eat in silence to feed the soul. For lunch the women are allowed to eat slices of hardtack [sea biscuits] and a handful of raisins, figs or dates or a piece of cheese. The men get three hardtacks. Water is the drink at this meal. For dinner we have vegetables and bread and butter. The vegetables are not many, but they manage to vary them; sometimes they give us macaroni, sometimes beans and sometimes corn, but we never eat meat, I suppose they think that our souls abhor meat.

Mrs Tingley and those who live at the homestead are well fed. They have meat and chicken on Tuesday and everything money will buy. " [*San Francisco Examiner*, **Nov. 17, 1902**]

In closing, Baron incidentally added something concerning Tingley.
You probably see plain enough ... that I am not an educated man. I have had very little schooling. I am twenty-six years old and I was taken from an institution for abandoned infants in Harlem. When I was three years old Mrs Tingley, who was then Mrs. George W. Parent, came one day and took me away. She says she adopted me, but she has never shown me any proof of the adoption.

Until I was twenty-one years old I went by the name Harry George Parent. It is my belief that I am the son of George W. Parent. I know that I look like George W. Parent and I act like him. Perhaps Mrs Tingley is my mother, but that is something I will have to prove. She told me that I was the child of very poor people and that they were dead. When I asked her where they were buried she would not answer. When I asked her what my real name was she said that I was Henry Baron, that my mother was a German and my father an Englishman. Now I shall try to find out the truth.

Tingley had brought Cuban children into the country; they were being held at Ellis Island at this time. Concerns had been expressed about the conditions they might be living under when brought to Point Loma. Immigration Commissioner Sargent was coming to do an investigation. The reporter for the *San Francisco Examiner* then commented:

> Baron told his story in a straightforward apparently truthful manner, displaying a remarkable memory for dates and the minute incidents of his life. He will leave in the morning for Los Angeles unless he decides to remain here until the arrival of Immigration Commissioner Sargent for the purpose of giving his testimony in the proposed investigation of conditions at Point Loma.
>
> All the gates of the Raja Yoga school are closed. Nobody is allowed to pass the guards. Mrs. Tingley denied herself to all visitors by advice of her lawyers, and the brotherhood silently awaits the coming of Commissioner Sargent.
>
> Apparently the organization is about to engage in a struggle with powers more aggressive and better armed than any that have heretofore assailed them. To meet this assault they have intrenched themselves in their stronghold and await the issue calmly yet with a grim defiance that bodes no good to their enemies in the event of a triumph for the Purple Mother. [**Nov. 17, 1902**]

On another occasion Baron specifically stated, as others have, that all guards were uniformed and armed and that no one could leave the premises unless they received direct permission from Tingley.

Frank Marshall Pierce (1847-1926) volunteered in the Union Army during the Civil War. In the Tingley vs Times-Mirror court case [see section titled: **Trouble In Paradise**], it was mentioned that he led military-style drills to guard the perimeter of the property at Point Loma. G. de Purucker met Pierce in Geneva during the Crusade, on the evening of September 3rd, 1896. He stated "The tall bald man had a mustache and goatee, a rather military-looking man who strutted when he walked. That was [F.M.] Pierce . . ." [*The Eclectic Theosophist*, July/Aug. 1985, p.7]

BOYS' BROTHERHOOD CLUB NO. I AND CO. A OF THE "NEW CENTURY GUARD" AS THEY APPEAR IN THEIR UNIFORMS AND ACCOUTREMENTS.

[*The New Century*, 3:1, November 18, 1899, p.7]

Emmett Greenwalt in his book *California Utopia* wrote about Henry Baron and Tingley:

> She was equally unfortunate in trying to rear a boy from an orphan home. An injury to this head appeared to affect his mental development and ultimately contributed to his death, but not before he caused her considerable embarrassment by periodically · running away. **[p.13]**

Greenwalt circumvented and whitewashed the entire case involving Tingley's allegedly adopted son Henry Baron and does not even mention his name. Greenwalt purposely dismissed Baron by saying he had mental problems and was not of sound mind. The reporter for the *Examiner* certainly had a different and personal observation of Henry Baron. Greenwalt's book is full of similar biases, always in favor of Katherine Tingley.

In addition to identifying as "Harry George Parent" and "Henry Baron" he registered as "Henry Olson" at the Albemarle Hotel at the time of his escape from Point Loma. He was known by yet another name when he died, November 15th, 1913. The following appeared in *The Los Angeles Times*:

> Charles Morgan, also known as George Parent, who claimed to be a son of Mme. Katherine Tingley of Point Loma, died at the County Hospital . . . of mastoiditis originally caused by the bursting of his ear-drums by the noise of gun-firing while he was in the navy. Morgan had been in the hospital about two weeks. Prior to that time he was employed cutting lumber for Renshaw, Jones & Sutton . . . He was 35 years old. [**Nov. 17, 1913**]

According to Greenwalt, Henry Baron came from the Shepherd's Fold, a charitable institution for unwanted children operated by the Episcopal Church. This institution was known for its cruelty and abuse of children. It had been found to be the most despicable place to raise children."Rev. Mr. [Edward] Cowley of Shepherd's Fold infamy, [was] convicted by a jury of nearly starving a little boy to death, and sent to prison for a year." [*The Sun* **(NY), Nov. 1, 1882**]

Countess di Brazza's Efforts

By October 1897 the Tingleys found another location a little further north and closer to where Philo worked as "clerk in the White Star Steamship company's office in New York". [*The Independence Daily Reporter*, **Independence, KS, June 20, 1896**] They moved into a picturesque red brick house with gabled roof in an exclusive neighborhood on Ninety-fifth street and Boulevard, now called west Broadway. [*Vanity Fair*, **Vol. 3, Oct. 1897**] All the other Tingley associates living at the di Brazza residence were likely also ejected. This latest residence provided them the opportunity to be together once again. Those who had resided at the di Brazza home were Philo and Katherine Tingley, Joseph Fussell and Frank Pierce. There had been many recurring visitors, including H.T. Patterson, President of the Brooklyn T.S., Emil August Neresheimer, Claude Falls Wright and Alexander Fullerton.

Upon her return from the world tour, an Indianapolis journalist asked Tingley "Where has the money come from for your crusade?" She replied:

> Some of our party have paid their own expenses. Not one of us receives a salary. My expenses are not paid by the society. There

have been some voluntary donations. You know that some of the members of our society are very wealthy. Mr. Patterson is a man of large means who left an important business to go on this crusade, at the risk of sacrificing everything. He has done much to make our efforts a success. **[*The Indianapolis Journal*, Mar. 21, 1897]**

MRS. KATHERINE TINGLEY IN HER LIBRARY.

[*Vanity Fair*, Vol. 3:3, October 1897, pp.671-673]

Tingley deflected answering the question directly and completely avoided mentioning that her primary contributor towards the Crusade was Countess di Brazza. Shortly before the Crusaders' departure *The Commercial Appeal*, Memphis, TN, on June 7th, 1896 wrote:

> It was anticipated that the trip in all its features will cost something like $25,000, but this heavy expense is no barrier to the small band of faithful spirits, who rallied to the fund . . .

The Theosophical Forum: New Series published a financial statement detailing receipts and disbursements for the "Crusade of American Theosophists Around the World." The actual cost was presented as $28,127.90 **[3:1, May 1897, p.16]** In today's currency, the equivalent amount is approximately $969,000.

One month following their return, it was reported in *The Sun* (NY) that

> Countess De Brazzi intimates that she has given up all the cash she cares to in upholding the Tingley followers, having expended a large amount in that direction on the crusade around the world. **[May 1, 1897]**

Although not a member, di Brazza was devoted to the theosophical cause. Following the revelations about Tingley, she sought to assist the Aryan Branch following the resignation of its president, Claude Falls Wright. A few days later newspapers reported that Henry B. Foulke, who in 1892 claimed to be Blavatsky's successor, had been offered the presidency:

> [A]t Onset Bay, Spiritualist camp ground, the Presidency of the Theosophical Society in America [actually presidency of the Aryan T.S.] was offered last night. Countess Di Brazza, Dr. Gibier, and other disaffected Theosophists came on from New York and met Foulke, offering him the place. Foulke refused it unless they would make Onset Camp the headquarters and change their policy radically. He says they have departed from the faith and must reorganize, and declines to go into their factional squabbles, pointing to the death of William Q. Judge and failure of Kitty Tingley to keep up the esoteric work in the western hemisphere. [*The Sun* (NY), May 1, 1897]

On May 3rd, 1897, a similar report appeared in *The Barre Daily Times*:

> The Countess de Brazza, Miss Rosa Moore and Dr. Gibier, the leader of the disputed Aryan branch of the American Theosophical

society, of which Catherine Tingley is the president, and from which Claude Falls Wright and his faction of followers of the cult are understood to have separated this week, have arrived here for the purpose of tending to Henry B. Foulke the presidency of the Aryan branch.... [*The Barre Daily Times*, Barre, VT, May 3, 1897]
[See Appendix C for more information about Countess di Brazza]

In 1888 Foulke was elected president of Krishna T.S. in Philadelphia. [*The Path*, 3:2, May 1888, p.65] Krishna T.S. was chartered on May 17th, 1887. In a letter to "Editor Times" at the time of Foulke's claim to be Blavatsky's successor, Judge wrote "He is not a member of the Theosophical Society. . ." [*Lucifer*, 10:55, Mar. 1892, p.82]

Records found in *Ancestry* indicate that in November 1897, Foulke was arrested for ". . . ill-treating a boy . . ." by "committing an unnatural act". In February 1898 he was found guilty by a grand jury in Plymouth County, MA, and sentenced to eight months. He apparently offered to expose the Onset Bay mediums if he received a lenient sentence. While sitting in the Plymouth County Jail he explained in the *San Francisco Examiner*, April 17th, 1898, how he and others conducted fraud at Onset Bay, MA, and claimed "All this time, however, I was, and remained, a theosophist."

The Theosophical Society in America

On February 11th, 1898, Neresheimer wrote a letter "To The Members of The Theosophical Society in America" to address rumblings in the ranks. In an obvious reference to those involved in accepting Tingley as the new Outer Head, "and which had been thought to be the right path towards helping the spiritual regeneration" he wrote that they now "made it appear that members of the T.S.A. were not exercising perfect independence and freedom by tacitly admitting the spiritual help and guidance which this Society enjoys at the hands of its original Founders". At this point, a number of the participating Council members in March 1896, were seriously questioning their decision.

Tingley claimed to receive directions from the departed Blavatsky and Judge, and from 'a sacred source'. A few years after leaving Point Loma, Louis Fitch stated that members were "taught the succession of teachers—through Confucius, Buddha, Jesus Christ, Mohammed and now the greatest of all, Katherine Tingley" and that "[s]he claimed that she had the power to stay in the spirit world, but that she preferred to come back here as the savior of humanity...". [*The Sun*, (NY), Nov. 8, 1902; *The Birmingham Age-Herald*, July 16, 1906]

Neresheimer wrote that rather than "unsettle" members, the expressed concerns had in fact given them greater power "for the grand ideals which have to be given to it by the instrumentality of this organization." Neresheimer boldly claimed that under Tingley's leadership the Society was being raised to the next level:

> The whole body of the T.S.A. has in consequence risen to a much higher plane, which will make greater things possible in the future than have yet been accomplished. . . .
>
> The coming Convention will give an opportunity to solidify the members of the Society into such a unity of stability and force as will bring the cause of Universal Brotherhood forward with a bound, ... [*The New Century*, 1:19, 20, Feb.18, 1898, p.16]

One week later, at the convention of the Society at Chicago on February 18th, 1898, an orchestrated and unexpected maneuver by Tingley shattered the cohesion of T.S. in America.

> Mrs. Tingley's followers, overriding all protests, proclaimed a change in the name and constitution of the Society, and gave unrestricted power over the new body into her hands. She thus removed herself from The Theosophical Society; but she took with her nearly everything that had given it external manifestation: the majority of its members, its organization, headquarters, lists, records, press, magazines, and practically everything it owned. She left only its reality and its name. [*TQ*, 17, July 1919, p.15]

The *San Diego Union* reported on March 10th, 1898 that about seventy-five members gathered "for an 'informal conference' of the Theosophical Society in America . . . in Mott Memorial hall yesterday, says the New York *Sun* of Feb. 28." Vice-President, A.H. Spencer had called the meeting. He stated:

> "The proposition made by the followers of Mrs. Tingley was to merge the T.S.A. into the Universal Brotherhood, our society to be known as the literary department. The constitution of the Universal Brotherhood gives to Mrs. Tingley absolute power over

us all. We are to give up to her all the records and archives of the T.S.A. and to forswear our constitution. It is our belief that this is directly contrary to the constitution of the T.S.A. and opposed to all the principles of Theosophical study. One of the fundamental principles of the Theosophical society in America is freedom of speech, thought and action within the limits of the law, and we cannot maintain that and put ourselves absolutely in the power of one person. . . .

". . .Our representatives were howled down at the convention and the resolution merging the T.S.A. into the Universal Brotherhood was rushed through without debate or discussion. . .

"After the convention a number of us held a meeting at the Palmer House in Chicago and repudiated the action of the convention. We declared the whole thing null and void. Three members of our executive committee and E.A. Neresheimer voted for the resolution. We decided that by their revolutionary action they had vacated their offices in the T.S.A. Today we want to ask the opinions of you members of the T.S.A. on this matter."

Mr. Hargrove and Mrs. Kcightley made speeches and a number of the other members spoke. They did not say anything about Mrs. Tingley save that they would never submit to her rule and would certainly oppose any scheme to merge the T.S.A. into the Universal Brotherhood. By an unanimous vote the Palmer House resolutions declaring the action of the convention null and void were indorsed. Mr. Spencer then read the constitution of the Universal Brotherhood to the meeting to show them what they might expect if they had to exist under it. The constitution refers to Mrs. Tingley as the "leader and official head" of the organization. She can do or undo anything, and the act or acts of committees are not valid unless approved by her. She is appointed for life, and has the privilege of appointing her successor. She also has power to appoint and displace at will all officers of the Theosophical Society in America.

"Why, it's not a constitution at all," said Mr. Spencer. "It's a recital, clause after clause, of the absolute power and dictatorship of Mrs. Tingley." [**Mar. 10, 1898**]

Four lawsuits were brought to the Supreme Court. Spencer sought to have a Receiver appointed to prevent removal of all the books, records, archives, money and property of the T.S. in America; Julia Keightley and Hargrove sought to examine all books and records, including membership lists of the E.S.; Julia Keightley sought to prevent Neresheimer applying for a Receiver for the Theosophical Publishing Company; Hargrove sought to examine the accounts and financial records of the Company for the School for the Revival of the Lost Mysteries of Antiquity. They were all struck down on the basis that:

> It was perfectly competent and legal for the Society . . . to attach itself to and become part of a larger body formed for similar purposes, and to transfer its records and archives to such larger body if this was done pursuant to resolution regularly adopted.
> [*The New Century*, **1:29, Apr. 30, 1898, p.8, quoting** *"The Evening Post* **of April 25th"**]

The Theosophical Society in America had to rebuild from scratch.

George Coffin, President of the Blavatsky branch of the Theosophical Society in Washington, one of the branches that dissociated immediately from the new organization, made the following statement to *The Washington Post* after the convention:

> "If Catherine, autocrat of all the Russians, were living to-day, she would be green with envy at the recent achievement of her namesake, Mrs. Katherine A. Tingley, in seizing the reins not only of spiritual, but temporal power, as well over the affairs of the Theosophical Society in America, of which she has recently proclaimed herself 'leader and official head.' Arrayed in a royal purple robe she issued her 'proclamation' to the delegates at the last annual convention, announcing that she had founded a new organization called the Universal Brotherhood. A committee of delegates was appointed to draw up resolutions, which, being ready-made, were promptly reported, as well as a cut and dried 'constitution' for the new Brotherhood. The constitution of the Theosophical Society in America plainly required that no change or amendment could be made unless each of the 150 branch

societies had a printed copy of the proposed change at least two months before the convention met, but a trifle like this was not allowed to stand in the way of the royal Katherine, and resolutions, constitution, and all were submitted to the convention, a yea and nay vote was taken viva voce, and, although there was a formidable protest of nays from the minority, the constitution of the Brotherhood was declared adopted amid the enthusiastic demonstration of a hypnotized majority, which rivaled the performance at the celebrated council of Nice, 1,500 years ago, when Arius was voted down and the dogma of Christ's divinity declared for the first time.

"All this was accomplished the first day of the convention, within four hours' time after it came together. An appropriate sequel to this achievement was the ceremony of crowning the 'leader and official head' the second day with a laurel wreath bedecked with purple ribbons. This was entirely befitting the dignity of one who had just been invested—without regard to law, 'tis true, for what regard for law has an autocrat? —with the following amazing powers, and this by American citizens, hitherto presumed to be sane and law-abiding.

"Art. IV of the so-called constitution provides that their [sic] shall he one 'supreme office,' in which shall reside 'paramount authority' called 'leader and official head,' and proclaims Katherine A. Tingley such 'leader and official head' for life, with power to appoint her successor. The Pope of Rome is always elected by the college of cardinals, so in this respect Mrs. Tingley has greater power than the Pope. She is invested with the following powers: To appoint all officers from highest to lowest, and to remove them at her discretion; to issue charters to branch societies and cancel them; to issue diplomas to individual members and cancel them; to appoint an executive committee and declare any of their acts null and void; to appoint a treasurer and finance committee and to declare their acts void and of no effect; to declare the by-laws or branches null and void; to disapprove by-laws framed by her 'cabinet,' and to disapprove any amendment to the 'constitution.'

"As if this were not enough to satisfy the craving or any human being the 'leader' is invested further with the power to "appoint agents for any purpose and endow them with whatever power she may elect to delegate.' It is to be hoped that under this section she will not delegate that New York business man to set fire to the New York headquarters with a can of coal oil, for she herself has said he would do so if she 'ordered' him.

"The crowning touch of humor in the 'constitution' is found in the provision empowering the 'leader' to call a congress of delegates from the branches, and giving her at the same time 'the power to prevent the discussion of, or action on, any subject which, in the judgment of that officer (the leader), is against the welfare of the brotherhood.' On this point the comparison of the veto power of the President of the United States with that or this autocrat is inexpressibly funny, for Congress can and does pass laws over his veto by a two-thirds vote, but this 'official head' can stop any discussion of, or action on, any subject by her 'congress,' so called.

"The amazing thing is this, that prominent lawyers, judges, doctors and business men joined in adopting this marvelous 'constitution,' and signed the document. But sober second thought has led several branches and many members to repudiate it. Branches at Washington, Cincinnati, Dayton, Brooklyn, Staten Island, Colorado Springs, and elsewhere have condemned the unlawful procedure, and will continue to conduct the Theosophical Society in America in the future as in the past, along the lines of scientific thought and research, which demands the utmost freedom of thought and the highest exercise of reason and common sense.

"No organization which has its inception in an unlawful act and in brutal disregard of the rights of a minority can hope to command public respect, even though miscalled universal brotherhood and liberty loving, self-respecting Americans will regard as dangerous or ridiculous any society with numerous ramifications which sets up and accepts an autocracy in defiance of the organic law of the land and the spirit of free institutions." **[Mar. 6, 1898]**

Trouble in Paradise

Aside from the hijacking of the Theosophical Society in America, the most pivotal event to be explored and exposed occurred in the early 1900s. It was the court case of Katherine Tingley vs Times-Mirror Company. This court case defined the parameters under which Tingley and her followers could proceed with their agenda at Point Loma. The case was based on the article, titled "Outrages at Point Loma", that appeared in the *Los Angeles Times* on October 28th, 1901. In this article Mrs. M. Leavitt, "a believer in what she terms 'the true school of theosophy'" recounts how her friend Mrs. Holbrook, "a well-to-do eastern wom[a]n" had to be

> rescued from the roost on Point Loma by her husband with the aid of an officer [a deputy sheriff] and a gun, and now hovers at the point of death from the abuse she says she received while confined in the "Homestead."

She described how she and others were being treated there:

> During the day time she was worked in the field like a convict, forced to plant trees, hoe corn and perform all sorts of hard labor, and at night she was shut up in a cell and guarded as if she were a raving maniac.

She revealed that Mrs. Minnie [Wilhelmine] Neresheimer [1853-1917], Emil A. Neresheimer's wife,

> has been forcibly separated from her husband and is also in the Tingley's clutches, and not allowed to speak to him. She is forced to live alone in a little tent in the grounds that surround the crazy institution. Armed men guard this place of horror, and, Mrs. Leavitt says, solitary confinement, hard labor and starvation are resorted to by the Tingley managers as punishments upon those who disobey their iron rules.

Evidence to substantiate most of what is said about Minnie Neresheimer's case can be corroborated. Although evidence regarding Mrs. Holbrook is not as readily available, it has been established that she was listed as a resident at "Lomaland Headquarters of the Universal Brotherhood" on the U.S. Census dated June 1900, married for thirty years. She was an enthusiastic participant to form a Branch in Wilkinsburg, PA, that was chartered on October 1st, 1895. [*The Path*, **10:8,** **Nov. 1895, p.260**] Elliott Holbrook, her husband, was president when Hargrove did a lecture tour in the area at the request of W.Q. Judge in late 1895 to early 1896. Ida Holbrook died April 3rd, 1905 at fifty years of age.

Minnie Neresheimer had apparently been quite seriously injured when she was attacked and robbed one afternoon in December 1896 as she rode home in her buggy. Two men stepped out of the woods by the road; one grabbed the horses while the other jumped into the buggy. A struggle ensued and he "grasped the frightened woman, who was almost exhausted, by the throat, and with a sudden jerk pulled from her ear a beautiful sapphire earing." He also grabbed her purse containing $100. She hurried to Flushing to notify the police, fainted, and was taken to "Prendeville's hotel where restoratives were given her." She was brought home, "suffering from shock." [*Brooklyn Daily Eagle*, **Dec. 22, 1896**] One week later it was reported that "Dr. C.B. Story, who is attending Mrs. Neresheimer, says that her injuries are more serious than was at first supposed, and that she will be confined to her bed for several weeks." [*Brooklyn Daily Eagle*, **Dec. 28, 1896**] Minnie was a small woman who never had much stamina. The manual labor she went through, together with the restricted diet, as depicted by others, would have been difficult for one of the "well-to-do eastern women."

A few months prior to the "Outrages at Point Loma" article (October 1901), *The New Century*, in the 'Point Loma News' section, noted that "E.A. Neresheimer . . . has been absent several weeks in New York City, undergoing a serious operation . . . he expects to arrive here [Point Loma] . . . by the 14th of August, to remain permanently." However, shortly after Mrs. Holbrook's rescue, Emil Neresheimer also took his wife away from the Homestead. [**4:18, Aug. 7, 1901, p.7**]

One of the conditions for Minnie's return to Point Loma was that Emil build a house on the grounds so she would have more independence and not have to live in a tent, as had been accurately reported. By March plans were drawn with architect Wm. Quayle & Co. to build a house on the best site on the peninsula, projected to cost $5600 to $6000. It was to be located near the Point Loma Invalid's hotel, also known as the sanitarium. [*Evening Tribune*, **San Diego, Mar. 13, 1903; July 1, 1903**]

At about the same time, the location of the proposed sanitarium on the grounds was announced in *Universal Brotherhood Path* in November 1902:

Land has been purchased for the erection of an up-to-date Sanitarium, southeast of the Homestead. The site is a beautiful one overlooking the bay, city and ocean, as well as the Homestead grounds. The building will be unique and beautiful, and will have every convenience and appliance known to medical and hygienic science; all this, together with the incomparable climatic conditions for conferring robust health, should make the Loma Sanitarium second to none. [17:8, p.540]

It was reported in April 1903 that architect Quayle had "completed the plans for the new sanitarium to be erected at Point Loma, the cost of which will run up into the hundreds of thousands of dollars." [*San Diego Union*, **Apr. 9, 1903**] Progress on the project appeared in the *Los Angeles Express*:

Articles of incorporation of a large hotel for invalids have been filed here, the project being to erect and operate a large sanitarium on Point Loma near the Universal Brotherhood of the Theosophists. The incorporators are Dr. J.C. Hearne, Clark Thurston, D.C. Reed, G.W. Fishurn and E.A. Neresheimer. The capital stock of the company is $50,000, of which $19,600 has been subscribed. [**Nov. 6, 1902**]

The sanitarium was to include medical and surgical facilities, and a training school for nurses, with the intention to give diplomas. To facilitate its function, a ferry line was to be built to run between San Diego and Roseville, operated by the Universal Brotherhood. [*Los Angeles Times*, **Nov. 7, 1902**]

Neither the "large sanitarium" nor ferry line was ever built. It seems it was a ploy to give hope to the citizens and politicians of San Diego about the possibilities that existed if Tingley and The Universal Brotherhood were respected and supported. A good part of Tingley's strategy at the time was to keep the Society for the Prevention of Cruelty to Children away from investigating her and her compound.

Dr. Joseph Carter Hearne (1851-1917)

Dr. Hearne was one of the incorporators for the proposed sanitarium on Point Loma. He eventually went on his own with a similar project at the corner of Fourth and Ash streets in San Diego.

NEW OFFICE OF DR. J. C. HEARNE, NOW BUILDING.

[Snapshot taken October 2022. Dr. Hearne's name is still above the main entrance door.]

Dr. Hearne was born in Kentucky, educated at the University of Missouri and Jefferson College in Philadelphia, graduating in 1872. He worked in Philadelphia and then Missouri; he was a particularly noted surgeon. He moved to San Diego circa 1890, became involved in public affairs as well as attended to a large private practice. [*San Diego Union and Daily Bee*, **Apr. 5, 1903**]

The *San Diego Union and Daily Bee* ran an article on January 1st, 1905 titled "New Office Building For Dr. J.C. Hearne." It was reported that construction had begun, described as having a "frontage of 100 feet on Ash street, and 25 feet on Fourth" and constructed of "hollow concrete building blocks, with a rough rock finish." The basement would contain the boiler, engine room, workshop, storage rooms, etc.; first floor reception parlors, library, rooms for surgical and medical purposes; second floor rooms for patients requiring constant care of a physician; the main roof was to have a "sun parlor, 21 by 51 feet inside dimensions." And the cost for this building: $12,000. In an article August 25th, 1908, also by the *San Diego Union and Daily Bee*, Dr. Hearne's institution was referred to as a "sanitarium."

In October 1909 Dr. Hearne made a plea for student nurses:
> Because of the continuous increase in the volume of business at the Hearne Hospital, several student nurses are needed at once, and applications from any young women desiring to take the course in the Hearne Training School for Nurses may be made personally to Dr. J.C. Hearne at his offices, corner of 4th and Ash streets. [*San Diego Union and Daily Bee*, **Oct. 31, 1909**]

He was listed as "manager and owner of the Hearne Training School for Nurses" in *Who's Who on the Pacific Coast* in 1913. [p.261]

In 1909 Dr. Hearne paid nearly $10,000 for "a five acre tract at Point Loma" and "is planning to have a home there on the Italian villa style." [*San Diego Union and Daily Bee*, **Oct. 31, 1909**]

Tingley managed to attract large sums of money for her extravagant plans. One such sum came by way of a bequest from the estate of Baronness Alice Frederica Malcolm who, "when [she] was over here" was hosted by Mrs. Tingley who "induced her to look into their work." [*The Sun* **(NY), Mar. 24, 1900**] The Baroness left £5000 ($25,000 at the time) to "The Trustees of the School for the Revival of the Lost Mysteries of Antiquity, recently founded or about to be founded in America." [*New York Times*, **Mar. 24, 1900**] However, the structure, which was proposed to be built in stone, was not constructed.

A lengthy article which appeared in the *San Francisco Call* on August 5th, 1900 includes:
> Of the thousands of dollars which have poured into the treasury of the brotherhood members of the society declare there has never been a published statement; and under the constitution the brotherhood treasury is little different from the private purse of the leader, so absolute is her control of it.

It was also understood that those who intended to remain permanently on the site were made to "convey properties and money" to Katherine Tingley, not to a general fund. The supposed ideal was to have everyone made equal in the name of brotherhood.

Numerous properties were amassed during the early 1900s. An article in *The Hanford Sentinel* (Hanford, CA), writing of the fiscal worth of the building and land holdings in 1906, claimed:
> The total value of the tract and buildings is estimated at $2,500,000. The theosophists are possessed of other property worth close to $9,000,000. [**Aug. 14, 1906**]

Some of these properties she considered as her own and sold through her De Westcotte Company, which she incorporated on September 21st, 1906.

No records have been found to indicate that Minnie Neresheimer returned to the Homestead before the construction of their residence was completed. According to one source the Neresheimers returned to Point Loma, after an extended eastern trip [*Evening Tribune*, **San Diego, June 9, 1903**], just in time for their house to be ready for occupancy in early July 1903. [*Evening Tribune*, **San Diego, July 1, 1903**] Emil taught music to the children in the Raja Yoga School. Then they moved to Denver, Colorado in 1904. [*Richmond Times Dispatch*, **Nov. 6, 1911**] The Neresheimers had lived at Point Loma for three and half years in total.

Minnie was never a member of the Universal Brotherhood but she had been a member of the Aryan Theosophical Society in New York, having joined March 5th, 1889. W.Q. Judge and William C. Temple were her endorsers. **[Edmonton TS Archives]**

The *Los Angeles Times* article (October 28th, 1901) continues: Mrs. Leavitt was clear about how Tingley managed to get her followers to do what she wanted them to do.

> Mrs. Leavitt claims that through a strong hypnotic power, Catherine Tingley works her will on sensible people. The "Universal Brotherhood," or in other words, Catherine Tingley, is an off-shoot of the theosophic society, which became disjointed some four or five years ago. Mrs. Tingley was formerly—the theosophists say—a common, dollar-taking spirit medium.
>
> She couldn't agree with the theosophists, so she branched off and set up her trap on Point Loma. She distributes literature throughout the East, and even in foreign countries, saying the Universal Brotherhood Homestead, located in the most beautiful spot on earth, offers to those who wish to retire into a quiet, thoughtful life, a home in which they may live peacefully and an atmosphere of soul-study and pure thoughts.
>
> Only people with money happen to get these pamphlets, says Mrs. Leavitt. When people answer her enticing advertisements in person Mrs. Tingley exerts her influence over such as are spookily inclined; and the almost incredible things which have taken place prove that once in the lair it is almost impossible to escape.
>
> Mrs. Leavitt says there is nothing taught at Point Loma but insane ceremonies; that the girls who are placed there to be educated are put to work at the most menial tasks, each one kept separate in a guarded cell and forbidden to speak to anybody else, and that the poor little children are quartered in a miserable building some distance from the main institution, and are continually on the verge of starvation—for Mrs. Tingley openly states that children are fed too much for their spiritual good, and must eat but little, so that they will be more etherial. Mrs. Leavitt says she knows personally of a case where both parents and children are victims, and the children have been taken away to the child-pen and are never allowed to communicate in any way with mother or father. For, says Mrs. Tingley, they will grow up purer if away from the bodily and affectionate influence of the parents!

The children are never allowed to speak to anybody except when they are selling trinkets to the visitors who come to the gates. The young lady prisoners make fancy work, which they sell to strangers. Purple robes are worn by the women, and a sort of khaki uniform by the men. [*Los Angeles Times*, Oct. 28, 1901]

Katherine Tingley vs *Times-Mirror* Company

Tingley's response was to sue the *Times-Mirror* Company for libel and to "recover $50,000 damages as a result of the publication of an interview with Mrs. M. Leavitt in the Los Angeles Times in October, 1901." The trial began on December 17th, 1902 in the Superior Court of San Diego county, and ran until January 12th, 1903. The Judge was Elisha Swift Torrance (1846-1926), who exposed his prejudice from day one. [*Los Angeles Times*, Dec. 17, 1902]

Minnie Neresheimer was one of the individuals called to testify. However, every question she was asked in relation to her statements was objected to by the plaintiff (Tingley's lawyers) "on the ground that the answer would be irrelevant and immaterial" and every single objection was sustained by Judge Torrance.

She was sworn on behalf of the defendant, Times-Mirror Company, and testified as follows, by Mr. Shortridge:

> I am the wife of Mr. E. A. Neresheimer. I reside at Point Loma, and before coming to Point Loma, we maintained a country home in Bay Side, Long Island. We formerly lived in New York city. **[2287, p.572]**

> Q. When did you give up your home in New York City?
> Mr. Andrews: Your Honor, the question is objected to.
> The objection was sustained by the Court, the defendant excepted, and the same is numbered, Exception No. 382 **[2287-2288, p.572]**

> Witness (continuing): My husband is a member of the Universal Brotherhood. I am not a member.
> Q. How long has your husband been a member of that organization?
> The plaintiff objected to the question on the ground that the answer would be immaterial, which objection was sustained, the

defendant excepted, and the same is number Exception No. 383. [2289, p.573]

Mr. Shortridge: State whether or not prior to October 28th, 1901 you were denied or cut off from the usual and ordinal association and communion with your husband?
The plaintiff objected to the question on the ground that the answer would be irrelevant and immaterial which objection was sustained, the defendant excepted and the same is numbered. Exception No. 388, [2294, p.574]

Questions were continually denied and sustained; Judge Torrance would not allow any examination of the witness. It appears that Judge Torrance had a twisted sense of the purpose of the case. Mr. Shortridge tried to explain the reasoning for the questions but Judge Torrance stated:

> The fact that that allegation is placed in the answer, does not establish the proposition that it is material. It is wholly irrelevant to the issue that could be raised in this case. It has nothing whatever to do with the case. It does not in the least degree tend to establish the truth of a single statement in this libelous article. It is not plead—if it could be claimed that these facts would find to mitigate damages, or tend to show a lack of actual malice or ill will on the part of the defendant, it is not pleaded for that purpose, because there is no intimation that the defendant had any knowledge of these things at the time this libelous article was published. The fact that it appears in the answer does not establish the proposition that it is material or relevant to the case. If a motion would have been made to have stricken this out, it would have been stricken out from the answer by the Court. You cannot inject an issue here merely by pleading it in the answer, unless it appears to be a material issue in the case. [2297-2299, p.575]

Mr. Shortridge: But is it not stated here that she was forcibly separated from her husband?

Judge Torrance replied:
> Yes sir, but there is nothing to show she was forcibly separated from her husband. We are not here to inquire about the relations between Mr. and Mrs. Neresheimer. This is not a divorce

proceeding between these parties. It is immaterial for the purposes of this case . . . We are here Mr. Shortridge, to ascertain the fact whether these matters charged in this libelous article are true. **[2300-2301, pp.575-576]**

Judge Torrance would not allow Mrs. Neresheimer to answer any of the questions so there was nothing for the defense to work with. He stipulated the purpose of the case:
> We are only inquiring into the question as to whether these alleged defamatory charges made against Mrs. Tingley are true or are not. **[2321; p.581]**

This example is cited to demonstrate the extent of prejudicial interference by Judge Torrance in the simple cross-examination of a witness for the defense. Depositions were given equally prejudiced treatment, sometimes worse.

The Sun (NY) reported that much evidence concerning Tingley's career in New York was "Kept Out of Her Libel Suit".
> In Mrs. Tingley's libel suit against the Los Angeles *Times* Judge Torrance today continued to rule out any evidence in New York depositions bearing on the woman's record when she was a spiritual medium and massage operator in that city. **[Dec.30, 1902;** ***The Birmingham Age-Herald*, Dec. 30, 1902]**

Judge Torrance's charge to the jury at the end of the lengthy trial removed all doubt of his bias. *The Los Angeles Times* on January 13th, 1903 included the following:
> The amount sued for was $50,000, and the court's instructions called for judgement in a "substantial" amount. After wrestling with the question for four hours and a quarter, the jury decided, by a vote of 10 to 2, that $7500 was "substantial" enough, as they did not deem that the plaintiff, according to the evidence, had a reputation that could be damaged more than that amount by the publication complained of, or that she suffered in any other way to an extent entitling her to recover a large sum.
>
> The plaintiff manifested great disappointment when informed of the verdict, as she had counted on receiving nearly if not all of the

amount sued for. Her counsel also were depressed, one of them, Mr. Andrews, remarking: "This is a defeat for both sides."

The parties to the defense do not look upon it as a defeat. The battle is not fought out. An appeal will be taken to the Supreme Court, where the lower court will be reversed, if serious error is sufficient for reversal.

There are ample grounds for claiming that serious error was committed by Judge Torrance, in numerous rulings in the case, justifying an appeal. The court at various stages of the case not only ruled against defendant in a manner indicating unquestionable bias, but even showed animus on more than one occasion, amounting almost to passion, and clearly departed from that judicial equipoise, which should mark the conduct of a just judge.

The court was manifestly unfair from the start, and ruled almost uniformly against the defense in excluding important evidence material to that side of the case. . . .

The lengthy charge of the court in the jury bore heavily against the defendant, and amounted to something more than a judicial charge, which should be only a statement of the law from the court to the jury. It was more in the nature of an argument than an impartial statement of the law for the jury's guidance. It was the charge that turned the scale for the jury. [*The Los Angeles Times*, **Jan. 13, 1903**]

In his closing statement, Samuel Shortridge, lawyer for the defense, on January 10th, 1903 asked:
> Who is the plaintiff in this case—whence did she come? Is her past not shrouded in mystery? . . . Who is the plaintiff of unknown past?

Mr. Andrews, one of Tingley's lawyers objected to the inference that Tingley had an unknown past. Shortridge responded that "Mrs. Tingley's past was unknown because it was not allowed to be shown to the Jury." [*Los Angeles Herald*, **Jan. 11, 1903**]

Shortridge questioned Tingley's reason for the law suit:

> Vindication! Why did she not ask it of the publisher? Why does she not arise and ask for it now. Gentlemen, I say to you again that the object of this suit is money—money, and not vindication. She asks for damages for what! For name, fame, and reputation!
>
> .... If she had desired vindication alone, she could have had it in a criminal action.
>
> .... She has gone too far; she has protested too much; she has denied everything and with a malignant heart has sought to blast the reputation of every person who has testified against her; she has shown the cunning and the vindictiveness that is the reverse of everything that is divine. It is money that she craves—money that she has grasped at every stage of her life, as far as it is revealed by the record, but this is shrouded in darkness. . . . [*Los Angeles Herald*, Jan. 11, 1903]

The Tingley vs Times-Mirror court case ultimately defined how future cases were handled. Judge Torrance's obvious bias toward Tingley by not allowing a proper scope of questioning witnesses, allowing absolutely *no* questions about her past nor how she treated people, emboldened her in future litigation. And she wasted no time.

Katherine Tingley vs Ernest W. Schmidt, et al

On January 11th, 1903, the *Los Angeles Herald* printed a lengthy article titled "Another Suit Against Otis" about a surprising development that occurred in the Superior Court of California in San Diego during the final days of the Tingley vs Times-Mirror court case.

While Samuel M. Shortridge, lawyer for the *Times-Mirror* in the $50,000 libel suit initiated by Tingley, was presenting his closing argument on January 10th

> [A] sheriff's deputy stepped in the courtroom and served upon Harrison Gray Otis, president of the Times-Mirror company, a summons in an action for $75,000, brought by Mrs. Katherine Tingley, alleging that he is a party to a conspiracy with his city editor, Henry E. Andrews; a Times reporter named Lanier Bartlett;

Mrs. M. Leavitt, the woman who gave the interview upon which the pending libel suit is based, and E.W. Schmidt, to blackmail and extort money from the plaintiff.

Tingley's new libel suit, delivered in the court room, during the ongoing original lawsuit, was based on a letter she received from Schmidt, dated "March 29, 1901. Confidential" which she received nearly two years earlier. It read:

> Madam Catherine A. Tingley, H.U.B., Point Loma: Dear Madam—You once, on the festival of laying the foundation stone of your temple, just as you were starting east, divided your bouquet and gave me some. I have those flowers pressed in sweet remembrance of that interview. I now wish to inform you that all your back past is in hand (from the time as Kitty Westcott you lived in Newburyport, Mass., till now), ready to publish to the public. How much is it worth to you to stop same? Let me know your views thereon at once, ere too late. Very respectfully, E.W. Schmidt, Special Agent. [*Los Angeles Herald; Los Angeles Times; San Diego Union and Daily Bee; Birmingham Age-Herald*, **Jan. 11, 14, 1903**]

Tingley assumed Schmidt was associated with the *Times-Mirror*. During his testimony in the ongoing trial, City Editor Andrews said he had met Schmidt in the fall of 1901, who had told him that Mrs. Leavitt had information concerning Point Loma. The Leavitt interview, upon which the $50,000 suit was based, was published October 28th, 1901.

General Otis stated concerning Schmidt:

> The words, "special agent," which follow Schmidt's signature, are repudiated . . . as having any possible reference to the Times, by which he says Schmidt was never employed or connected in any way whatsoever. . . has no knowledge of Schmidt beyond what was testified to by Mr. Andrews. [*Los Angeles Herald*, **Jan.11, 1903**]

E.W. Schmidt was 'special agent' for the insurance company he was working for at the time, Fidelity Mutual Aid association of San Francisco. In his sworn and notarized statement, January 10th, 1903, he stated that he had never had any connection with the *Los Angeles Times*, never claimed to have one, and definitely was not in conspiracy with H.G. Otis.

The *Los Angeles Times* of January 11th, 1903 wrote:
> Katherine A. Tingley wants money and she wants it bad. Despairing of getting $50,000 from the Times-Mirror Company, as a salve for alleged libel, she began a new action today by which she seeks to recover the modest sum of $75,000 damages for alleged blackmail conspiracy.
>
> This latest bluff of Mrs. Tingley is not taken seriously. . . The cause for action in the suit commenced today, a copy of the complaint being served on Gen. Otis in Judge Torrance's court about 4 o'clock this afternoon [10th], is based on the allegation that Mrs. Tingley in March, 1901, received a letter from one E.W. Schmidt, stating that he had in hand all her "back past," and asking how much it would be worth to her not to have it published.
>
> The complaint alleges that by the communication Schmidt and the other defendants meant to convey a threat that unless the plaintiff paid them a sum of money they would publish derogatory matter against her in the Los Angeles Times; that plaintiff refused to yield to the blackmailing demand, and in default of such payment October 28, 1901, H.G. Otis and co-defendants published a libel in The Times, thereby causing plaintiff to spend large sums of money in disproving said libel, wherefore she demands $75,000 damages.

The Los Angeles Times wrote that this complaint "is not taken seriously. It is a very weak and far-fetched, though none the less venal and vicious attempt . . . . perpetrated with malice aforethought" and reported that "Mrs. Tingley's other counsel refused to join with Hotchkiss in instituting so asinine a suit." **[Jan. 11, 1903]** One such counsel would have been Iverson L. Harris, Sr. (1860-1921), her personal attorney involved in all her other court cases. [*The Los Angeles Times,* **Sep.14, 1921**]

A.B. Hotchkiss filed the complaint as Attorney for the Plaintiff. [*San Diego Union and Daily Bee,* **Jan. 11, 1903**] and the complaint was issued by the District Attorney for Schmidt's arrest. "Constable Marks went to Los Angeles. . . to make formal service of the papers and bring Schmidt down." [*Los Angeles Times,* **Jan. 13, 1903**] Schmidt was in Court in San Diego on January 15th "on the charge of sending a threatening letter to Katherine Tingley". [*San Francisco Call*, Jan. 15, 1903] Unable to make bail, or find a lawyer, he spent the next few days in jail. In Judge Thorpe's court on January 17th it was argued by Sam F. Smith, Schmidt's lawyer, that the case was being heard in the wrong jurisdiction. The hearing nonetheless proceeded.

> Mrs. Tingley on the stand identified a letter said to have been written by Schmidt, which formed the basis of the charge. [*San Francisco Call*, Jan. 18, 1903]

Constable Marks testified next, and stated that in conversation with him, "Schmidt told him he had written a friendly letter to Mrs. Tingley for the purpose of warning her against others." [*San Diego Union and Daily Bee*, Jan.18, 1903]

At the end of the day, asserting the jurisdictional issue and lack of motive on Schmidt's part,

> Attorney Smith . . . moved that the case be dismissed, giving as his reasons that the court had no jurisdiction as it was proven by the prosecution that it had been committed in Los Angeles; that the prosecution had failed to prove any attempt on the part of the defendant to commit the offense as prosecution witness, and that the letter had been written in a friendly spirit, and for the purpose of warning the prosecuting witness rather than with any intent to extort.
>
> Judge Thorpe asked the prosecution if it had any other evidence to introduce. Judge Andrews [Tingley's attorney] said that there was none. The court then granted the motion of Mr. Smith to dismiss the case, and the defendant was released. [*San Diego Union and Daily Bee*, Jan.18, 1903]

Tingley then filed a writ of habeas corpus and had Schmidt returned; he was again discharged. The court jurisdictional issue continued; the letter had been written in Los Angeles so on February 13th Judge Conklin granted Schmidt, et al, a change of venue to Los Angeles [*Los Angeles Herald* and *Los Angeles Times*, Feb. 14, 1903] Tingley and her lawyers objected to Judge Smith's decision that "such cases must be prosecuted in the city in which the letter is mailed" [*Los Angeles Herald*, Feb. 20, 1903] but on August 28th, Judge Conklin struck "from the file the bill of exceptions filed by Mrs. Katherine Tingley [in March] on her appeal from the order granting a change of venue in her damage suit . . ." [*San Francisco Call*, Aug. 29, 1903]

Tingley was in Cuba for most of 1903. It was reported that Tingley left Point Loma on February 17th and it "was surmised . . . that Cuba is . . . the ultimate destination" as no one would say where she was going. [*Los Angeles Times*, Feb.18, 1903] The May 26th edition of the *Los Angeles Times* reported that she had been in Cuba "for several months"; she returned to New York November 29th, 1903. [*Los Angeles Times*, Nov. 30, 1903]. However, while she was away she had her lawyer republish the January 19th, 1903 summons in newspapers, on at least eight occasions between January and April 1903, and perhaps thereafter as well. She was determined to pursue Schmidt and Otis relentlessly. However, Cuba beckoned. *The San Francisco Call* of March 8th, 1903 reported:

> Katherine Tingley has secured for a Cuban Raja Yoga school the estate of the late General Sanchez, Governor of Santiago. . . and comprises 360 acres. The estate was occupied as his residence by the general.

It appears that the lawsuit did eventually fade way. *The Los Angeles Herald* reported that "[a] motion to dismiss the suit on the ground of delay in its prosecution" was presented in superior court in San Diego in December 1904. [Dec. 18, 1904] It was in fact dropped in early 1905. [*San Diego Reader*, Jeff Smith, July 2014]

Returning to Judge E.S. Torrance: Notably, he did not allow much factual evidence to be presented in the Tingley vs Times-Mirror case. This was his first case as Judge in the Superior Court of California. His reputation was in question before he was elected to office. On October 23rd, 1902 he received a "Strong endorsement by the San Diego Bar"

> In view of the exaggerated, unfounded, and in some instances, as we believe, malicious attacks which have recently been made upon the character and reputation of Judge E.S. Torrence, we, the undersigned members of the bar of San Diego county, consider it our duty to publicly express our confidence in him as a man and as a judge.

This endorsement was signed by 39 members of the bar. His name was placed on a ballot for election and on November 6th it was reported that he had won his place to sit on the bench of the Superior Court. Three other judges were elected: W.R. Guy, W.R. Andrews and N.H. Conklin. All three became very influential in sustaining Tingley's agenda at Point Loma. [*The Record*, **National City, CA, Oct. 23, 1902; Nov. 6, 1902**] And thanks to Judge Torrance in particular, although Tingley's was a very questionable victory against the *Times-Mirror*, she used it to spin her narrative of having attained success, and it seemed to provide encouragement to pursue numerous other litigations.

However, one year later, in January 1905, the Los Angeles Bar Association filed impeachment proceedings against Judge Torrance and an arraignment was filed citing his "alleged unfitness . . . to continue on the bench" and calling for an investigation and his removal. It was claimed that over at least the previous two years, he exhibited

> scandalous misconduct both on and off the bench, drunkenness, misdemeanors in office, willful misconduct and willful neglect of the duties thereof, and conduct unbecoming a judge of the Superior Court of the State of California. . . . frequently [drank] intoxicating liquors and caroused with litigants and lawyers representing litigants having actions and proceedings pending in his court. . . . was very profane, and would curse and abuse upon the public streets . . . reputable attorneys and other citizens of the State of California. . . . [*The Los Angeles Times*, **Jan. 17, 1905**]

The hearing by the committee appointed to investigate the charges began on February 4th, 1905 and ended February 10th. [*Los Angeles Herald*, **Feb. 5, 11, 1905**] They determined that he should be reprimanded but concluded that "from the facts found by us as herein presented . . . there is insufficient evidence to warrant impeachment proceedings." [*Los Angeles Herald*, **Mar. 2, 1905**]

The Neresheimers

The Neresheimers had been at Point Loma three and a half years when they "left the colony in 1904 and came to Denver. Mrs. Neresheimer was with him in the colony, and it has been reported that it was through her that he severed his relations with it." He denied having severed ties "and declared that he was still a loyal follower of Mrs. Tingley." It was announced in late 1911 that "E.A. Neresheimer, millionaire, will sell his beautiful home here" and that "he and his wife have planned to leave for Point Loma as soon as his business affairs were closed up" and return to live there "until the end of their days." [*Richmond Times Dispatch*, **Nov. 6, 1911**; *The South Bend Tribune*, **(IN), Nov. 15, 1911**; *Los Angeles Times*, **Oct. 16, 1911**]

Neresheimer was involved with irrigation and dam projects in the Denver area that came under investigation by the grand jury in Weld County in 1911. One year later it was reported that returned indictment after indictment led to "much money... turned back into the coffers of Weld county and a number of men... atoning for their crimes in the state penitentiary." [*Weekly Courier*, (CO), Oct. 11, 1912]

Then on October 7th, 1912, in Weld County, "the Grand Jury heretofore empaneled and sworn herein, have returned to the Court in open session a True Bill [i.e., sufficient evidence to warrant criminal charges] of Indictment against the said defendants..."; they being the men in charge of affairs: Neresheimer and four business partners, including Milton Smith, now his son-in-law. [**District Court Record for Weld County**] They were "indicted on four counts": guilty of conspiracy to commit larceny, embezzlement, and to obtain property by false pretenses. Bench warrants were issued for their arrest and bonds were fixed at $5000 each. They were accused of diverting $1,300,000 in bonds, the property of the Denver-Greeley Irrigation District, and obtaining control. [*The Fort Collins Express*, Oct. 10, 1912; *Albuquerque Journal*, **Oct. 8, 1912**] Neresheimer was obviously concerned about the possible outcome; he transferred titles for his personal properties to his wife and his son.

Several court procedures later, the hearing was set for December 2nd, 1913. Transcript of District Attorney George A. Carlson's decision reads that he:
> files herein his motion to dismiss the above entitled cause, . . . and is granted leave to dismiss the said cause... Whereupon it is ordered by the Court that the said defendants, . . . in this said indictment specified be discharged and go hence hereof without day, and that both they and their respective sureties herein be fully and finally released. [**District Court Record for Weld County**]

Carlson ran for Governor of the State of Colorado in 1914, and served as Governor for two years: 1915-1917.

E.A. Neresheimer is listed in the Denver City Directory as late as 1918. The announcement of 1911 of their plans to return to Point Loma seems to have been premature. The following was repeated in various papers at the time.
> A New York friend of the family is reported as saying that revelations in the suit of George L. Patterson, of Newcastle, Pa., against Mrs Tingley to recover $300,000 left by his mother, a

disciple of the "Purple Mother," led Mrs Neresheimer to appeal to her husband to quit the colony. [*Richmond Times Dispatch*, **Nov. 6, 1911**]

Harriet Patterson-Thurston died, July 25th, 1910. This court case was a turning point for a number of people.

Minnie Neresheimer died on August 17th, 1917 in Los Angeles. Emil wrote in his "Reminiscences" that "it was not until March, 1919, that I was again able to return to Point Loma". He remarried in November 1919 "in the large oriental room of Madame Tingley's home". [*San Diego Union & Daily Bee*, **Nov. 30, 1919**] He is listed in the 1920 San Diego Directory as vice-president of Theosophical University (which was established in December 1919), resident of Point Loma Homestead; and in the 1927 Directory he also holds the position of treasurer of Point Loma Homestead. He eventually became disillusioned with Tingley:

> The "Leader and Official Head", who even from the very beginning had frowned upon any differences of viewpoint from her own, had meanwhile expelled not only individuals, but had dissolved whole branches throughout the country, and abroad. . .
> As a result of her unsympathetic attitude, and that of others who followed her lead, the membership began to decrease rapidly, and thus most of the results of Mr. Judge's efforts to build up the Society throughout the country were lost. [**Reminiscences**]

Neresheimer "left Point Loma with my family early in March, 1929". He released "Some Reminiscences of William Q. Judge" in February 1932. [**Reminiscences**] He died at his home in Santa Monica on April 17th, 1937. Emily, his second wife, died in Los Angeles on September 21st, 1955.

Chapter Four

Revelations

There was obvious disenchantment within the society as illusions shattered and historical background was uncovered. Much effort was made to suppress information about Tingley prior to her involvement with the Theosophical Society. During the Katherine Tingley vs Times-Mirror Company court case in 1902-1903 significant evidence surfaced surrounding her life in New York City around 1892-1893.

John Morgan Pryse (1863-1952)
John M. Pryse stated under oath that Tingley "made passes over me with the apparent endeavor to hypnotize me. Many others have told me she did the same thing with them." **[Tingley vs Times-Mirror, 1457, p.365]**. He elaborated that this occurred "at a convention once" and at "the other occasion" **[1479, p.370]** which he elaborated "was a display of her ability to do so." **[1481, p.371]** Pryse stated:

> Her teacher in hypnotism was a man by the name of the Rev. McCarty [McCarthy], having a school of hypnotism in Harlem. He told me that she was his pupil; that he developed her clairvoyance and hypnotic powers, and that he considers her now, to use his own terms, the greatest black magician on the American Continent—which I do not believe. **[1459, p.365]**

Charles P. McCarthy (1826-1899)
Charles P. McCarthy was born in Ireland and died in New York City on November 25th, 1899. He founded a Universalist church in Philadelphia in 1862. In 1880 he gave up the ministry to follow the science of hypnotism and in 1892 Rev. Charles P. McCarthy opened a school for hypnotic study. *[New York Times*, **Nov. 27, 1899]** After opening his Academy he was called Dr. McCarthy and advertised his business as "Dr. McCarthy's Séance, Academy of Hypnotism". *[New York Tribune*, **April 7, 1892]**

McCarthy's home and working address was within minutes of where Tingley lived at the time. She took McCarthy's hypnotism classes after he advertized that his Academy was open for business. It is very likely that they

knew each other prior since McCarthy often dealt with mediums and gave lectures on the subject. The *Chicago Daily Tribune* wrote:
> Mrs. Tingley was in Boston for a few years, and then she made her appearance in New York. There, under the direction of Prof. Paul McCarthy, Mrs. Tingley studied hypnotism. As the professor once stated, 'he greatly improved her psychic gifts.' There can be no doubt of Mrs. Tingley's power of hypnotism, and she used them with great advantage. **[July 8, 1906]**

In 1896 McCarthy in an interview about his school of hypnotism stated: "I have devoted the last forty years of my life to the study of this science . . . ." [*The Atlanta Constitution*, **Atlanta, GA, Feb. 23, 1896**]

Edward W. Parker (1842-1908)
Another theosophist's testimony to consider is Edward W. Parker. He joined the T.S. in 1886 in St. Louis, Missouri. His endorsers were Elliott B. Page and Dr. J.D. Buck. He was a friend of W.Q. Judge and on the American Board of Control. He was a civil war veteran; a banker and financier who was instrumental in the building of the first hospital in the area in 1888 [*The Encyclopedia of Arkansas History and Culture;* **St.Vincent Health System, Mission and History**]; he established a banking and brokerage firm, E.W. Parker & Co. in 1888; he helped finance the publication of Blavatsky's *The Key to Theosophy,* for which Blavatsky sent him a copy with a signed inscription of appreciation (Sep. 27th, 1889); he built a hotel in Boston, MA; he amassed a large collection of books on mysticism, Asian beliefs and Hinduism, which he had arranged to be donated to the Manly P. Hall Theological Library in Los Angeles upon his death.

Following Tingley's takeover of T.S. in America, Parker "made inquiries into her character and life." During his testimony in the Tingley vs Times-Mirror Supreme Court case in January 1903, he stated:
> I stopped in Newburyport, Massachusetts between three or four days in August 1899, to make inquiry as to her career there, and I talked with various people who knew her to the number of about twenty. **[2198; p.550]**

When asked why he replied:
> Because I was simply endeavoring to ascertain her general reputation in the hope of opening the eyes of some good deluded men and women, friends of mine, who asked me to ascertain the facts. **[2214-2215; p.554]**

One in particular was Dr. Alfred A. Walton, who had spent his childhood and youth in Newburyport.

At the proceedings of the U.S. Board of Special Inquiry at Ellis Island in November 1902 regarding the Cuban Children case, Parker presented a letter dated November 9th, 1899 from Tingley's first husband, Richard Cook, whom he had contacted as part of his investigation. It (Exhibit D) was quoted in a newspaper report of the day's court proceedings:

> I married Kate Westcott, in 1867 at Savannah Ga. She came there from Montreal, after she had either been expelled or had run away from Ville Marie Convent. We had been lovers since we were children of about 12 years. I was surprised to see her there and immediately wrote to her father in Newburyport asking his permission for me to marry her. He replied that she was of age and could do as she chose; that he would have nothing more to do with her, anyway. We were married and lived together two months. At the end of that time I found out that she was visiting a Boston woman who was in Savannah, and whom I knew was a woman of evil reputation. I told her that she must either leave her alone or leave me. The result was we separated. I eventually came to New York.
>
> In 1874 I began suit for a divorce. She then lived in Sixth avenue, in New York. In talking of the prospective suit with her I agreed that I would bring my action on grounds of desertion, to avoid scandal. When the time came to serve the papers we could not find her at the Sixth avenue address, and I wrote to her brother in Newburyport asking where she was. He replied that she was dead. Some time later I received a letter from her asking me to call on her at the address given in New York and found she was married again. [*The New York Press*, **Nov. 8, 1902**; *New York Herald*, **Nov. 8, 1902**]

In answer to questioning about his findings Parker stated that Tingley had a "very bad" reputation in Newburyport, and that

> she had commenced a dissolute career at twelve years of age. That she had separated families. That she had lived in a home of ill fame in Boston. [**Tingley vs Times-Mirror, 2201-2202, p.551**]

He further testified that he had been given names to follow up with by Charles P. McCarthy. Parker testified that he had spoken with Charles P. McCarthy, who knew her and was "an opponent of Mrs. Tingley's". **[2226, p.557]** At the time of the court case, Parker was an active member of the society that "Mr Fullerton is the General Secretary [of] in this country." **[2207, p.552]**

Dr. Henry Hugo Reuthling (b. August 1862 - ??)
Dr. Henry Hugo Reuthling, a personal friend and neighbor of Katherine Tingley, testified that he met her "in the Fall of 1893," that her business "was a magnetic healer and medium", that she claimed to have the powers of a hypnotist **[Tingley vs Times-Mirror, 1346-1348, p.337]** and, based on his own personal experience, that Mrs Tingley had a bad reputation as a fraud in the neighborhood. **[1366, p.342]** He continued: "Her general reputation was a low one, a low reputation . . . in the first place, she was very untruthful." **[1401-1402, p.351]** "She had that reputation among all people that had any dealings with her. . . . Her reputation among the people she had dealings with was that of an untruthful and unreliable woman, and as a fraud." **[1406-1407, p.352]**

In a report in *The Sun*, Reuthling is quoted as stating at the hearing at Ellis Island:
> Mrs. Tingley invited me to her house on the pretext of meeting her husband. . . . She told me she could cure ills by passing her hands over persons and by massage. Her patients were mostly men. She locked herself in the room with them.
>
> She practiced hypnotism. She tried to hypnotize me. Her methods were indecent. I was very indignant. *[The Sun* **(NY), Nov. 8, 1902]**

The New York Tribune on November 16th, 1902 wrote that while he was living next door in 1892, Tingley "was known as a masseuse and hypnotist."

In his Tingley vs Times-Mirror court testimony he stated:
> I called at her home one time on an invitation from her. I found the rest of the family absent and she seated herself very close by me and commenced to speak to me very rapidly, staring at me intently and making suggestions which I considered improper —
> . . . . I found her speech improper and suggestive. . . . I saw very plainly that the woman had impure intentions.

When questioned further:

> Q. What do you mean by the use of the word impure?
> A. Well, I mean by that her suggestions were of a sexual nature, that is what I mean to say.
> Q. What did you understand from her language and conduct?
> A. Nothing else could be understood but what the woman wished.
> . . . Well, no woman would directly ask a man to do a certain thing. . . I understood it very plainly to be a desire for sexual intercourse. [**Tingley vs Times-Mirror, 1353-1359, pp.339-340**]

In reference to her healing cures:
> Mrs. Tingley herself explained to me how she had cured sick people, for instance how she had cured a sick brother, Westcott, by treating him by magnetism, but he died very soon after he got in her house. [**1350, p.338**]

George W. Westcott was Katherine's younger brother, born April 13th, 1853. He was the only family member who actually had anything to do with her. As mentioned earlier, in 1880 George lived with Katherine and her then husband George Parent. George Westcott died in a Boston hospital May 28th, 1893. He suffered from morphine poisoning and died of heart failure. [*Massachusetts Death records.*]

Seizing the Opportunity

When it became obvious that W.Q. Judge's health was failing, the opportunity to capture the Theosophical Society in America was seized.

One is left to wonder whether the scheme to hijack T.S. in America was planned before Judge's death, possibly before Judge was at Mineral Wells with Tingley. How else to explain the speed with which this scheme was executed. Tingley took over as Head of the E.S.; orchestrated the mysterious 'mahatma' charade; announced plans to establish the 'school'; and amassed funding and enthusiasm for the world tour—all within a three-month period. Since there is no evidence that Judge ever appointed Tingley to anything, this seems to have been planned in advance. If Tingley was as good a psychic as her associates claimed, it would have been easy for her to determine the state of Judge's health. This might also explain why Tingley never visited Judge after his return to New York in early 1896. Judge allowed very few visitors near the end; one would expect that his supposed 'successor' would have been one of them.

There has never been any material evidence to support that William Q. Judge ever appointed Katherine Tingley to any position in the Theosophical Society in America and yet she kept repeating that after meeting Judge it led "eventually to his appointment of me as his successor in the leadership of the Society." [*Splendor of the Soul*] The only so-called evidence presented has been innuendo, contrived and circumstantial at best. A very influential yet mostly overlooked individual who was closely involved with the ascension of Tingley to leadership of the Esoteric School after Judge's death was none other than Frank Marshall Pierce, her loyal supporter throughout the years. He helped orchestrate the hijacking of the Theosophical Society in America by influencing others to streamline the process to position Katherine Tingley. It seemed this duo had a broader scheme in mind—to be fulfilled in future. Pierce was the covert power in the background, at least until February 1898 at which point Tingley seized total control by forming The Universal Brotherhood.

The *Sterling Daily Gazette* later described the following:
> On Jan. 13, 1898, at her home in New York, she established the Universal Brotherhood and at the convention of the Theosophical Society a month later in Chicago the constitution of the Universal Brotherhood was adopted and the Theosophical Society was merged into it. Mrs. Tingley was elected as President for life, with power to appoint her successor. [*Sterling Daily Gazette* (IL), July 11, 1929]

There is no evidence that Pierce was ever a member of the Theosophical Society during Judge's lifetime, or that he ever attended any meetings. But he had the motive, the desire, the admiration for Tingley, and the opportunity to convince those close to her to band together and appoint her as their new leader—all within days of Judge's death.

Pierce was an Engineer, whose primary income in his early years came from selling "drills for blasting." In 1898 his company advertized in the *New York Tribune* as "Frank M. Pierce Engineering Company, Contracting Engineers" and listed Power Plants Designed & Installed; Electric Railways Financed, Built and Equipped; Rice & Sargent engines and other high grade engines and boilers. The address was Havemeyer Building, 26 Cortlandt St., New York. However, by 1893-94 there were clear signs that his business was in severe financial difficulty.

Frank and Maria married March 26th, 1874 and lived with her parents, Henry and Mary Bullwinkle. Mary died December 15th, 1886; it appears that Frank and Maria continued to live with Henry, who died on June 3rd, 1893. The New York City directory for the year ending July 1st, 1893, lists Francis M. Pierce as living at 51 West 87th. Because Henry died without a will, Maria applied to Kings County Surrogate's Court for "Letters of Administration" to deal with the estate, which mentioned, "no real estate". She is shown as "Petitioner" and "resident of Sherman Square Hotel in the City of New York", where according to the 1893-1894 NYC directory, Frank was also living. The directory to July 1st, 1895 shows him living at The Gerlach Hotel. Frank struggled financially; sometime in 1895 he moved in with the Tingleys and Joseph Fussell at 373 West End Avenue, the di Brazza residence, where he did not pay rent.

In October 1898 Fussell wrote about him in *The New Century Path*:
> F.M. Pierce in point of time is one of the newest members but a new force came into the work when he joined it. He is one of those who seems to understand the occultism that lies in daily life and who carries out the philosophy in all that he does even more than many older students, commanding respect and evoking love in all.
> **[2:3, Oct. 22, 1898, p.6]**

Pierce later admitted that Fussell was his best friend, and named him as his 'nearest relative' when hospitalized from January 24th to December 16th, 1918 at the Battle Mountain Sanitarium in Hot Springs, South Dakota, a U.S. National Home for Disabled Volunteer Soldiers. The "disabilities when admitted" include "neurasthenia, habitual constipation, fanatic, arteriosclerosis, arthritis, defective vision". He was readmitted from July 13th to October 13th, 1925. **[Ancestry]** Pierce died March 27th, 1926 at Point Loma. **[*Theosophical Path*, 30:5, May 1926, p.499]**

Following the Leonard/Falls Wright wedding ceremony on May 3rd, 1896, it was suspected that Tingley was the new "Mahatma". Reporters would go to her residence and try to have an interview. During one such attempt, the reporter was met by a servant who disclosed that:
> Mrs. Tingley is at her office, No. 144 Madison avenue. However, the servant said if I wanted to see Mrs. Tingley I had better call before June 16, for then Mrs. Tingley started on a trip to California, and perhaps for a trip around the world. Mrs. Tingley expects to return in a little less than a year. . . .

Pierce's close involvement was demonstrated a few days later:

> In order to obtain a personal interview with Mrs. Tingley I called at her house again Wednesday evening. This time I met Frank M. Pierce, president of the Pierce & Miller Engineering Company, the offices of which are in room No. 1,006, Havemeyer Building, No. 26 Cortlandt street. It appears that Mr. Pierce is interested in theosophy, and resides with the Tingleys. While Mrs. Tingley remained out of the parlor, Pierce appeared for her. Before we commenced our conversation Mr. Pierce drew a pair of portières together. . . During our talk Mrs. Tingley stood on the stairs, but did not make her appearance to the parlor. [*New York Herald*, **May 17, 1896**]

The H.P.B. Branch had a number of reporters among their members. It's not clear if the reporter who went to interview Tingley was a member of the H.P.B. Branch, but may have been surprised when Pierce answered the door and then proceeded to personally handle the interview. Pierce was obviously a closely involved participant in the intrigue.

A strong alliance between Frank Pierce and Katherine and Philo Tingley is further evidenced by their applications for passports a few weeks before the departure of the Crusaders on the world tour. On June 5th, 1896, Frank M. Pierce signed his Passport Application form and his Oath of Allegiance. Philo B. Tingley signed as Notary Public and Katherine A. Tingley witnessed. On his application, Frank stated that his permanent residence was 373 West End Avenue, NY City and that he was a Contracting Engineer. He asked that his passport be sent to 26 Cortlandt St., New York, his business address.

On June 6th Katherine A. Tingley signed her passport application form. She specified that her passport be sent to 373 W. End Ave. Frank M. Pierce signed her application as witness and also specified this as his residence address. Pierce also witnessed Philo's application, both again using the same address. Philo provided his date of birth, December 9th, 1857, and Katherine gave hers as July 6th, 1850, thereby removing three years off the actual date. Even under oath it was common for her to vary the year of her birth. On her last passport, issued April 30th, 1928, she claimed to have been born in 1852. Tingley employed the services of Dr. Maretta Dixon, a dermatologist, for facial treatments. Dr. Dixon advertised:

Every lady engaging to have this wonderful work accomplished is guaranteed to have from ten to twenty-five years taken off her looks. [*San Diego Union & Daily Bee,* Oct. 28, 1907]

It apparently gave Tingley the confidence to incrementally remove years from her actual year of birth.

All three passports were issued on June 11th, 1896, two days before departure. Philo and Frank demonstrated little interest in theosophical teachings; Katherine herself had been a member only since October 1894, and none of them could afford the "crusade" trip around the world.

On their return from the Crusaders' tour Tingley is quoted as saying that Pierce was "A New York business man, who did quiet but effective work, which will bear fruit in the future." [*The Indianapolis Journal,* Mar. 21, 1897] Pierce was the business manager of the organization in the early days; there was no man Tingley trusted more. She appointed him as a member of her Cabinet in 1896 and as Secretary General of the Universal Brotherhood upon its inception in 1898. He was the general supervisor of all that happened at the International Theosophical Headquarters, Point Loma, with the authority to stop any improvements.

The transcript of Pierce's testimony during the Tingley vs Times-Mirror court case includes questioning about his position of General Secretary.

> Q: Who, if anybody, has power to terminate it or bring it to a close?
>
> A: Myself, no one else that I know of, during good conduct. Katherine Tingley, the plaintiff in this action, has not the power to terminate my Secretaryship as long as I perform my duties properly. [3205, p.802]

When questioned further

> Q: Is there any other person, any committee, board or group of persons associated with you, that has or had the power of terminating your Secretaryship or your membership of the cabinet?

Pierce responded:

> A: No further than I have stated that I know of and that is myself. [3211, p.803]

It becomes evident that Tingley and Pierce were equally into this scheme.

At eighteen years of age Pierce enlisted in Pittsfield, MA, as a Private in Company K, Massachusetts 8th Infantry Regiment in the Union Army during the Civil War. He would eventually use his military experience to head military-style drills on a regular basis, with guns, at Point Loma to guard the perimeter of the property with its three and half foot high fence. He said it was to keep out the jack rabbits and cotton tails. [3201, p.801] He stated, "I am familiar with all the grounds, buildings and conditions at Point Loma and that includes the entire grounds, the Colony, the Homestead, the School of Antiquity and the Lotus Home." [3182, p.796]

The *Journal of San Diego History* interviewed Iverson L. Harris Jr. in the summer of 1974. He recounted his early experience at Point Loma:

> We would get up in the morning about 5:30 and we would go out and have calisthenics, physical drill. In those days, we even carried guns. We had military drill because the Secretary General of our Society at that time, Frank M. Pierce, was a Civil War veteran and thoroughly believed in military discipline. We had some of the discipline, we learned to march and so forth. We learned the manual of arms. . . . We would go out and do a gun drill. . . . Then at about seven o'clock, we'd all march to breakfast in the community dining room where we all ate together. . . .
>
> But I must say that until Dr. De Purucker took over we had no technical training in Theosophy at all. . . .[20:3, Summer 1974]

NEW CENTURY GUARD SENTINELS OF RAJA YOGA SCHOOL, LOMA-LAND, IN LINE FOR DUTY

[*The New Century*, 4:15, June 21, 1901, p.10]

Taking Control

Like H.P.B., Judge did not appoint a successor; it was a test, left to the wisdom of the members. It was however known by those closest to him that Judge regarded Hargrove "as my own son". **[The Future of the Theosophical Publishing Co., by Julia Keightley, Feb. 27, 1898, p.4]** James H. Connelly [1840-1903], a good friend of H.P. Blavatsky and W.Q. Judge, was an American journalist who worked on some of the best newspapers in the country and was on the staff of nearly all the prominent papers in New York city. He assisted Judge on *Notes on the Bhagavad-Gita* and *The Yoga Aphorisms of Patanjali*. In an article titled "Theosophy's New Leader" about the annual convention, April 26-27, 1896 and the selection of Hargrove as president of T.S. in America, he wrote:

> [I]t was made known, with unquestioned authority, that Mr. Judge had expressed strongly his wish that Mr. Hargrove should succeed him. Under these circumstances the 230 delegates present, representing 99 branches in all parts of the country, ratified the selection without any dissent. **[*The Dispatch*, (Moline, IL), May 11, 1896]**

Perhaps Judge had Hargrove in mind to also head the Esoteric School when urged to mention to Hargrove in 1895 that he was needed in America.

Frank Pierce, the nearly forgotten man, was quietly involved at every step. Tingley informed Neresheimer which committee members could participate in the decision-making process; he was instrumental in convincing them that she was the person Judge wanted as his successor. Tingley ascertained that the Head of the Esoteric Section overrode the President, then declined the presidency. Joseph H. Fussell worked at T.S. headquarters and had access to all of Judge's records; Emil August Nereshiemer was one of the executors of Judge's Will. The other individuals who participated in installing Tingley as head of the E.S. were Ernest T. Hargrove, James M. Pryse, H. T. Patterson, and Clement Acton Griscom, Jr. The actions of Pierce and Neresheimer were essentially responsible for Tingley's rise to power. However, next to Tingley herself, Pierce was the most powerful person in the organization.

The easiest to hoodwink was Hargrove. He was interested in Neresheimer's daughter, which tended to make him vulnerable to influence (he and Aimee married on January 17th, 1899). He likely also felt intimidated by the others since he was the youngest and newest member. Not only was Hargrove rather naive at the time, he only met Tingley for the first time five or six days after Judge's death. Patterson was already on board, having been a regular visitor at the Tingleys. The Griscoms might not have known Tingley very well, if at all, as she was not a regular at T.S. meetings and events. Genevieve Griscom was psychic herself and had received personal training from Judge. Judge occasionally stayed with the Griscoms in Flushing, Long Island, sometimes for weeks at a time, instead of going home to Brooklyn, and would explain occultism to her. Clement Griscom was extremely busy with his involvement in the ocean liner enterprise and various other businesses. James Morgan Pryse at first was supportive, until his brother John explained to him why he was not, and James saw and read some of Judge's alleged diaries.

These individuals were among the E.S. members living close enough to attend a meeting at Headquarters on Sunday March 29th, 1896. A statement was read to those in attendance, informing them "of the authenticity of the new 'Outer Head'" a copy of which was then mailed to all E.S. members. A few days later a circular marked "Strictly Private and Confidential" was sent to the E.S.T. members globally, 19pp, dated April 3rd, 1896.

The circular included an introductory statement and a verbatim transcript of the March 29th meeting. It opened with "This is done according to the directions of the late Outer Head, William Q. Judge." From a review of events it seems more to have been at the direction of Katherine Tingley. As noted in *The Theosophical Movement 1875-1925* (pp.667-671), Judge's "private papers" are alluded to as "proofs" of selecting Tingley, but nowhere is it confirmed that they were in "Mr. Judge's own handwriting," adding:

> The much-proclaimed and never-produced "private papers of Mr. Judge" bear a rather remarkable likeness to "private notes" of Mrs. Tingley. [p.671]

Neresheimer and Wright had been "consulting" Tingley for a year or more before Judge's death and accepted "messages from the Masters" received through her by psychic means (trance), one in particular from March 1895 concluded with, "Under no circumstances must Mr. Judge know of this." [p.669] From the inception of the Esoteric School of Theosophy by H.P.B., members were strictly forbidden from seeking occult instruction from a second source; they apparently forgot, or more likely, were compelled, to ignore this rule.

The chosen participants became the supporting cast. Since Hargrove was likely to be the new President, they made him the front man to answer questions from the media and general membership, and to defend the narrative that was being presented. He had only been in the country since the fall of 1895, travelling and lecturing most of that time and not closely involved with matters at headquarters. It was mostly he who had to defend the supposed necessity to conceal the identity of the new "Mahatma" for an entire year; the more he defended Tingley and the narrative the more he became embedded into the scheme.

> Katherine Tingley had insisted that her identity must remain unknown for a year to all except the "Council of Guardians". To all others she wished to be known only by the name of "Promise".
> **[Reminiscences]**

And newspapers asking questions about the 'adept' were lied to and told 'he' was of foreign birth.

Everything was orchestrated to happen very quickly—within a few weeks of Judge's death. According to Neresheimer:

> What was done by Katherine Tingley during this interval and transition stage was nothing short of genius in her versatility, bold and precise action, and her making use of her collaborators in the best possible manner. **[Reminiscences]**

He added that Tingley immediately took over the Headquarters, "where she went daily, directing and supervising all the various activities of the different departments of the Society." He claimed that

> [a]fter she had taken the place of "Outer Head" I was forcibly struck by the great difference between her and Mr. Judge, who, to my observation, had at all times been consistent in word and act with the philosophy and teaching he promulgated.

A somewhat irreverent article printed in *The Birmingham Age-Herald* (July 16, 1906), taken from the New York *Sun*, included the following:

> . . . Mrs. Tingley convinced many of the members that while Hargrove was all right as the nominal president, she was really the secret head of the organization, the adept whose identity was not to be revealed until one year after the death of Judge.

Tingley had gone to Ville Marie Convent, a Jesuit school in Montreal for five years (1862-1867), was trained in hypnosis, lied about her past, abandoned her first husband, deceived her closest friend Countess di Brazza and many others. Her parents (Capt. James P.L. Westcott and Susan Chase Westcott) and her older brother, James W. Westscott, wanted nothing to do with her—there had to be reasons why.

A New Direction — Point Loma

At the Evening Session on the first day of the Second Annual Convention of T.S. in America, held at New York City April 26-27, 1896, James Morgan Pryse spoke on Judge's emphasis that "placing Theosophy before the children . . . [was] one of the most important activities of the Society." Claude Falls Wright spoke next about the founding of a School for the Revival of the Lost Mysteries of Antiquity. Katherine Tingley followed, still unrevealed as the mystery 'mahatma', about such a school being "the opportunity of the nineteenth century"and exclaiming "Oh God, my God! Is there no help for us?" [p.26] Volunteer subscriptions that very evening collected $4250 toward building of the school.

This announcement had obviously been planned well in advance of the convention. On May 8th, 1896 *The Franklin Democrat* (IN) reported:

> The site of the new school of theosophy has already been decided upon. In fact, it is said that a mahatma, or something of the kind, has been guarding the chosen spot carefully for many years, to prevent the intrusion of profane feet. The exact place is a secret, known only to the illuminati. But it is known that the site is on a mountain in the west.

On June 1st, 1896 *The Sun* (NY) wrote a lengthy article about the Crusade which was leaving June 13th. Hargrove gave an outline of the stops, culminating with their arrival in San Francisco (February 11th, 1897), then from there:

> Our most important business on this trip from San Francisco will be to dedicate the site of the School for the Revival of the Lost Mysteries of Antiquity. The place has already been chosen, but we are not ready to make it public yet. One reason for this is that the purchase of ground has not been consummated yet, and we do not desire to have to pay ten times as much for the property as it is worth.

Neresheimer wrote in his "Reminiscences" that while he was in Dublin with the Crusaders in August 1896, a few days before his return to New York, Tingley instructed him to "purchase a tract of land" at Point Loma before their arrival at San Francisco. He added that he followed up with Griscom and Rambo. A newspaper article later reported that the crusaders arrived in Bombay on October 25th, 1896 and it was supposedly while in India that Tingley had a vision of a site, complete with buildings and gardens, revealed to be in Point Loma. [*Los Angeles Times*, **June 16, 1897**]

A different version of the story was recounted by G. de Purucker on April 26th, 1930. He stated that he met Tingley for the first time in Geneva, Switzerland where he was living and while the Crusade was on tour. When she realized G deP had lived in San Diego she asked him the name of the peninsula in the area, telling him that she had never been there but had seen it. It was Point Loma. He drew a map of the San Diego area, Tingley immediately sent a telegram to Neresheimer, who transmitted it to Rambo and Griscom. [*The Eclectic Theosophist*, **July/Aug. 1985, p.8**]

Clement A. Griscom Jr., whose health was breaking down as a result of overwork, was advised by his physician to take a rest and was recommended a sea voyage. He decided to sail to Honolulu to meet the Crusaders on the final leg of the world tour. He combined this with the opportunity to complete the purchase of the Point Loma property. He arrived in San Diego on January 9th, 1897 and together with Edward Rambo, who arrived from San Francisco on the 15th, they proceeded to examine the properties on the point. In Griscom's own words, written January 23rd, 1897:
> [Rambo] proceeded with the collection of data, the names of property owners, their addresses and circumstances, the values of land, and in many cases, offers and specific prices for property in the neighborhood were obtained. [*Theosophical News*, **1:34, Feb. 8, 1897, p.3**]

The *San Diego Union and Daily Bee* reported on January 27th, 1897:
> Mr. Rambo, acting on the instructions from Mr. Griscom, concluded the purchase of 120 acres on Point Loma, paying $12,000 therefor. The deeds were filed yesterday afternoon ....

Griscom had left for San Francisco on the 24th, sailed for Honolulu on the 26th on the *Australia* and encountered storms which extended the time at sea; the ship pulled into port in Hawaii on February 2nd. The Crusaders arrived early on the morning of February 4th on the *S.S. Alameda*, having left Sydney, Australia seventeen days earlier. Griscom met them and then left with them for San Francisco that evening. [*The Honolulu Advertiser*, **Feb. 5, 1897**]

Speculation was expressed in the newspapers surrounding the reason for the purchase of these lots on Point Loma. Among the guesses: the laying of a telegraph cable from San Diego to Japan via Honolulu for the Pacific Cable Company of New York, or creating terminals for International Navigation Company and/or Union Pacific railroad. *The San Francisco Call* clarified the matter when it reported on January 31st, 1897:
> The reasons for the purchase of 132 acres of land near Point Loma, San Diego, by G.A. Griscom of New York, . . . is made for the purpose of establishing on Point Loma a school for the revival of the lost mysteries of antiquity.

By mid-June the purchase of additional lots increased their holdings to 235 acres, covering over a mile of ocean front property on Point Loma. [*San Diego Union & Daily Bee*, **June 15, 1897**]

The Crusaders had sailed into San Francisco at the end of their world tour on February 11th, 1897. Before heading to New York, the cornerstone of the future school was laid. An elaborate ceremony was held on February 23rd with invited guests and onlookers estimated to number one thousand people. [*San Diego Union*, **Feb. 24, 1897**; *Fort Wayne Daily News*, **Mar. 13, 1897**] Among the dignitaries invited:
> President Philip Morse of the Chamber of Commerce, Mayor Carlson, Judges Hughes and Torrance of the Superior Court, and others will be present in their official capacity . . . [*New York Times*, **Feb. 23, 1897**]

Two years later, while attending the congress held at the site of the future School for the Revival of the Lost Mysteries of Antiquity at Point Loma, Tingley "rededicated" the cornerstone. When asked when it would be built, she responded "When the masters order." $35,000 had been raised by then. [*The Sun* (NY), **May 1, 1899**]

The article continued:
> While attending the congress at Point Loma Mrs. Tingley put up at a hotel about a quarter of a mile from the grounds where the meetings were held. She drove over at each meeting in an open

carriage, behind an undertaker's team of snow-white horses. She dressed in loose flowing robes of royal purple, and had her little dog by her side; the coachman was dressed in white, and wore a purple badge with the word "Loyalty"on it. No one was allowed to address her as she went along, but all heads were bared. She was met at the gate of the grounds (a large triumphal arch) by her "cabinet" with uncovered heads, and at that moment four trumpeters, stationed on the prayer tower (an old well derrick), sounded to the four quarters of the world a proclamation of universal brotherhood. Preceded by the President, Mr. Neresheimer, she entered the auditorium and ascended the platform, the audience standing with bowed heads. [*The Sun* (NY), May 1, 1899]

Following are excerpts from the closing statement by Samuel Shortridge, lawyer for the defense at the Tingley vs Times-Mirror court case, presented on January 10th, 1903:

We see full grown men proud to surrender their individuality; willing to become her subjects; willing to appear as servitors in her royal retinue. Whether we call the men feeble-minded, and woman earnest and sincere, the fact remains that the power this woman exercises is extraordinary and repugnant to the spirit of America. It goes back to the dark ages and to foreign countries. It seems that she snatched the scepter and grasped the crown from the dead, she claims to be the successor of Mme. Blavatsky and William Q. Judge—a successor self-appointed. She has taken her seat upon the throne and American citizens are proud to do her bidding. It is extraordinary. She is vested with life-tenure and with power to appoint her own successor, and with power to cast into outer darkness such members of her organization as come under her displeasure. It is a power autocratic, un-American and un-Christian. Yet revolting as it is, there are those who seem proud to be her subjects. No despot that sat at Constantinople, ever claimed to extrude such power over men and women as Mrs. Katherine Tingley does, and strangest of all, does it with their consent. . . .

We have a right to speak of her as a colossal fraud and a monumental fake. [*Los Angeles Herald*, Jan. 11, 1903]

[*San Francisco Call*, August 5, 1900]

Chapter Five

The International Brotherhood League

Within weeks of her return to New York on April 4th, 1897 following the Crusaders' world tour, Tingley introduced another grand plan. On April 29th she launched "The International Brotherhood League" and converted the headquarters of the Theosophical Society in America at 144 Madison Avenue into the "Headquarters of the War Relief Corps".

I. B. L. and War Relief Corps Headquarters—the General Committee on the steps.

[*The New Century*, 1:45, August 27, 1898, p.7]

In August 1897 she opened an aid station in Harlem at 58 West One Hundred and Twenty-fifth Street. A committee included Anna M. Stabler, Solomon F. Hecht, Daniel N. Dunlop and other members of the H.P.B. Branch. Dr. Herbert A.W. Coryn, who had joined the American Section in 1895, became physician-in-chief in charge of the nurses' training class which met on Monday and Thursday evenings. [**New York Times, Aug. 19, 1898**]

Complaints among theosophical members were that the society had been converted into a charitable organization and that Theosophy was no longer the focus. The President of T.S. in America, Ernest Hargrove, and the President of T.S. in Europe, Dr. Archibald Keightley, resigned in August and November respectively, as did numerous individuals, including Julia Verplanck Keightley. [*The Sun* (NY), Dec. 28, 1897] Membership across the country plummeted.

Work Room at Headquarters, showing the ladies making up goods, Dr. Coryn instructing nurses, and the General Committee holding a meeting in the background.

[*The New Century*, 1:45, August 27, 1898, p.7]

Cuba had been fighting for its independence from Spain for some time; "the U.S. joined in to help its neighbor." [*Time*, Jan. 22, 2015] The Spanish-American War was officially fought from April 21st to August 12th, 1898. A Notice from "Editor" [Tingley] appeared in *The New Century*, September 1898 issue. It read in part:

> . . . I am now making preparations in connection with the International Brotherhood League to go to the Philippines or to

Cuba, and am arranging for *The New Century* to be carried on during my absence . . . . **[1:49, Sep. 24, 1898, p.2]**

General William Ludlow, a member of the Aryan Branch since 1891, was the probable liaison regarding these proposed excursions. He was a firm believer in Theosophy and contributed articles to *Theosophical Quarterly*. He wrote:

> Theosophy embraces every department of thought and knowledge, physical, mental and spiritual, and constitutes in itself a complete philosophy on all planes of existence. **[23, Jan. 1926, p.211]**

He also happened to be Genevieve Griscom's father/Clement Griscom Jr's father-in-law.

Ludlow had an impressive military career. He graduated from the University of the City of New York, and the United States Military Academy in 1864, and was commissioned in the Corps of Engineers. He served in engineering and scientific capacities in various regions of the USA. Among his achievements: he oversaw the mapping and data collection in the Black Hills of South Dakota, including Yellowstone (1870s); served as Engineer Commissioner in Washington, DC (1886-1888); served as military attaché at the Embassy in London (1893-1896); served as Chairman of the Nicaragua Canal Commission (1895; in August he was promoted to Lieutenant Colonel); then in 1898 he commanded the 1st Brigade of Henry Lawton's division during the siege of Santiago, Cuba, in the Spanish-American war.

> [H]e was promoted to Major General of Volunteers in September and in December was appointed Military Governor of the city and Department of Havana remaining in that post until April 1900 and contributing much to the rebuilding of the city. While in Havana he was promoted in January 1900 to Brigadier General, United States Army. . . .
>
> In May 1901[he] was ordered to the Philippines . . . but soon returned to the United States on sick leave. He died on August 30, 1901 . . . and was buried with full military honors . . . Arlington National Cemetery. **[Arlington National Cemetery.net/wludlow]**

His death was attributed to tuberculosis contracted in Cuba. He had a distinguished career in military and civil engineering. His integrity was always regarded as beyond question.

American involvement in the war officially ran from April to August, 1898. Soldiers wounded as a result of the fighting between the Spaniards and Americans in Cuba were being brought to Camp Wikoff, the military installation at Montauk on Long Island, NY, to be treated. On August 4th Major General Samuel Young was ordered to take command of the installation "referred to in all orders of the War Department [as] Montauk Point Camp." [*The Brooklyn Eagle*, Aug. 4, 1898]

On August 19th and 21st the International Brotherhood League made preliminary visits to what was to become "The Brotherhood Hospital at Montauk" to make arrangements and to determine what was most urgently needed. On August 23rd Dr. Coryn and a few assistants went as an advance party to set up camp. Tingley, F.M. Pierce and a number of others arrived the next day.

> The International Brotherhood League . . . continued in operation for three weeks. Rest and aid was given to exhausted soldiers. Many, just convalescent, or thought to be so, leaving camp on furlough and making for the depot (in some cases a walk of two and a half miles), were utterly exhausted by the time they had reached our hospital, which was located on the main road from camp, and within a short distance from the depot. [*The New Century*, 1:48, Sep. 17, 1898, p.7]

The exact location was described:
> The tents were pitched on the road leading to the main camp from the railroad station, and near a branch of the road leading to another part of the camp. . . It was about 300 yards from the railroad station, and nearly all the troops as they came into or left the camp had to pass our tents. It was a march of from one to three miles from the station to the various divisions of the camp . . . .
> [*Universal Brotherhood*, 13:7, Oct. 1898, p.399]

It was reported in local newspapers that the theosophists had
> established a relief tent about three-quarters of a mile from the Montauk Point depot. There are four female and seven male nurses in attendance, and there are twenty sick in the tent. [*The Birmingham News*, Birmingham, AL, Aug. 30, 1898; *Democrat and Chronicle*, Rochester, NY, Aug. 31, 1898]

The site eventually consisted of seven hospital tents and a wooden structure for a kitchen. The I.B.L. tents were near the perimeter of the base and were apparently met with "considerable opposition from some quarters" as well as "incidental" obstacles while some were "*placed in our way*." However, the same article acknowledges the assistance of General Wheeler and other officials. [*The New Century*, 1:47, Sep. 10, 1898, p.7; *Universal Brotherhood*, 13:7, Oct. 1898, p.401-402] General Wheeler was commander of Camp Wikoff from August 19th to September 4th, 1898. [https://aaqeastend.com/contents/camp-wikoff-national-military-park-proposal-revised-10-16-17/] When back in the United States, Wheeler commanded the convalescent camp of the army at Montauk Point, now a state park in New York. [*Harper Encyclopedia of Military Biography*, T.N. Dupuy, C. Johnson, D. Bongard; HarperCollins Publishers, 1992; p.794]

General Ludlow arrived at Montauk from Santiago, Cuba on the transport ship *Mohawk* by August 25th. *The Brooklyn Eagle* wrote that day that "Brigadier General William Ludlow, who recently arrived at Montauk from Santiago, has been ordered to report to Washington." [Aug. 25, 1898] He visited his wife at the residence of C.A. Griscom Jr. on August 27th while on his way from Camp Wikoff to Washington with General Russell Alger. [*The Brooklyn Eagle*, Aug. 28, 1898] General Alger was appointed Secretary of War in the Cabinet of U.S. President William McKinley on March 5th, 1897. General Alger had gone to Montauk Camp to do a personal inspection following a complaint about deplorable conditions. He found that things were better than expected and "with sanitary arrangements now being made, such as digging drains and filling in puddles, the camp would be in excellent condition." [*The Sun*, (NY), Aug. 27, 1898] (Secretary of War Alger closed the military encampment at Montauk on October 9th, 1898.)

An article in *The Sun* mentioned that Tingley sat at the entrance of one of the tents. Presumably, General Ludlow and General Alger would have gone past the International Brotherhood League's location. Tingley and General Ludlow, a long-standing member of the Aryan Branch of T.S. in America, would have known each other. General Alger was likely introduced to Tingley on this occasion. Plans to provide relief services elsewhere were obviously discussed, as shortly after, Tingley announced that she expected to go to the Philippines or Cuba.

The September 17th, 1898 issue of *The New Century* included a copy of a letter Tingley had written to President McKinley under heading "Report of the War Relief Corps" [1:48, p.7] explaining that one of the purposes for establishing the International Brotherhood League was to collect necessaries to distribute around Santiago and that since the war had ended a hospital had been set up at Camp Montauk instead. In light of various connections, arrangements to go to Cuba inevitably followed.

A "new crusade" was announced in the November issue of *Universal Brotherhood*. The *New York Herald* of October 18th, 1898 reported that the American Evacuation Commission was appealing "for help for the sufferers from the War, in Havana." In the November *Universal Brotherhood* issue, it was stated that the International Brotherhood League had obtained recognition from President McKinley and was provided with "free transportation for all supplies and workers." [13:8, Nov. 1898, p.459] They were hoping to leave for Havana no later than November 15th, however departure was delayed until February, and to Santiago rather than Havana.

In November 1898, General Ludlow
> submitted to the War Department a report upon the subject of the transportation of troops by sea. The management of transportation for the troops destined for Cuba will be governed largely upon the recommendation of this board. [*Evening Star*, **Washington, DC, Nov. 10, 1898**]

It was reported in the November 28th issue of *Evening Star* that:
> The Secretary of War has approved the regulations for the army transport service prepared by the Ludlow board.

Spain gave the U.S. control of Cuba when the war ended. On December 12th, 1898:
> By direction of President McKinley, Major-General William Ludlow, United States Volunteers, was today appointed Military and Civil Governor of Havana city. He will in addition to his executive duties, command all the troops within the city limits. . . . In Havana he will have charge of the reorganization of the Guardia Civile and the Orden Publico into a municipal police force, and will establish a civil government there. His principal task will be cleaning of the City. In this work he has had much experience, and understands modern methods of sanitation for municipalities. [*The Sun* (NY), **Dec. 13, 1898**; *Evening Star*, **Washington, DC, Dec.13, 1898**]

Tingley and the I.B.L. could not have travelled to Cuba on the military U.S. Transport *Berlin* nor entered Santiago on behalf of the International Brotherhood League without the involvement of General Ludlow and the consent of Santiago's Governor, Brigadier General Leonard Wood, who had led the 2nd Brigade, Cavalry Division, Fifth Army Corps to victory at Kettle Hill and San Juan Heights. [https://en.wikipedia.org/wiki/Leonard_Wood] Wood was promoted to governor of Santiago later in 1898 following the departure of commander General Samuel Young.

On Thursday February 2nd, 1899 Tingley and others, including Dr. Coryn and Frank Pierce, left New York for Santiago, Cuba, arriving Sunday afternoon, February 12th. In her letter dated March 6th Tingley wrote of the many difficulties the locals were enduring and that she had been approached by a number of children, some of them orphans, asking her to take them back with her. She wrote that:

> If General Wood will give me transportation for them, I shall take several children back to America to be trained at the Lotus Home, and then to return to be workers among their people. [*The New Century*, **2:22, Mar. 25, 1899, p.6**]

The April 8th, 1899 issue of *The New Century* printed an article from the *Springfield (Mass.) Republican*:

> The party left Cuba on the "Seneca," Ward line, March 20. They found they were to be assigned to the funeral ship "Roumania," now the "Cook," and so Mrs. Tingley brought the party home at her own expense. [**2:24, p.7**]

They arrived in New York on March 27th, 1899. Two Cubans are mentioned as having returned with them. One was "Santiago Macco, . . . a son of General Macco," who had become their interpreter, and "Ricardo de Preval, a little Cuban boy."[*Los Angeles Times*, **Apr. 10, 1899**] *The New Century* issue of April 22nd, 1899 names those present on the train leaving Weekawken station in New York heading to California for the Congress at Point Loma on April 4th, among them:

> Mr. F.M. Pierce, Mrs. Richmond-Green, Mr. Neresheimer, Mr. Patterson. Mr. Iverson L. Harris, Maceo the son of General Macco (Cuban), The Leader [Mrs. Tingley], other Cubans. [**2:26, Apr. 22, 1899, p.6**]

"Senorita Antonia Fabra, of Cuba", is also mentioned in the *Los Angeles Times* [**Apr. 10, 1899**] and in *The New Century* 'Antonia Fabre' is mentioned as part of the delegation attending the Universal Brotherhood Congress in Stockholm, Sweden. [**3:3, Dec. 2, 1899, p.5**]

Bringing children from Cuba to Point Loma was a means to rescue some of them from difficult circumstances, and evolved into an opportunity for publicity when the children of officials were also brought to the Raja School once it had been established. Orphaned children certainly awakened the sympathy of well-intended individuals and the newspapers.

Tingley's determination to bring more Cuban children to Point Loma resulted in numerous difficulties with the Gerry Society (the Society for the Prevention of Cruelty to Children). This society may also have become involved in June 1896 concerning the so-called disappearance of Flossie. The allegation by Richard Cook of maltreatment of his daughter was likely being used in the Cuban children interventions.

When it was revealed in May 1896 that Tingley was 'the unknown mahatma', an interviewer from the *New York Tribune* asked her about "other members of her family", obviously with Flossie in mind. Tingley responded, without referring to her by name:
> The only other person who might have been counted as one of my family was a girl whom I cared for during many years, and who some people thought was my own . . . .

The reporter followed up with:
> But it is said that you also had a daughter whom you placed under social treatment for mental trouble?

Tingley's response:
> This is the same girl. She is not my daughter as I have already told you. I took her from an institution where she had been partially maintained by a relative of limited means. It is true that for many years I cared for her and in all ways treated her as my own child, feeling for her the same love that a mother would feel for her own offspring. But after taking a physician's advice, and being urged to it by my husband and some of my friends, I sent for her relative—who was then in a better position to look after her than formerly—and was obliged to make it clear that I could not assume the responsibility of her future. The whole matter thus

came to an end, as the child was sent back and is now in the home of her relatives, and is well cared for, though, of course, she is debarred from some of the luxuries with which I was able to surround her. In justice to the child it should be made known that she is not and never has been in any home for mental treatment.
[**May 18, 1896**]

Tingley completely contradicts her first husband, and father of Flossie, as to why he had removed Flossie from Tingley's care in November 1895 when she was almost fifteen years old. If Tingley did in fact ask Richard Cook to take his daughter back, the timing of relieving herself of the responsibility of having Flossie, and the well-known state of Judge's health at the time, could imply anticipatory planning.

The question of the treatment of children at Point Loma arose during a contentious court case in 1902 involving custody of two boys between their father, who wanted to remove them, and their mother who insisted on keeping them at Point Loma under Tingley's care. The I.B.L.'s success at Montauk, which Tingley built upon to bring Cuban children to Point Loma, was examined. Upon inquiry to the military officials Tingley had named, letters of response regarding I.B.L.'s involvement at Montauk indicated that perhaps Tingley's claims were exaggerated. None of them apparently had any recollection of work done by the International Brotherhood League. One did respond that many people went to Montauk to help the soldiers. [*New York Herald*, **Nov. 13, 1902**] However, indirect interactions through couriers, which Tingley mentions in *Universal Brotherhood*, had been normal communication procedure; no one individual or group was necessarily memorable to the officials involved.

General William Ludlow must have been instrumental with Tingley's excursion to Cuba on a military transport ship, yet he is not mentioned in any related reports in *Universal Brotherhood* or *New Century*. He is yet another theosophist who has been dismissed from the annals of Point Loma history.

Chapter Six

Point Loma Homestead and Colony

Dr. William Partridge (b.1858- ??)
Another individual dismissed from Point Loma history was Dr. William Partridge. He graduated as a Homeopathic Physician from the Pulte Medical College in Cincinnati in 1888. He studied under Dr. Buck. He was a well-known newspaper man and at thirty-seven years of age was the Financial Editor of the *Cincinnati Tribune* and worked for the broker firm of W.E. Hutton & Co. He was listed in the *Official Register and Directory of Physicians and Surgeons* in California as of 1896. He was also a lecturer on Theosophy and spoke at the San Diego Lodge in April 1897. In May 1897 Dr. Partridge, his wife Martha, and their two surviving children moved to Point Loma.

> Dr. and Mrs. Partridge of Cincinnati . . . moved into the cottage on the Theosophical society's grounds yesterday afternoon. Dr. Partridge is one of the leading members of the society in Cincinnati, being associated with Dr. Buck, the leader. It is understood that he will be the local representative of the American society, and in charge of the buildings and grounds. The cottage has just been completed, and is the first of several of the kind.
> [*San Diego Union & Daily Bee*, **May 21, 1897**]

Also in May 1897, Martin A. Oppermann of Pennsylvania, purchased forty acres of land, adding to the original 120 acres. [*San Diego Union & Daily Bee*, **May 21, 1897**] Oppermann built himself a residence there:

> A contract for the erection of a cottage on the land lately purchased by the Theosophists at Point Loma has been awarded by Martin A. Oppermann, and building will begin this week. [*San Diego Union & Daily Bee*, **May 26, 1897**; *The Internationalist*, 1:1, **Oct. 1897, p.19**]

Another sixty acres purchased by Edward Rambo in June, adjoining "the government reservation" extended their property "over a mile of the ocean front of Point Loma, and altogether. . . 235 acres."

It was hinted by a man intimately connected with the recent dealings of the society on Point Loma that the work on the buildings had been purposely delayed in order to prevent the rise of real estate in the vicinity until the Theosophists had secured all they wanted. They intend to buy three hundred acres to complete the plans on the scale outlined.

This article also noted that Dr. Partridge:
> [I]s in charge of the domain for the Theosophical Society, and occupies one of the small cottages erected for that purpose. [*San Diego Union & Daily Bee*, **June 15, 1897**]

In October 1897 Dr. Partridge reported:
> [T[he work of the new Home Hotel is being pushed rapidly, that the foundation of the building is completed, and the frame of the structure is raised. Messrs. Wood and Opperman, the proprietors, expect to have the building ready for occupancy by January 1st.
> [*The New Century*, **1:5, Oct. 28, 1897 p.6**]

Also in October 1897, *The Internationalist* reported that Dr. Partridge had been selected by the Directress [Tingley] as one "who would be in charge of or concerned with the care of the school buildings." [**1:1, Oct. 15, 1897, pp.19-20**] In June 1898, Dr. Partridge is described as "superintendent of the grounds." [*San Diego Union & Daily Bee*, **June 19, 1898**] However, it seems all did not work out as planned. On June 29th, 1898 the real estate transfer of the Partridge property on Ocean Beach, on the northern part of Point Loma, was recorded. The family is listed in the 1899-1900 San Diego City Directory, at an address in National City, a district south of San Diego. And in June 1900 Dr. Partridge and his family were living in Columbus, OH. His name seems to have been stricken from the historical records of Point Loma.

Dr. Partridge likely met Judge on numerous occasions in Cincinnati at Dr. Buck's home. Dr. Partridge was a strong advocate of the teachings and lectured at every opportunity. His departure from Point Loma came shortly after the February 1898 convention where the name and constitution of T.S. in America were changed to Universal Brotherhood and Tingley assumed total control over all aspects of the organization.

An article in The *Sun* provided an update and change of plans for the school:

Mrs. Tingley's pet project, "The School for the Revival of the First [Lost] Mysteries of Antiquity," it is said, has so far fallen into desuetude [inactivity] that the building which was only begun at Point Loma, . . . is to be completed and turned into a sanitarium by Dr. Loren A. Wood, . . . to whom it has been turned over. [*The Sun* **(NY), Dec. 28, 1897**]

Neresheimer's summary version: The future at Point Loma included plans for a great Congress to be held there in 1899. Dr. Lorin F. Wood arranged with Tingley to purchase a tract, adjacent to the land already owned by the Society, to build a Sanitarium. He relocated with his family in the summer of 1897. Tingley asked that it be constructed to also accommodate guests who would be attending the Congress (April 4th, 1899). [Reminiscences]

The New Century announced in a September 1897 article that "A Wonderful Health Resort" was nearing completion, where "Both sick and well and those seeking rest and change will find it a most attractive place" referring to it as "a well managed hotel." **[1:1, Sep. 30, 1897, p.5]** The *San Diego Union & Daily Bee* reported that:
> A building permit was obtained yesterday by Wood & Oppermann for the construction of the Point Loma Hotel and Health Resort, on Point Loma. The cost of the building was estimated at $20,000. **[Oct. 1, 1897]**

The October 1897 issue of *The Internationalist* reported:
> Dr. Wood's plans are quite extensive, and include boating and bathing facilities in addition to the main building of sixty rooms, with all the outfit of a hotel of the first class, which is expected to be completed by the time winter travel sets in to Southern California, and which will be found a great convenience to our members and others . . . **[1:1, Oct. 15, 1897, p.20]**

The January 22nd, 1898 issue of *The New Century* mentioned that "the new hotel and sanitarium is rapidly nearing completion and Dr. Wood is east purchasing the furnishings." **[p.7]** By March it was being referred to as the Point Loma House. **[1:24, p.5]** A June article mentioned "the large and finely constructed hotel recently completed by Dr. L. Wood." [*San Diego Union & Daily Bee*, **June 19, 1898**] The San Diego Directory 1899-1900 listed it officially as the Point Loma Hotel. According to Emmett Greenwalt, the hotel-sanitarium was remodelled circa 1900 to become the Homestead. *[California Utopia: Point Loma: 1897-1942,* **photo]** There is no listing in the 1901 edition because "Universal Brotherhood and Theosophical Headquarters (The), Pt. Loma, information refused the Directory Co. by secy. Genl. F.M. Pierce."

[*The New Century*, 1:24, March 26, 1898, p.5]
[Photo of the original "Point Loma House", recently completed by Dr. Lorin Wood, while Dr. William Partridge was superintendent of the grounds. Notice the Egyptian designed roof with western style architecture.
"Elizabeth C. Mayer, President of the Musical and Dramatic Club . . . will open a Musical Conservatory" on October 13, 1898. – *The New Century*, 1:45, August 27, 1898, p.3]

[Photo of "Point Loma House", *The New Century*, 3:2, January 27, 1900, p.1]

Three years following the initial purchase of the property, the headquarters of the society was transferred from New York to Point Loma on February 13th, 1900. The move was made official in April 1900. The "New Cycle Unity Congress of the World" was declared open at the meeting of Point Loma Lodge No. 150 on April 13th, 1900. A Notice in *Universal Brotherhood Path*, included the following:

> After April 26th, the Central Office of the Universal Brotherhood will be moved to Point Loma, San Diego, California.
> All communications and letters for the following:
> Katherine Tingley, Leader and Official Head,
> F.M. Pierce, Secretary General,
> Secretary E.S.T.
> should be addressed to Point Loma, San Diego, Cal. [***Universal Brotherhood Path*, 15:2, May 1900, p.120**]

Remodeling of the Point Loma hotel-sanitarium (right) to become the Homestead, and construction of the Temple (left), about 1900. Note steel superstructure for glass domes and spheres.

[*California Utopia: Point Loma: 1897-1942*]

[Point Loma House was officially completed February 18, 1898 and within two years Katherine Tingley ordered the roof replaced with huge domes of aquamarine glass for a more opulent, Turkish/Greek appearance. Note: February 18, 1898, was also the date of the Chicago Convention where the name and constitution of T.S. in America were changed to Universal Brotherhood.]

EAST ENTRANCE OF THE RÂJA-YOGA ACADEMY AT THE INTERNATIONAL
THEOSOPHICAL HEADQUARTERS, POINT LOMA, CALIFORNIA

[*The Theosophical Path*, 24:5, June 1929, p.343]

[On March 2nd, 1900 it was announced that "the Point Loma House has changed hands having been purchased by the Universal Brotherhood organization by which the property as a whole has been taken over." [**San Diego Union and Daily Bee**]

The building permit (issued October 1st, 1897) for the Point Loma House/Hotel would have been registered in the name of the Theosophical Society in America at the time, and now Tingley was transferring the titles of all lands and buildings of the Theosophical Society in America to Universal Brotherhood, over which she maintained absolute control.]

On September 16th, 1900, the *Los Angeles Herald* ran a long feature, "Weird and Wondrous City of Esotero; Strange Things are Going on in the Home of Mystery." The entire article was also included in the transcript of the Tingley vs Times-Mirror court case. [pp.144-157] Excerpts are included here:

The ethics of Universal Brotherhood, in theory, is beautiful. As practiced under the direction of She-who-must-be-obeyed, it is not beautiful. [602, p.151]

It is about two and a half years since She, by a political move worthy of a ward boss rather than the exponent of a profoundly pure philosophy, seized control of the Theosophical society in America and declared Universal Brotherhood, leaving the minority high and dry with little left but their name. [603, p.151]

The constitution, prepared and printed before the convention, shows the well-laid scheme. It declares that there shall be one supreme office, in which shall reside paramount authority regarding all matters which concern the welfare of the Brotherhood, the title of the person filling this office being Leader and Official Head; that the Leader and Official Head of [604, p.151] this organization is Katherine A. Tingley; that the person filling this office shall serve for life or until her or his resignation; that the person filling this office shall appoint her or his successor.

Continuing, the Constitution provides that the Leader and Official Head shall have sole power to appoint all officers and agents, with power to remove any or all of them at her discretion; to declare the policy and direct the affairs of the Brotherhood; to cancel or suspend the [605, p.152] charter of any subordinate lodge, and to suspend or dissolve the membership of any person; that the treasurer shall receive and disburse all moneys as directed by a finance committee, whose acts are void and of no effect when disapproved by the Leader and Official Head; that the leader and Official Head may call a congress at such time and place as she may designate, for the consideration of any matters connected with the welfare of the Brotherhood; the Leader and Official Head to have power to [606, p.152] prevent the discussion of or action on, any subject which in her judgment is against the welfare of the Brotherhood.

The self-planned, self-executed apotheosis of Katherine A. Tingley was the signal for hundreds of men and women to withdraw from the organization. Others follow the ignis fatuus of a hope that the society might be wrested from this control. On they sped, urged by faith and devotion to the cause, sinking deeper and deeper into [607, p.152] the mire of mystery which lies under their crust of a much-vaunted charity and Brotherhood. [608, p.152]

An interview with F.G. Calkins, formerly president of Los Angeles branch of the Universal Brotherhood was included in the article/court transcript:
> I withdrew entirely from the organization about one year ago, after having become satisfied that Mrs. Tingley (who had by certain means gained complete control of the executive of the society) was diametrically opposed to the principles of theosophy, for the promulgation of which philosophy the society was organized.

> Her methods seemed to me intensely Jesuitical and correspondingly unjust. I was satisfied her methods were working a great injury to the sublime philosophy, the study of which was discouraged, with the apparent purpose of inducing members to look solely to her for the truth (?) which they were obliged to accept or be branded a "disloyal". **[Tingley vs Times-Mirror, 611-612, pp.153-154]; [Tingley vs Times-Mirror, *Los Angeles Herald*, Sep. 16, 1900, "Inside Facts Concerning the Dream City of Esotero", 576-628, pp.144-157]**

The "Black Magician" Period

Frank Pierce directed the shows at the Fisher Opera House (later renamed Isis Theater) where elaborate expositions of theosophy were featured. He was so enthralled with Tingley that he wrote a little story involving her. Albert Smythe, editor of *The Lamp* (published 1894-1900) wrote:
> As an Esotericist of the Universal Brotherhood I had placed in my hands on the 15th December, a brochure, 16pp. octavo, wire-stitched, published by F.M. Pierce, at 144 Madison Avenue, New York, and titled *FACTS*.

Smythe writes that it is a realistic melo-dramatic romance depicting Katherine Tingley as the heroine.
> There are only five characters in the little drama. Pierce leading heavy-weight, in the words of Mr. Gilbert, "as mild a mannered man as ever cut a throat or scuttled a ship." Katherine, the heroine, a dear creature, whose reputation is being shielded (not without

reason) by the hero. [*The Lamp*, 3:11 (35), Jan. 15, 1900, pp.191-194]

Throughout this period, the narrative being pushed to the membership was that a new cycle was coming and that with new leadership, change was also coming in their society. The constant threat used was that if you disobeyed Tingley's authority you were putting yourself at risk of being banished from the "White Lodge" into the "Black Lodge" and to join forces with the "black magicians". Benjamin F. Hilliker, a member of the Los Angeles Lodge, admitted in evidence that Tingley made statements at meetings with reference to the disaster that would follow and pursue anyone who left the society.

> She said there were dark forces and light forces. The dark forces would pursue those who left the society and they would be subject to all manner of malady, such as insanity, go crazy, generally go down, personally and mentally. [*Tingley vs Times-Mirror*, 1862, p.466]

Albert Smythe, now editor of *The Canadian Theosophist* (1920-1947), wrote that Daniel Nicol Dunlop (1868-1935)

> was associated with Mrs. Tingley as her secretary for some time after her return from the world Crusade and his intimacy with her methods and practices caused him to change his opinion of her at the time when in 1899 he was at Point Loma. [16:5, July 1935, p.141]

Smythe wrote that he and Dunlop "were both expelled from the Universal Brotherhood at that time" during what they referred to as the "black magician period". Dunlop stated that "in spite of official declarations, freedom of opinion is not permitted" and that "all those who disagree with official attitude are accused of 'venomous hatred' when all that those so accused wish to do is get at the facts." [*CT*, 3:4, June 1922, p.57]

Alice Cleather described how, after undergoing an operation in New York in August 1899, she was "isolated... under the pretence of affording me an opportunity to conquer a dreadful 'elemental,' by which the Leader declared me to be possessed... It was diabolical." [*The Lamp*, 3:12 (36), Feb. 1900, p.206]

James Morgan Pryse (1859-1942)
James Morgan Pryse joined the T.S. at Los Angeles in July 1887. He eventually entered the printing business with his brother John, which led to setting up the H.P.B. Press in London and the Aryan Press in New York. He authored several books and was a devoted and enthusiastic worker in the Movement. In July 1897 he wrote a letter to the Editor of *Theosophical News* updating readers about his recent extensive lecture tour:

> From personal observation I can report that the Theosophical Movement is on a sounder basis and making more rapid progress than ever before. And I have had ample opportunity for such observation, having just finished a tour of eight months' duration, travelling 15,000 miles, visiting a third of the Branches of the T.S.A., and delivering about 100 public lectures, besides attending an equal number of T.S. and E.S.T. meetings. [2:5, July 19, 1897, p.1]

T.S. in America had flourished under Judge's leadership and was continuing to flourish until Tingley, through the constitution of a new organization, Universal Brotherhood, declared absolute power, confiscated all the assets of T.S. in America, and instituted her domination.

A few years later Pryse is said to have lost faith in Tingley and left the organization. He wrote several excellent books, many of them published by his brother, John. Even before he had written his works, Judge wrote of James: "That he is a man who lives and works unselfishly for the T.S. is a fact that is recorded in the unimpeachable books of Karma." [*CT*, 12:2, Apr. 1931, p.56]

Robert Crosbie (1849-1919)
Another individual who became disappointed by Tingley's actions was Robert Crosbie. Crosbie was born in Montreal, Canada, and eventually moved to Boston where he met W.Q. Judge when Judge spoke there. He joined the T.S. on June 5th, 1888 and was one of the earliest members of the Esoteric Section. He was an enthusiastic supporter of Tingley early on, claiming that he believed the information originating from New York. He moved to Point Loma in 1900, apparently at Tingley's request.

Shortly after it was announced that Tingley was Judge's successor, the *Boston Daily Globe* interviewed Crosbie and wrote:

> Pres. Crosbie of the Boston branch said yesterday, when asked about Mrs. Tingley's antecedents: "Why, we never think of such a thing as that, any more than we would think of asking where a man got his clothes made."

He was then asked: "How did she happen to be chosen to her present position?" and responded:

> "Her fitness was recognized—that's all that was necessary. For a position like that there couldn't be any such thing as an election. When she was recognized as the leader she became the leader. She has the inner vision, which is like a spiritual X-ray, and which enables her to see at a glance the aura, or spiritual light, which surrounds every person."
>
> Mr. Crosbie said that Mrs. Tingley has not only very fine psychic powers, but she has also the true mahatmic vision, and she is in direct communication with the invisible powers which control the Theosophical movement. **[May 19, 1896]**

When he and his wife moved to Point Loma, as required of those taking up residence there, all their assets were turned over to the organization. However, it has been said by others and written elsewhere that such assets in fact went to Tingley. When the Crosbies "quietly left Point Loma" in 1904, none of their assets were returned; they were now penniless. They rented a house in Pasadena and he found work as a bookkeeper. Conflicting reports circulated about their departure. In the register of members, a note next to his name reads "Bad conduct" and "Expelled 1904".

Crosbie joined the re-formed T.S. in America, under Hargrove, in 1906. However, when discussion arose about changing the name to The Theosophical Society in 1907, he left the organization. [The revised name was made official at their convention in April 1908.] Crosbie and seven associates wrote the "Declaration of the United Lodge of Theosophists" and on February 18th, 1909 The United Lodge of Theosophists was established.
[Biographical Notes, **compiled by Wane Kell, 1998]**

As an added note, in this same time period, Mrs. Elizabeth Spalding was also very captivated by Tingley. When asked if anyone ever questioned Tingley, she responded that no one would think of doing such a thing. She declared that they recognized, and did not doubt, Tingley's great wisdom.

Must Have Absolute Control!

In 1906 the well known journalist, writer and medical doctor, George Henry Picard (1850-1916), wrote an insightful sympathetic article. An excerpt from "Practical Theosophy at Point Loma" reads:

> It is a favorite notion of the theosophists that every essential moral lesson which can be taught to adults may be taught also to children.
>
> The so-called theosophical movement in this country was started more than a quarter of a century ago by that really remarkable and little understood woman, Helena P. Blavatsky, who left the world a system of philosophy and of evolution which seemed to possess few of the elements requisite to secure popular acceptance. At the death of Mme Blavatsky the cult languished and was lapsing into obscurity when Mrs Tingley was proclaimed by a small and rather unorthodox wing of theosophists as the dead priestess' successor.
>
> The new leader realized immediately that theosophy as Mme. Blavatsky taught it was no longer possible. She it was who planned the transition from mere abstract intellectualism to something which has the form of practical philanthropic activity, a change from the original base which was not effected without leaving behind that part of the Blavatsky following which preferred theory to practice.
>
> The ultimate result of the advance movement in the ranks of theosophy was the foundation of Point Loma. This became the Mecca toward which all those who were willing to show by their conduct that they had no other motive in their profession than to render help to humanity by lives of unselfish devotion to the principles which they profess turned hopefully. Thus it is that the activities at Point Loma, in addition to the daily duties of home life comprise the practical diffusion of lofty ideas through lectures, literature, music and the drama. Many magazines, pamphlets and books are issued and an immense correspondence is carried on. It is claimed that branches of the organization are to be found all over the world. [*The Topeka State Journal*, **July 28, 1906**]

Those who had worked with Judge viewed Tingley's strategy quite differently. John Morgan Pryse, a close associate of both Blavatsky and Judge, determined that Tingley's leadership was destroying the society. Under title "Theosophists In A Revolt" the *New York Times* reported:

> There is a revolt on in the Universal Brotherhood, formerly known as the Theosophical Society of America, because of the methods employed by Mrs. Katherine Tingley, the head of the movement in America. The rebels are led by John M. Pryse . . . who has issued a circular in which he charges that Mrs. Tingley has usurped power and is conducting the society for her own purposes to the detriment of the organization.
>
> Mr. Pryse, in his circular, declares that no member of the society can truthfully claim to be an occultist, and that it is not necessary to have a leader in the organization. One lodge, the White Lotus Theosophic Society, has already seceded, and others will likely follow. [*New York Times*, **Jan. 26, 1899**]

Dr. Franz Hartmann, obviously disturbed by the new direction set at the February 18th, 1898 convention in Chicago, declared in his letter to the editor of *Theosophical Forum: New Series* in March 1898, nearly one year earlier than John Pryse, that

> The freedom from dogma necessarily includes the freedom from enforced belief in the authority of any particular person, whose assertions have to be considered infallible; the freedom from spiritual tyranny and the exclusion of any dictator or autocrat in matters of faith. – I have, as I said, never desired to meddle with society matters, but as my silence would probably be mistaken for consent I am bound to express my opinion in view of the great stroke of policy performed by Mrs. Katherine A. Tingley, of New York, by which she has formed a new church of her own, usurped dominion over the so called T.S. in A. and E. etc., and made herself Pope, King and dictator in one.
> **[3:7, Apr. 1898. p.11]**

Many followed Tingley because of their Oath in the Esoteric Section, taken when Judge was alive. Many were convinced, because they trusted what they were told, that Judge had chosen Tingley as his E.S. successor; they would have felt obligated to endorse her. On May 17th, 1896 Hargrove announced at a meeting in Chickering hall, New York, "She was appointed by Mr. Judge, and we are going to sustain her. . . . ." [*Boston Daily Globe*, **May 18, 1896**] The whole idea was well contrived and most of the members lost sight of reality. Slowly they eventually realized the rashness of their actions and either quit or were kicked out of the Universal Brotherhood, while others just kept silent even though they could have exposed Tingley as a fraud. A lengthy article in *The San Francisco Call* included the following:

> The leader and official head blandly states that this is a "weeding out time"; that under the strain of the end of the century many could not get beyond the door, which was closed upon them, thus retarding their development. . . .
> Bit by bit the pedestal upon which Katherine A. Tingley poses as a goddess is crumbling away. [**Aug. 5, 1900**]

When the E.S. was started by H.P. Blavatsky in 1888, and the subsequent Inner Group, the Oath taken was to their Higher Self. After February 1898 when the Universal Brotherhood replaced T.S. in America, Tingley enacted the E.S. Oath to her personally, not to the Higher Self. Annie Besant did the very same thing when she became President of the Theosophical Society in 1907, headquartered in Adyar, Madras, (Chennai).

Annie Besant O.H. [Outer Head] wrote in a private Esoteric Section members-only publication:

> Those who are ready to subordinate themselves to the common good are called upon to give themselves to this great service, and to let go, *for the remainder of this life*, the petty interests of the personal self. These will be allowed to bind themselves to me by the essential part of the old pledge of the Esoteric Section, at first laid down by the Light-bringer H.P. Blavatsky, with an additional clause to meet the requirement of the time, and they will form the Esoteric Section once again. But none should take this pledge who is not prepared to carry it out *to the full*, nor should any take it with a mental reservation of any kind. No one will take it save of their own free will; but once taken, it binds; those who take it and then, when the test comes, break it, fall under the stern condemnation: "Thou hast not lied unto men but unto God."
>
> This pledge runs: "I pledge myself to support before the world the Theosophical Society, and in particular to obey, without cavil or

delay, the orders of the Head of the Esoteric Section in all that concerns my relation with the Theosophical movement; to work with her, on the lines she shall lay down, in preparation for the coming of the World-Teacher, and to give what support I can to the Society in time, money and work." [*The Link*, Aug. 1911, pp.42-43]

Besant and Tingley each proved, by demanding unquestioned obedience to them, that they were *not* occultists.

Louis S. Fitch (1872-1962)
Louis Fitch, among others, described the absolute control Tingley wielded with the inhabitants of the Homestead and Colony at Point Loma. He was hired as bookkeeper in June 1900 and lived at Point Loma from August 1900 to March 1901. On the witness stand at the Board of Special Inquiry at Ellis Island in November 1902 regarding the Cuban children, he testified about his position.

He stated that after a long conversation "with me alone" Tingley told him that 'Spots' had employed him—the spaniel dog that she claimed Judge had given her. She told him "I know that Mr. Judge's spirit is in Spots, directing this movement." [*The Sun*, (NY), Nov. 8, 1902]

A summary article in the *New York Tribune* reported:
> Mr. Fitch told of the rites and beliefs which Mrs. Tingley was fostering, and the dog known as the "purple inspiration," which Mrs. Tingley told him contained the spirit of William Q. Judge, the head of the American Theosophists, who had left her the dog on his deathbed. Mrs. Tingley had said she was guided by its inspiration. [**Dec. 9, 1902**]

As to his position:
> Mr. Pierce, the treasurer, told me, he wanted me the first thing to forget all the bookkeeping I ever knew. In the School of Ancient Mysteries the mysteries, he said, meant truth, and that was the truth they were after out there. Therefore I know nothing of bookkeeping. I only saw what they wanted me to see, and I got $75 a month... [*The Sun*, (NY), Nov. 8, 1902]

It was also reported that:
> Mrs. Tingley . . . had asked him if he understood bookkeeping, and when he said he did, she told him to forget it—forget all he knew about bookkeeping or had overheard, and a knowledge of how to keep books would come to him from a mystic source. [*The Hartford Courant*, Nov.11, 1902]

He found it difficult to do his job. "I never brought the books to balance in all the nine months I was there. I was always called off, sometimes by Mrs. Tingley herself." [*The Sun*, (NY), Nov. 8, 1902; *The Birmingham Age-Herald*, July 16, 1906]

In his testimony at the Tingley vs Times-Mirror case, he stated that he was also their photographer, ran errands for Mrs. Tingley, guided visitors and did guard duty. [877-878, p.220] He claimed that Tingley exercised control over every aspect of the members "in the minutest detail." [889, p.223] Summarizing the day in court in December 1902, a reporter wrote concerning Fitch:
> He said the pledge of the Esoteric Society of Theosophy was very binding, members taking oath to obey the leader in all things, the leader being Katherine Tingley. Mrs. Tingley had absolute control over everything and everybody and she exercised this in the minutest detail. She regulated where all the members should lodge, what they should eat and where they should eat at; whom they should have conversation with; whom they could walk or talk with and whom they must not speak to or look at. [*The Montgomery Advertiser*, Dec. 21, 1902]

The *Los Angeles Times*, summarizing the day's events in court, reported:
> Mrs. Tingley, Fitch says, was inclined to late rising. Her breakfast was invariably served in her room, very generous in quantity and quality. She sometimes appeared at the evening meal, but most of her meals were served in her room. Mrs. Tingley wrote a great deal herself, but she had educated people there who, Fitch says, did her reading for her and "filled her up with what she was to write." [Dec. 21, 1902]

Again, from his testimony at the Cuban children hearing, reprinted a few years later, he stated:

> What caused me to show up the whole thing was that I found that they taught the succession of teachers—through Confucius, Buddha, Jesus Christ, Mohammed and now the greatest of all, Katherine Tingley. She claimed that she had the power to stay in the spirit world, but that she preferred to come back here as the savior of humanity. . . I believe she is bent on going down to posterity as a second Christ, if not a greater. She will stop at nothing to gain her ends. [*The Sun*, (NY), Nov. 8, 1902; *The Birmingham Age-Herald*, July 16, 1906]

Further to "Spot", an article that appeared in *The Hanford Sentinel* (Hanford, CA), detailed the morning ritual of greeting the rising sun "on the hill known as 'the sacred ground'" and Spot's influence:

> There is a short reading, perhaps from the "Chita" [Gita], perhaps one of Spot's letters, which this inspired dog contributes regularly.
> . . .
>
> Excommunicated Tingleyites state that in her dog Spot Mme. Tingley found the reincarnated soul of William Q. Judge, . . . Spot is carefully tended and has several suits of clothes to protect him from the changes in the weather, for if he should die the intelligence of William Q. Judge might reappear in some animal thousands of miles from Lomaland and the Universal Brotherhood would lose one of its most valued advisers. [**Aug. 14, 1906**]

Other reports concerning Spot consistently include similar details, which Tingley, under oath in court in 1903, denied ever expressing. One is left to wonder if she was deliberately making fools of everyone or if she actually believed her own narrative. Either way, transmigration into a lower species upon death is not part of theosophical teachings, and insinuating that Judge commingled with Spot is misleading at best!

The Cuban Children & Commodore Gerry

Further to the Board of Special Inquiry concerning the Cuban children held at Ellis Island in November 1902, Commodore Elbridge T. Gerry of the Society for the Prevention of Cruelty to Children, expressed concerns about what morals the children might be exposed to under Tingley's care. He claimed "there is no question that the cause of public morals has been furthered through the presentation of the 'Lotus Buds' [children] matter."

He stated that he understood the Los Angeles *Times-Mirror* was being sued by Tingley for libel and that he wished the *New York Herald* had been attacked, adding "[t]he society would have been happy to supply it with all the ammunition at its disposal" regarding Tingley's past. [*New York Herald*, **Nov. 8, 1902**]

Elaborating on his reasons for requesting a rehearing before the Board of Special Inquiry, Commodore Gerry added:
> Understand, there is no personal animus in this case. We are not vindictive. The whole affair resolves itself into a question of public morals, and the newspapers... have always in the past been ready to support the cause of sound, sane public morals. [*New York Herald*, **Nov. 8, 1902**]

The Lischner Document

Dr. Hyman Lischner (1880-1967)
Dr. Lischner was born in Kiefr, Russia on October 27th, 1880, came to America in 1895 and became a U.S. citizen August 3rd, 1904. He graduated from the New York Homeopathic Medical College and Flower Hospital on May 6th, 1905. Dr. Lischner was listed in *The Practitioners' Digest and California Register of Physicians and Surgeons* as having registered there in 1909, and living at Point Loma. [**1:2, Jan. 1910**] His specialty was diseases of children. His wife, Frances (nee Rieger), was also a medical doctor. She graduated from the New York Medical College and Hospital for Women in 1909, and was registered in Los Angeles in 1914.

Dr. Lischner claimed he was a "co-member" of the Point Loma organization and had been closely involved for many years. In all likelihood he knew Katherine Tingley in New York and she invited him to Point Loma, offering offices in the Isis Theater. The *San Diego Union and Daily Bee* reported that he "decided to locate in San Diego and ... opened offices in the Isis theater building." [**Jan. 30, 1910**] According to the County Directory, he still had his practice at these offices in September 1917.

Dr. Lischner issued a 38-page pamphlet, dated May 8th, 1931 and titled *Some Correspondence Between Dr. G. de Purucker, Dr. J.H. Fussell and Hyman Lischner, M.D.*, which he distributed together with a letter dated May 28th addressed "To a Fellow Theosophist". In this letter he described having "had the opportunity of observing . . . for over thirty years" and that "inconsistencies in the every day life of the 'Leader' . . . forced themselves upon my conscience and resisted all my efforts at 'explaining them away'." He wrote that Tingley had banned *The Mahatma Letters to A.P. Sinnett*, *Letters of H.P. Blavatsky*, and *The Real H.P. Blavatsky* by William Kingsland. However, "some three years ago" Neresheimer gave him copies when Lischner asked for more information about H.P.B. His letter included the following:

> My nature was just beginning to timidly rebel against what I was gradually becoming aware of as priestly authority parading under the guise of "successorship", ceremonialism, emotionalism, "lying for the good of the Cause"[Jesuitical!], and other doctrines and pretensions, "passed on" to the "devoted" and "privileged", by word of mouth and by various means of suggestion that were radically and shockingly different and contrary to public and published professions—all in the name of Theosophy and H.P.B.

He went on to explain why he had compiled the 38-page pamphlet which he included with his letter:

> A sense of duty to the Theosophical Movement and to H.P.B prompts me to take the liberty of sending you a copy of some correspondence that has passed between Dr. de Purucker, Dr. Fussell and myself . . . . **[Letter and pamphlet, Edmonton T.S. Archives]**

Dr. Lischner was Tingley's physician; he wrote that he had frequent opportunities to get to know members of her household and her "cabinet" after her cerebral apoplexy [stroke] in 1925. **[See Appendix G for full text of May 28, 1931 letter; See theosophycanada.com for full text of the pamphlet, May 8, 1931, 38pp.]**

Interestingly, Tingley reportedly resided chiefly in Europe from 1925 until her death in July 1929. It seemed to coincide with the loss of her appeal in the California Supreme Court in June 1924 when an earlier verdict was upheld. Dr. George Mohn left his home in Los Angeles and took up residence at Point Loma. In 1918 Mrs. Mohn filed a suit charging that "by the exercise of . . . improper and undue influence, [Tingley] did induce [him] to turn over and transfer to [Tingley] personal and real property. . . of the value of about $250,000. . . ." and also that Tingley "had caused an estrangement between herself and husband." The case dragged on for years. Mrs. Mohn was awarded a judgment of $100,000. [*Los Angeles Times*, **Mar. 2, 1918;** *San Bernardino County Sun*, **June 29, 1924;** *Dictionary of American Biography* **(1936), p.562]**

One year later, Dr. Lischner is mentioned in an article in *The Canadian Theosophist*. William C. Clark (1878-1945) was president of Orpheus Lodge, Vancouver, BC. Details of his visit to California in 1932 were included in the September issue.

> On his return journey besides once more looking up the Pryse Brothers and the U.L.T. at Los Angeles he met Dr. Hyman Lischner an ex-member of the Point Loma Society and now a member of the U.L.T. It was the pamphlet published by Dr. Lischner containing his correspondence with D[r]. de Purucker and Dr. Fussell which threw added light on the claims to Successorship, etc., made by them, which made so deep an impression on some Students. [*CT,* **13:7, Sep. 1932, p.211]**

Chapter Seven

Conclusion

During the last few days of Judge's life he gave specific instructions to Hargrove as to what needed to be done. Others closest to him were not made aware of these instructions; Hargrove was the only one directed to carry them out.

The first instruction: Judge told Hargrove to take over control of the *Forum*. The New Series of *Theosophical Forum* was initiated by W.Q. Judge in May 1895 following the independence of the Theosophical Society in America. Judge wrote in issue No.1 – May 1895 that it was entering upon a new life and era, adding:

> The Forum will be sent in future directly to each member, and all are requested to read it with attention so that suggestions may be made tending to render it of greater value to members, and perhaps even to Branches. It will in a sense, though as yet not officially, be the organ of the Society for notices, changes, news and other matter. **[p.1]**

Judge's introductory statement does not indicate any intention to develop a school. Rather, it is clear that the revitalized magazine was designed to be instructive, with a "definite and rigorous application of theosophical theories." **[p.1]** It does not point to a School for the Revival of the Lost Mysteries as promoted by Katherine Tingley as a teaching facility.

Hargrove wrote: "It was Judge's aim always to make every Branch, every department of the Work, and every individual member, self-supporting, materially, morally and intellectually." [*TJC*, **Part 2, p.285**; *TQ*, **July 1933, p.34**] Tingley did the complete opposite; she controlled every aspect of their lives and eventually closed most Branches.

In San Diego alone there were three active Branches, chartered in 1888, 1889 and 1890. They were still active in 1897 but after February 1898, when Tingley founded the Universal Brotherhood, Branch reports dwindled and by 1900 these Branches had all died. After the purchase of the Fisher Opera house in March 1902, the only meeting place for theosophists in the area was in the (renamed) Isis Theater "where public lectures were held at 8: p.m." on Sunday nights. [*San Diego Union and Daily Bee*, **July 27, 1902**] That was still the case in 1918. [*San Diego Union and Daily Bee*, **Jan. 1, 1918**]

Tingley controlled who was allowed to lecture and where, advising
> Universal Brotherhood Lodges needing lecturers should not apply to other Lodges or to the members direct, but should send in their request to the central office. [*Universal Brotherhood*, **13:6, Sep. 1898, p.351**]

Further restrictions appeared in the September 24th issue of *The New Century*
> NOTICE: Will all the members of the Universal Brotherhood Organization and the International Brotherhood League in America please remember that the only authorized lecturers in the field are Sidney Coryn and Lucius Cannon for the district adjacent to his home. I have already made this announcement in the Universal Brotherhood magazine and in the New Century, and I hope that members of both organizations will hereafter take notice and remember that no person desiring to lecture are to be recognized, except the two mentioned in this announcement. Please have this notice placed upon the bulletin board in the respective lodges. [*The New Century*, **1:49, Sep. 24, 1898, p.6**]

Lucius H. Cannon was from Milwaukee. Brahmana T.S. was chartered there on November 7th, 1888 and he was the secretary in 1893 and 1894. Several former Branches of T.S. in America became newly affiliated Lodges of the Universal Brotherhood, including this one.

Arrangements were occasionally made for visiting lecturers, for example Albert Smythe, who did a lecture tour to Universal Brotherhood Lodges starting in New York City on January 1st, 1899 "reaching Point Loma at the time of the annual Universal Brotherhood Congress" in April. [*Universal Brotherhood*, **14:10, Jan. 1899, p.582**]

The second instruction: Judge told Hargrove to attend to *The Path* which was due for a name change to *Theosophy*, starting with the April 1896 issue. Judge wanted Hargrove to take over the magazine's lead articles, "The Screen of Time" which were usually written by Judge, a clear indication that Judge wanted Hargrove to take over.

The third instruction: Judge told Hargrove to take over his office desk, located on the third floor, and which was Judge's personal property.

Hargrove explained in one of his articles in *Theosophical Quarterly*:
> It was on February 3rd at 6 p.m., that he arrived in New York, driving from the station to the Lincoln Hotel, where he had decided to stay until a suitable apartment could be found for him. He was far more ill than when I had left him at Aiken some three weeks earlier: he was much weaker, his cough was more frequent, his digestion gave him greater pain, he could barely whisper. But he insisted upon my spending an hour or more with him daily, while he went over details of the Work in its many ramifications. When he could, he whispered his comments or directions; at other times he wrote notes on scraps of paper,—such as: "*Forum.* If possible relieve C.F.W. of the *Forum*, and take entire charge of it, either at once or by degrees." "*Path.* You must attend to it. Articles to come are yours and Buck's. I can't finish mine I fear. I have Miss Hillard's. You must write Screen of Time." He thought of everything; I must have a desk at 144 Madison Avenue, then our Headquarters; so another note says: "Your desk is to be in Correspondence Class room, 3rd floor. Desk belongs to W.Q.J. Use it." He was indefatigable, unconquerable; and the explanation was simple: his zeal, springing from so great a love for the Work that so long as he could think he must think first of that, always of that, and then, from the same source, find strength to pass on to others, by some means or other, the thought he willed into action. I can imagine a dying mother, unable to move, still tending her little one like that. [*TJC,* Part 2, p.291; *TQ,* 32, Jan. 1935, p.203]

Why did Judge want Hargrove to take over the *Forum* when it was already under Claude Falls Wright's control? Judge knew, although he apparently did not approach Wright nor Neresheimer, that they had been 'consulting' Tingley, in spite of their pledge in the E.S.

It is important to note that Judge allowed few visitors. During his last days, one is left to ponder why did he not want any visit from his personal secretary Claude Falls Wright or Joseph H. Fussell, or any other staff member, or his supposed 'successor'? Neresheimer may have visited him.

Hargrove continues:
> No matter how ill, he always got up and dressed as usual, refusing to stay in bed; but, with rare exceptions, he could not receive visitors. He sent for Mrs. Griscom, wanting to see her, and he saw Mr. Griscom, so loyally devoted to him, several times. [*TJC*, Part 2, p.291; *TQ*, 32, Jan. 1935, p.203]

The following incident becomes more important than first realized and is mostly overlooked by historians, perhaps because of preconceived biases against Hargrove. It clearly indicates, if one accepts as did Blavatsky, that Judge was able to receive and transcribe letters from the Masters.

Hargrove wrote in *Theosophical Quarterly*:
> While Judge was at the Lincoln and I was spending part of every day with him, reporting on what had already been done to carry out his instructions, upon what remained to be done, and receiving further directions from him—every branch of the work being covered—I did not realize that he was dying. I did not even think of it as a possibility: he was so intensely alive in heart and mind, so vibrant with energy. Nor did I realize the extent to which his long illness had frayed his nerves; if I had, I should not have allowed myself to become rather discouraged at times by my inability always to please him. His patience and self-control were really marvellous, but I knew that my inexperience and stupidities were occasionally a trial to him, and then doubtless I looked as well as felt crestfallen.
>
> This childish reaction was stopped completely by a letter which I received, addressed to me at 144 Madison Avenue, postmarked February 20th, the envelope of which was in Judge's writing. The "letter" itself was in a modified script which I well knew, and read as follows:
>> Ernest—Never mind his nerves which have been exposed a long time. He is really pleased with what has been done and especially with the way you did the Screen. △
>
> I had the grace to be ashamed of myself for making such a message necessary, or, if not necessary, for having drawn on the

> compassion of one whose generosity is unending but whom I might have spared. [*TJC*, **Part 2, p.292;** *TQ*, **32, Jan. 1935, p.204**]

This envelope, with a letter inside, appeared on Judge's desk in the third floor office. It certainly was not delivered there personally. Some of the letters received by Judge were also meant to be read by Hargrove. It was also clear to Boris de Zirkoff that Judge did write "By Master's Direction" under the guidance of his (and Blavatsky's) Master and without the influence from any medium, specifically Katherine Tingley. The △ is the symbol designating "signed by Master".

Further indication that Hargrove was the closest theosophical member to Judge is evidenced in Judge's letter from Aiken, SC, December 19th, 1895:

> On your return to New York, Griscom wants you to stay with him till you find your own place. That place will be with me, as we are going to take a small house or a flat. . . . we shall have the satisfaction of being together. [*TJC*, **Part 2, p.286;** *TQ*, **31, July 1933, p.35**]

When the Judges finally moved into their apartment Hargrove moved in with them into his own room. Judge called it their "home". A room for Hargrove was a requirement by Judge because he wanted him near. Neresheimer even mentioned it briefly in his "Reminiscences" that during the last days of Judge's life Hargrove lived with them.

In Hargrove's words:

> It was a relief to Judge when, finally, an apartment had been found for him (he hated hotels), and his furniture had been moved into it. It was on the third floor of 325 West 56th Street. He, Mrs. Judge and I drove there on the afternoon of February 22nd. From that day he grew weaker and weaker. Some two weeks before his death his doctor warned him that unless he would consent to give up all work, he would throw away his only chance to recover. Judge consented, but the first effect of such a change in his whole life's practice was to make his condition worse: there was danger of an immediate collapse. His cough was incessant; he could no longer lie down; he would doze with his head on his arms on the back of a chair. Absolutely uncomplaining, he never lost his magnificent power of endurance and self-control.

> On the morning of March 19th, I had gone to the T.S. Headquarters at 144 Madison Avenue as usual, although much worried by Judge's appearance (as already stated, I occupied one of the rooms in his apartment). In the early afternoon I received a telegram: "Go to Twenty-Ninth Street railroad office; get full particulars all Florida resorts, trains, tickets, sleepers; then come home.—W. Q. Judge." When I returned, he whispered that if he could "only get to some place where he could sit in the midst of sunshine and flowers", he might yet perhaps recover. Not long afterwards, while I was sitting by the sofa on which he half sat and half reclined, watching him as he dozed, the "Rajah" suddenly came to the fore, and with his unmistakable force said, among other things: "There should be calmness. Hold fast. Go slow".
> **[*TJC*, Part 2, p.292; *TQ*, 32, Jan. 1935, p.204]** [See Appendix: "Life In a Borrowed Body" for details re 'the Rajah'; also see https://www.theosophycanada.com/files/the-judge-case-volume-ii.pdf pp.487-493]

Judge's last words have erroneously been assumed to be advice for the executive of the society whereas they were clearly instructions for Hargrove. It becomes evident that although Hargrove was accepted by the executive as the one to succeed Judge as President of the Theosophical Society in America, they were hoodwinked into believing that he was not destined to be the Outer Head of the Esoteric School. Neresheimer had been meeting regularly with Tingley, sitting blindfolded before a painting of the "Rajah" with her seated beside him

> and we both maintained absolute silence for some fifteen minutes of meditation. This, she had said, was for the purpose of preparing the requisite Occult atmosphere, and so making it possible for us, the more effectively, to consecrate our efforts. **[Reminiscences]**

When Neresheimer came across the symbol and the notes mentioning "Chela", he assumed it was Tingley and went directly to her to determine how to proceed. Clearly she covertly seized the position of Outer Head of the Esoteric School.

Hargrove was perhaps naive or even intimidated by the older members to accept their vision of the future with Tingley at the helm. She concocted the plan that the identity of the 'Great Unknown' had to be kept secret for one year, which meant that she needed someone acting as president to answer problematic questions from the press. And Neresheimer made it easy for Tingley to step in and take control.

Indications are that Clement and Genevieve Griscom eventually realized from Tingley's actions that they had been swayed and regretted acquiescing to events shortly after Judge's death. Clement withdrew from active participation in the society's councils and committees shortly after the return of the Crusaders. Hargrove was only twenty-five years old, and the Griscoms were both twenty-seven when Judge died; everyone else was older.

Hargrove closes with:
> The debt we owe him is beyond calculation. The existence of the Society to-day is due primarily to his labour and sacrifice, and to the light he passed on. H.P.B. had hewn a track through primeval forest, and, to do so, had been obliged to use dynamite and axe. Judge turned her track into a paved road: he was the great consolidator. Both built their own memorials: H.P.B., her *Secret Doctrine* and *Voice of the Silence*; Judge, that living nucleus, one of the fruits of which is the thirty-two years' existence and growth of the THEOSOPHICAL QUARTERLY, and the continuance, so far into the twentieth century, of the Work of the Lodge which Masters inaugurated in 1875.
>
> Gratitude is never easy to express, but the least I can say is that I personally owe him, directly or indirectly, all that I value in life.
> [*TJC*, Part 2, p.293; *TQ*, 32, Jan. 1935, p.205]

Closing Words

In a letter to Judge H.P.B. wrote:
> Well, I have raised a 'Frankenstein' [the T. S.], and he seeks to devour me. You alone can save the fiend and make of him a *man*. Breathe into him a soul if not the spirit. Be his Savior in the U.S. and may the blessings of my SUPERIORS and yours descend on you. Yours—the 'old woman,' but one ready to offer you her *inner* life if you begin and proceed with the work. . . . But as the ranks thin around us, and one by one our best intellectual forces depart, to turn *bitter* enemies, I say—Blessed are the pure-hearted who have only intuition, for intuition is better than intellect. . . .

> Yours ever, H.P.B. [*Letters That Have Helped Me*, p.282; *Irish Theosophist*, 3:9, June 1895, pp.156-57]

In this letter H.P.B. confirms Judge's connection with the Mahatmas when she writes "my SUPERIORS and yours".

In the tribute issue following the death of Æ (George William Russell) the editor of *The Aryan Path* indicated that he had in hand an unpublished letter by Æ dated October 17th, 1922.

> Æ couples a condemnation of the Theosophical Society, "which seems to me now in some moods to be a nursery of the Black Art," with words of appreciation of "that great and wise man, William Q. Judge whose very memory seems to have been forgotten by present day Theosophists. I think he was a true adept in that sacred lore and I have never found in those who came after H.P.B. and Judge the same knowledge, wisdom and inner light." [*The Aryan Path*, 6:12, Dec. 1935, p.722]

THE END

Appendix A

The Cloakmakers Strike and The Blizzard

The timing of two events is critical in order to substantiate Tingley's story: the dates of the blizzard in the New York region, and the cloakmakers strike. She wrote in *The Gods Await* [p.62] that she saw Judge for the first time when a storm was brewing, "an ordinary snowstorm that gave little warning of the tremendous blizzard . . ." New York newspapers 1893 and 1894 were checked to find a storm that would fit Tingley's story; it also had to tie in with the cloakmakers' strike she refers to.

A lot of time and effort was dedicated to researching the cloakmakers strike, a compelling story in itself. Some of the more extensive details have therefore been added as this appendix for the benefit of those interested in learning more about the tragic circumstances at the time.

By the middle of August 1894 trouble was stirring at the Central Labor Union involving the cloakmakers. Strife arose between two unions.
> A victory was announced for Joseph Barondess over the Socialists. The Socialists succeeded in organizing a cloakmakers' union on Socialistic principles, in opposition to the old Cloakmakers' Union, No.1, of which the old Barondess was manager. They also succeeded in forcing him to resign his office, and tried to bring the old union into their fold. But as a preliminary they demanded that Barondess be blacklisted. This so angered the old cloakmakers that they re-elected Barondess as manager. The cloakmakers' delegates announced yesterday that the new Socialist cloakmakers' union had become tired of the Socialists and wanted to return to old Union No.1. [*New York Times*, Aug. 13, 1894]

This set the stage for the beginning of a bitter strike to follow between the owners and the workers which lasted into spring of 1895.

By late August the cloakmakers and the clothing cutters went on strike.
> About 1,000 cloakmakers, who work for Freedman Brothers of Broadway and Prince Street and contractors dealing with the firm,

> struck yesterday for an advance of wages .... Nearly thirty clothing cutters employed in B. Schleestein's shop at 217 Greene Street, struck yesterday morning for an advance of $2 a week. They won. Twenty cutters in the shop of Lippman & Sons, at 198 Greene Street, also struck for an advance of $2 a week. [*New York Times*, August 28, 1894]

A few days later, it was reported that others in the clothing trades also wanted an advance of wages. The general perspective was that
> This is the beginning of what will probably be the largest strike in the clothing trades that has taken place in New-York, as it will include, besides the finishers, the tailors, basters, cloakmakers, and suitmakers. . . . New York is one of the largest clothing manufacturing centres in this country and more clothes are made here than in London or any other large city in Europe. More that 80 per cent of the clothing workers are Hebrews, mostly from Russian Poland." [*New York Times*, Sep. 3, 1894]

A few days later the Knights of Labor tailors decided to strike as well which added about 4,000 more men to the already 8,000 out of work. "The Knights of Labor say they have 15,000 men on strike." [*New York Times*, Sep.7, 8, 1894] The next day the strike grew when
> The Overcoat and Sack Coat Makers' Union, No. 30, of the United Garment Workers, representing the cheaper grade of the clothing trade, held a meeting at Liberty Hall yesterday and declared a general strike in all the branches of that trade. About 5,000 hands will be affected. [*New York Times*, Sep. 9, 1894]

This strike was a heavy burden on all who lived on the East side of New York City and there was much suffering. An article in the *New York Times* examined the poverty-stricken Hebrew congregation "the purliens of the east side to the corner of Orchard and Broome Streets."
> There were all sorts and conditions and types and ages of men gathered on the worn and cracked steps that first led to the forlorn synagogue and then went higher to the wretched room in which the Executive Board of the cloakmakers sat on a few battered chairs round a splintered pine table, and in an atmosphere of poverty conferred over a situation well-nigh desperate. There were gentle-faced young men who spoke as if they were too tired to

talk, and who, therefore, looked in silence with a dreamy thoughtfulness on the little restaurant that challenged them with its cheap luxuries across the way. There were middle-aged men, fathers of families, in coats of prodigious gloss, so prodigiously threadbare were they. Intended by nature to be big and broad and wholesome, they looked instead like a group of figures from a life-size picture of a famine. There were venerable old patriarchs whose tangled white beards, whose melancholy, wistful faces, whose sunken and famished eyes told with a sorrowful eloquence how heavily the hand of need bore them down in a land old exile and of strangers.

One of the men explained that their situation was not well understood and spoke for the men:

"But the last year the average pay of a tailor or an operator in the cloakmaking trade was $4 a week for just exactly twenty weeks out of fifty-two. . . .

"Remember that in the very best times we do not work more than six months in the year, and have during the other six months to live upon what we save while we have work.

"The men employed in those shops realize that the times promise to be good; that there is work to be done; that it must be done right now and that, if the men who are going to do it want to get their wretched circumstances improved, they must ask for that improvement now. [*New York Times*, Sep. 13, 1894.]

The friction between workers and owners only increased when the cloakmakers gave them a list of demands. Thousands of strikers took to the streets one night in a protest parade. Before a permit was received the police ordered them to disperse and they refused. [***New York Times***, Oct.12, 1894]

In November some relief came from manufacturing firms from other cities like St. Louis and Chicago offering jobs to cloakmakers if they moved to their cities. Three firms in Chicago asked for 300 cloakmakers. It was stated by a cloakmaker who received a letter from a fellow-workman, that $5 a day was made by good workmen. [***The Evening World***, Nov. 24, 1894]

In spite of all this help there were thousands of starving cloakmakers in New York City.

> Over four hundred families of strikers were helped yesterday at the relief depot, at 112 Ludlow street, groceries and provisions enough being given to last until tomorrow. Coffee, tea, and bread and herrings will be issued tomorrow between 8 A.M. and 12 M. George W. Jones, who is in charge of the relief depot, said more funds and supplies are needed. [*The Evening World*, **Nov. 24, 1894**]

Many families of the striking cloakmakers were utterly destitute.

> Extreme destitution prevails among many families of the striking cloakmakers. Delegate Langendorf, of the Relief Bureau of the Cloakmakers' Union, at 98 Clinton street, told a reporter for *The Evening World* today that fifteen families, who were in the greatest want, had received dispossess notices several weeks ago. He secured money to pay their rent for a month, and had obtained adjournments of their case, but now he is unable to get any more money or adjournments.
>
> The cases of twenty-five striking cloakmakers who have received dispossession notices will come before Civil Justice Goldfogle, Monday morning.
>
> There was not even a loaf of bread in the relief depot, at 98 Clinton street, this morning, but the applicants were few owing to the fact that to-day is the Hebrew Sabbath. [*The Evening World*, **Dec. 22, 24, 1894**]

In reference to the proposition of the anonymous donor's suggestion for others to follow his lead and personally support families, Joseph Barondess of the Cloakmakers' Union responded:

> "The treasuries of the labor organizations are exhausted, and with all the kindness and sympathy they have shown for the strikers, they are not in a position to do much for us at present.
>
> "It is dreadful to think of the cold Winter months that are now upon us, without any hopes for the settlement of the cloakmakers' troubles, at least for the next two months. The suggestion of 'A Subscriber' is the most practicable one that has been made. 'The

Evening World' is the only evening newspaper that could bring about such a systematic plan to assist the striking cloakmakers who are in such dire want. I can only add that 'A Subscriber' has the gratitude and appreciation of humane people in general and the striking cloakmakers in particular...."

Desperation persisted:

There was a crowd at the relief depot at 98 Clinton street, this morning, clamoring for bread, and George W. Jones, who is in charge of the place was compelled to cut each of the few loaves of bread in two in order to relieve as many of the poor cloakmakers as possible." [*The Evening World*, **Dec. 24, 1894**]

Then on Wednesday December 26th a severe storm hit New York City. This is the only storm that fits the criteria Tingley presented when she claimed to have first seen Judge standing outside the perimeter of the crowd that was waiting for food at the soup kitchen she was managing. The next day *The New York Times* reported:

[T]he first real snowstorm of this season visited this section yesterday afternoon. The snow swirled in and out among the high buildings where the drafts of air were the strongest and beat down upon the unfortunate passers with cutting and chilling effect.

Beginning, as it did, at a little before 6 P.M., the storm increased in intensity and volume until at midnight but few conveyances were running, and it was with the utmost difficulty that pedestrians were enabled to keep upon their feet." [*New York Times*, **Dec.27, 1894**]

The Evening World reported:

The severe storm which has been raging since last night along the Atlantic coast from Maine to Florida will be followed by a cold wave, which Signal-Service Officer Dunn believes will cause a drop of 20 degrees in the temperature within the next twenty-four hours.... The storm is central over this immediate vicinity, and covers a radius of from 500 to 600 miles....

When the snow began to cover the town last night with a fine white powder every one confidently believed it was going to be a decent self-respecting sort of arrangement of flakes. There was a difference this morning, and the snow worked itself in easy stages first to hail, and then to a cold, miserable, beating rain, which drenched everything in sight.

And here is where the snow did a very bad thing. It blocked up the sewers; it formed itself into basins and troughs to hold the fickle rain, and the slush made tempting floating islands in these miniature ponds, on which the unwary pedestrian put his faith and his foot, to his intense disgust and sorrow, believing the stuff to be the top of a cobblestone which had been raised from the depths like King Arthur's sword. . . .

As for umbrellas, the City Hall Park at 8 o'clock was a perfect Bay of Biscay of them, and there was a dado of them on the Broadway side of the Post-Office, with their ribs stripped and shorn of the covering and with their handles broken by the wind. An umbrella this morning was not the good thing it is usually supposed to be. [*The Evening World*, **Dec.27, 1894**]

Tingley stated that Judge was using an umbrella at the time she saw him, we can only imagine what happened to it. In Brooklyn where Judge lived:

The storm hampered the Brooklyn trolley lines considerably. Snow-ploughs were out before daybreak and sweepers were used continually. . . . A trolley wire broke from the weight of ice on Classon Avenue, just below Myrtle, and blocked the cars going in both directions for half an hour. . . . On some of the routes the water and slush in the street was sufficiently deep to prevent a car from passing through, and traffic was entirely suspended until the plough reached the scene. The employees of the sewer department were out early in the day relieving chocked-up sewers and removing debris. [*The Evening World*, **Dec.27, 1894**]

The storm created much havoc.

New York was the first big city it struck, and here it lingered. During its stay it left a nine-inch enamel of snow, and then further discouraged the Street-Cleaning Department by wetting that layer with a half-inch rainfall. . . . In this city the wind attained a velocity of 35 miles per hour in some places, about 100 miles an hour in others, especially around street corners. . . . [*New York Times*, Dec 28, 1894]

On top of the storm there was bad news for the cloakmakers.
> The latest phase of the cloakmakers' strike was made public yesterday through a letter written by Daniel W. Richman, President, of the Cloak Manufacturers' Association, to the cloth commission merchants of the city, asking them not to sell goods to the cloak manufacturers who signed the articles of agreement presented last October by the striking cloakmakers. [*New York Times*, Dec 27, 1894]

People were dying in the streets: "A laborer forty-five years old . . . was found by a policeman ill from exposure . . . at 2 o'clock yesterday afternoon." He died before the ambulance came. Another man also died that night walking the streets on his way back from his church. The following morning a policeman saved two people on his way to the West Thirteenth Street station. Others were found wandering the streets during the storm because they had no place to go. [*New York Times*, Dec 28, 1894]

In Red Bank, NJ, it began snowing just before 6 o'clock, and "four hours later the snow was 5 inches deep on the level. Then the snow changed to rain, and a driving wind commenced to blow. During the night the velocity of the gale was fifty miles an hour . . . In the outlying districts the snow drifted badly, making the roads well-nigh impassable." Camden fared no better "electrical wires . . . were torn from their fastenings, and poles were blown down by the high wind . . . ." [*New York Times*, Dec. 28, 1894]

Across NY State places like Troy, Kingston and Syracuse up to two feet of snow had fallen, snow drifts delayed railroads, and street car lines and highways were blocked. Albany, Poughkeepsie, Newburg, among others, and outlying districts were also severely affected, as were several States. [*New York Tribune*; *New York Times*, Dec. 28, 1894; *The Sun* (NY), Dec. 27, 1894]

In New York City:
> Traffic was everywhere impeded, and to walk for a distance without getting the feet wet was practically impossible. The surface cars had such hard work in the morning in making their

trips on time that many of their usual customers patronized the elevated railway . . . . [*The Evening World,* **Dec. 28, 1894**]

The storm compounded the misery of the strikers. On January 1st, 1895, *The Evening World* reported: "Twelve Thousand Idle Men: Cheerless Outlook for Cloakmakers and Their Families. No Prospect for Work Until March at the Very Earliest."

> This is the third month of the strike of 12,000 cloakmakers and cutters. Over six hundred of them with their families enter upon the new year with hunger and want staring them in the face and no prospect of work until March. The Relief Committee of the conference of forty labor unions supplies them with bread, sometimes a little coffee and occasionally bologna sausage and pickled herrings, a few potatoes and onions, and once in a fortnight tea. The quantities are so small they do not relieve the sufferers.
>
> "God only knows what will become of these poor people if our supplies are cut off," said Manager G. W. Jones of the Relief Bureau, at 98 Clinton street. "We gave out 300 loaves of bread this morning and 100 pounds of bologna contributed by M. Zimmerman and G. Goldman. Adolph Kres, of Baltimore, sent a check for $20.95, and the Metropolitan Prepared Food Company gave us nineteen three-pound cans of corn meal mush. There was a rush for these supplies and we were nearly mobbed by the starvelings. . . ."
>
> A proposition has been made to Joseph Barondess, the leader of the cloakmakers to select from among the 12,000 strikers about 500 or 1,000 of the most able-bodied men, citizens of the United States, and send them in a body to the Street-Cleaning Commissioner as applicants for work in cleaning the streets. [*The Evening World,* **Jan.1, 1895**]

On January 3rd aid for the needy cloakmakers was on the way. "The Association for Improving the Condition of the Poor has conditionally promised $10,000 for the relief of the distressed cloakmakers." They were to be employed to remove snow and other street work. The wage was $1 per day. [*New York Times,* **Jan. 3, 1895**]

On Friday January 4th *The New York Times* reported:

> Striking cloakmakers began yesterday to enroll as street cleaners, under the conditions of the offer of the Society for Improving the Condition of the Poor to appropriate $10,000 to pay them for their work. . . .
>
> The men are to work only six hours a day, and for this they will receive $1.
>
> No evictions of strikers were reported yesterday, but several heads of families reported that they had certainly a shelter for only a few days more. The relief bureau disposed of large quantities of bread and bologna. [**Jan. 4, 1895**]

The Evening World was a bit more cynical about the work being done by the Cloakmakers.

> For twenty minutes they worked feverishly with picks and shovels, then they rested, lighted cigarettes and talked the situation over. When they resumed work they took things more easily, working the pick with one hand and manipulating the cigarette with the other.

The article continued, insinuating the men weren't working hard enough. Sub-titles "Different from Pushing a Needle" and "Phew! But This is Work!" claimed "there were twenty-five tailors who were bold enough to say they were willing to work", implying they were lazy while they were more likely weak from hunger. [**Jan. 4, 1895**]

And on Saturday January 5th:

> The snow shoveling brigade of the striking cloakmakers are not working today for the reason that they are observing the Hebrew Sabbath. They will resume work on Monday morning, and about 300 more will be added to the force of yesterday. [*The Evening World*, **Jan. 5, 1895**]

By Monday January 14th not much had changed with either the cold weather or the cloakmakers' needy situation.

> It was said at the Cloakmakers' Relief Committee's headquarters yesterday that 500 of the men would be at work on the streets to-day. This number represents the full quota of tickets which will be

issued every ten days. The cloakmaker holding one of these tickets is entitled to ten days' work. At the end of that time new men will have a chance to work and earn a little money, which will enable them to prevent for a time, at least, the dread and gaunt wolf of starvation from entering their humble quarters which they call home. [*New York Tribune*, **Jan. 14, 1895**]

At the end of the month their condition remained unchanged.

There is little change in the condition of the East Side cloakmakers, although the strike which was begun some four months ago is practically off. . . . Many of the cloakmakers have, however, taken advantage of the permission given to them to seek work wherever they could find it. While a number of them have obtained work, the majority are still idle, and there seemed to be as many unemployed men around their headquarters in Clinton-st. and No. 412 Grand-st. yesterday as usual. As the street-cleaning fund provided by the Society for Improving the Condition of the Poor was exhausted some time ago, and the trades unions relief bureau in Clinton-st. is closed, the cloakmakers are now compelled to depend solely on their own resources.

Secretary Rode, of the University Settlement Society, No. 26 Delancey-st., told a Tribune reporter yesterday that it was . . . in East Side life that the worst suffering was undergone. The University Settlement Society is still giving relief to some of the families of the cloakmakers, but it is also urgently calling on all the cloakmakers to seek work wherever they can get it to do. The society, Mr. Rode told the reporter, realized that there was no likelihood of there being sufficient work for all the cloakmakers this spring. The cloakmakers also realize it. The spring cloakmaking season will be at its height about March 1 and will end about April 15. [*New York Tribune,* **Jan. 30, 1895**]

There is no doubt about the timing of the cloakmakers strike and the blizzard of 1894-1895.

Appendix B

The Lotus Circle

W.Q. Judge once wrote "Our duty these days of trial and transition is to engage in propaganda, so as to place Theosophy before as many of the race as possible. To do that, the most common-sense, simple presentation of theosophy, free from vagueness and big words, is the best." [*The English Theosophist,* Feb. 1900, p.243] One method employed toward this end was "The Tract Mailing Scheme." It was reported in the June 1891 issue of *The Path* [6:3, p.95] that Judge had announced at the Convention that 260,000 tracts had been printed. Then it was reported in the November 1891 issue of *The Path* [6:8, p.264] that the "T.M.S. . . . has now incorporated the operations of that invaluable 'Press Scheme'." The March 1892 issue included the following:

> For some months past the Press Scheme has been growing in importance and value, more and more periodicals opening their columns to articles . . . . [6:12, p.417]

It was further explained in the September 1892 issue that

> This brings before the eyes of hundreds of thousands of readers scattered over an enormous territory the fact that elementary information on the subject of Theosophy can be thus procured, and opens up a channel of information to many who otherwise would have no idea how to procure a document. [7:6, p.199]

The success of the "Press Scheme" led to the creation of "The League of Theosophical Workers (L.T.W.)," a union-type operation for practical operations, based out of the Aryan Lodge Headquarters. It called for new members and volunteers willing to assist and "especially children, are wanted for the Lotus Circle." [**"The Lotus Circle" by Shawn Higgins, July 2023;** *The Theosophist,* **Vol. XIV, May 1893, pp.511-512**]

Elizabeth (Lizzie) Chapin started the New York Lotus Circle, described as a Theosophical Sunday School, in Brooklyn on October 30th, 1892 at the Aryan T.S., 144 Madison Avenue. Lizzie and Maude Ralston, who had both joined the Brooklyn Branch T.S. on November 13th, 1890, adapted old church songs and wrote theosophical stories for the children. This Lotus Circle became very successful.

In 1894, Elizabeth Churchill Mayer is mentioned as being in charge of "the Lotus Circle or unsectarian Sunday-school" at 144 Madison Avenue, "which is regularly attended by fifty or sixty children and some adults every Sunday afternoon." [*New York Times*, Jan. 1, 1894; *New York Tribune*, Apr. 2, 1894]

Anna Miller Stabler joined the Theosophical Society February 9th, 1890 after hearing disparaging remarks about Blavatsky and reasoning "that a woman who was the object of so much criticism must be remarkable." [***The World* (New York), June 19, 1893**] Her efforts and enthusiasm led to starting the H.P.B. Branch in Harlem on May 8th, 1891, the day Blavatsky died. It became one of the most active branches of T.S. in America at the time. In June 1893 Stabler started the Harlem Lotus Circle, which also became very successful.

A detailed article titled "The Lotus Circle" by Shawn F. Higgins, published July 5, 2023, provides the "Aftermath" following Judge's death:

> Katherine Tingley continued the Lotus Circle. Lizzie, Maude, and Stabler all remained involved. Lizzie became President of the Katherine Tingley Branch T.S. (607 East 14th Street, New York City) in September 1896, and ran that Branch's Lotus Circle. Maude assisted with the production of Tingley's children's play, "The First Crusade,". . . Stabler became the superintendent of Tingley's "Lotus Home For Children" in Pleasant Valley, New Jersey. All three would resign by 1898, after internal discord fractured the organizational structure of the American Theosophists. . . .
>
> Stabler seems to have grown weary with the Movement by 1899 . . . .
>
> Lizzie and Maude threw their support behind the Griscom-Hargrove Theosophical Society. . . .
>
> https://www.patheos.com/blogs/marginalia/2023/07/the-lotus-circle/

Appendix C

Countess Cora Ann (Slocomb) di Brazza Savorgnan
January 7, 1862 - August 24, 1944

Cora Ann Slocomb, only child of Cuthbert Harrison Slocomb (1831-1873) and Abby [Abigail] Hannah Day (1836-1917), was born in New Orleans, Louisiana.

Captain Slocomb enlisted in the Confederate Army for the Civil War, going out in 1862 in charge of the Fifth Company, Battalion of the Washington Artillery, New Orleans. [*The Slocombs of America and Their Alliances*, p.508] He became a prominent citizen and merchant in Louisiana. Many businessmen and aristocrats spoke French; Cora's parents wanted her to speak Parisian French. In 1869 the family visited England and a twenty-five year old french-speaking servant returned with them. Cora attended school in New Orleans until her father's death at the age of forty-one; Cora was eleven years old. She then studied with private tutors for two years and then at thirteen years of age, in 1875, went abroad to study German in Germany, French in France, eventually completing her education on the Isle of Wight in Southern England. She returned to America from England on December 14th, 1880. She eventually spoke four languages fluently: English, French, German and Italian.

Two versions were found as to when and where Cora met Count di Brazza. One claims that she visited Italy for the first time in 1887 when she met and married Count Detalmo di Brazza Savorgnan. [info taken from "Life of the Italian Woman in the Country" by Countess Cora Slocomb di Brazza, from "A Celebration of Women Writers" Mary Kavanaugh Oldham, ed.] A similar version: "Cora was born in New Orleans in 1860, she had studied painting in Rome, where she had fallen in love with the count Detalmo di Savorgnan Brazza, who came from Brazzacco and was the brother of Pietro, who explored Congo and founded Brazzaville. [Newsletter of September 2010 on the tourism website of Friuli Venezia Giulia] The second version, which appeared in The *Morning Journal-Courier* of New Haven, Conn., claims "Miss Slocomb and the Count first met in our own national capital. The count was an attache of the Italian legation at Washington eight years ago, when he met Miss Slocomb in Washington society." **[July 28, 1893]**

Details aside, Cora Slocomb and Count Detalmo Savorgnan di Brazza married in New York on October 18th, 1887. The Reverend Father Ducey of St. Leo's Church, officiated at the religious ceremony at 11:30 at the temporary home of her mother. Because the Count was Catholic and Cora Protestant, the marriage could not be celebrated in a Catholic church. A civil ceremony was performed at 10:30 by the Italian Consul, Gen. Giovanni Raffo.[*New York Times*, **Oct. 19, 1887]** The Count and Countess sailed to Italy in November 1887 [*The Times-Picayune*, **New Orleans, Nov. 11, 1887]** and "will pass the winter at the groom's Roman piazza." [*The Evening World*, **NY, Oct. 18, 1887]**

Daughter, Ida Anna (Idanna) di Brazza was born in Moruzzo, Udine, Italy in 1891. She died in 1940. No exact dates can be ascertained. **[Ancestry]**

The Savorgnan family was originally from Friuli-Venezia Giula and were considered 'Patrizi' (patricians) since their family was close to noble roman families and to the Pope. Detalmo was described as "unconventional . . . lover of Civil Engineering, scientist-inventor. Both believe that 'wealth is joy only because it offers the opportunity to do good to your neighbor; that of the poor was a cause that they shared with equal determination'." [**"The Courage and Passion of Cora Slocomb" by Luciano Morandini, translation]**

Countess di Brazza/Cora Slocomb was struck by the difficulties faced by the average citizen of the area where she lived in Italy, especially the women. She initiated a number of projects to improve their circumstances, including the following:

Lace-Making:
Within a few years of settling into life in Italy and wanting to improve the condition of the average individual, with the cooperation of some noble ladies "she organized upon her own castle grounds a grand industrial and agricultural fair to which all the peasantry were invited," complete with prizes. Then in 1891 she decided to introduce the industry of lace-making which eventually led to her establishing a lace-making school in Venetia where "10,000 peasant women and girls earn an honest and profitable livelihood . . . a boon to the working women." [*The Times-Picayune*, **May 15, 1893]** She saw it as an opportunity for independence and development. It

eventually led to the invitation to participate in the World's Fair in Chicago in 1893.

Violets:
Count Filippo di Brazza Savorgnan was described as a gentleman and violet fancier from Udine, Italy. He bred one that became known as the Conte di Brazza, for which he won the Royal Horticultural Society award in 1883. After the death of Count Filippo, Cora "strove to promote violet breeding and commercial cultivation in the countryside of Udine." It developed into an industry that provided money for the bridal trousseaux of the marriageable young girls. [**"The Violet in Italy" by Giulietto Fanin; The American Violet Society website**]

Coincidentally, Cora was always renowned for her fondness of the color purple.

Biscuits:
A brief bio of Cora Slocomb appears on www.biscottibrazza.it It includes details of how Cora brought further opportunity to the region.
> After moving from the US to Brazzacco in Friuli, Cora was particularly struck by the population's poverty and especially the women's submissiveness. With humanitarian spirit, she introduced female entrepreneurship to Brazza Castle by opening the first school of lace-making and founding a prize for creativity within the frame of the local agricultural fair that promoted farm work. Both her initiatives were later developed across Italy and the US.

In 1893, seeking another opportunity to improve the circumstances of the average citizen, the 'Brazza Biscuit' was born. It won first prize on the occasion of the first local agricultural show of Martignacco, north of Udine. The Newsletter of September 2010 on the tourism website of Friuli Venezia Giulia, includes the following:
> Thanks to her, the Cooperative Lace School was founded, exporting the local handicraft all over the world. From her capability to look far the biscuit of Brazza was born, the first example of industrial confectionery production . . . destined to become successful.

If the shortbread from Martignacco had such a great success, in fact, it was thanks to this great woman, to her highly creative mind and to her love for the land where she had chosen to live.

This shortbread biscuit stayed on the market until 1958 and the old recipe is still used on the occasion of festivals and events.

Countess di Brazza was also an author. *The Times-Picayune* article of May 15th, 1893 mentioned that she had "written a book on antique and modern lace, which is a complete and thorough history of the origin of lace-making" and included 200 patterns. *The Slocombs of America and Their Alliances* included the following:

> Countess Cora Slocomb di Brazza received [a] medal for the collection of antique lace, and another for her book especially written for the occasion entitled, *Old and New Lace in Italy: a learned treatise on textile art.* [p.509]

In 1896 Countess di Brazza (Cora Slocomb) published her first purely illustrated literary work titled *An American Idyl*, 244 pp. It was published by The Arena Publishing Company, Boston. The cover of her book was purple. It is described as "an ethnographic, ethonobotanical and biological treatise on the Indians of Arizona and Northern Mexico, written in the form of a novel. A romance set in Southern Arizona between a scientist and a local Indian girl while exploring the flora and fauna of the region. The emphasis is on how the Pima Indian tribes lived in harmony with nature and utilized plants and animals in a caring and concerned, 'Idyllic' way."

The website on the Castello di Brazza mentions [translated from Italian] that Count Detalmo di Brazza was appointed to the International Postal Union (he invented and patented the world's first postage meter in 1896 - *Meter Stamp Society Quarterly Bulletin*, Fall 1997). This allowed them to travel extensively. Cora's activity during these U.S. visits included work on behalf of the Peace Through Law Movement, which is referred to in *The Slocombs of America and Their Alliances* [p.509] as "the International Peace Arbitration Movement, . . . [with] offices in Washington, D.C., and Bern, Switzerland." She developed the Universal Peace Flag and the Universal Peace Badge* as part of a sophisticated system of peace education. They are displayed on the website of the international foundation that has been established in her name: [https://www.coradibrazza.com/index.html]   She participated in many expositions around the world between 1893 and 1905. She was also involved in various fund raising efforts. Two examples among many endeavors she supported: aid for the Greek Red Cross in 1892, and for the victims of the earthquake of Monteleone in Italy in 1905.

On April 11th, 1906 Countess Cora di Brazza Savorgnan, age 42, left Naples on the *SS Romanic* for Boston, accompanied by her 17 year old daughter, Ida. They arrived on April 23rd. On May 2nd Cora delivered an address at the first session of the annual meeting of the American Social Science Association at the request of the President of the Association. [*New York Times*, Apr. 11, 23, 1906; May 3, 1906]

On the website castellodibrazza.com the following details appear (translated from Italian). In 1906 her husband, Detalmo, wrote "Cora lost her reason in a day." She was transferred to a nursing home at the age 44. On June 8th, 1906 she was transferred to an apartment within a mental hospital in Imola where Detalmo visited her regularly until his death December 13th, 1920 [National Probate Index of Wills and Administrations, 1927 - London, England]. She was then transferred to Villa Giuseppina on the Via Nomentana in Rome and then in 1927 back to Brazza where she was assisted by a nun. Her nephew wrote "her memories stopped at 1906. She died in 1944 (August 24th) age 82, without realizing that the weekly visits by her daughter stopped at least six years earlier because of her death." Cora died in Rome, Provincia di Rome, Lazio, Italy. She was interred in the Metairie Cemetery. [Ancestry]

In his article "The Courage and Passion of Cora Slocomb" Luciano Morandini wrote that in 1906 the public life of Cora ended. He quoted Detalmo as having written in his memoirs, "No warning signs; Cora fell sick on a hot afternoon in May." However, some public appearances have been recorded. An interview with Countess di Brazza appeared in the *Muskogee Times-Democrat* (Muskogee, OK) February 6th, 1907 originating from Rome, reporting on Cora's plan to open schools to educate emigrants before they left for the United States. In the *Washington Herald* (Washington, DC) August 18th, 1907 a short article headed "Countess Di Brazza Ill, Stricken with Appendicitis While on Motor Tour in France." On April 17th, 1910 an article appeared in the *Washington Post* (Washington, DC) originating from Rome on the 16th, detailing "Notable Roman Gathering. When Americans Married to Italians Met Mrs. Roosevelt at Luncheon." Countess di Brazza is listed among the attendees.

It was speculated that Cora was affected by Paget's disease which causes thickening of the skull. However upon research, it seems unlikely as Paget's usually starts earlier in life and is characterized by multiple fractures in different bones and pain. There is no mention of such symptoms in her history. There are, however, records that such a sudden change usually occurs with people dabbling with the black arts. This does not seem to have been in Cora's nature. However, an article in *The Washington Post*, May 5th, 1895 described the Countess, in part, as follows:

> Born in New Orleans, educated in England, widely traveled, broadly cultured, versatile and brilliant in conversation, a keen student of political economy, and knowing how to remedy evils as well as to perceive them....

The actual reasons for her condition after 1906 remain unknown. Perhaps it may even have been the result of something inflicted upon her, from a distance.

The Barberi case, to which Cora expended much effort, is detailed within the main text, in Chapter 1.

* The *Pro Concordia Labor* flag was designed by Countess Cora di Brazza in the 1890s. It consisted of three upright bands, yellow, purple and white, with a complicated symbol in the middle consisting of clasped hands atop a shield representing "the insight that the task of developing humanity and creating a peaceful world must be a joint venture undertaken by both men and women who labor for these goals together.... The 'Universal Peace Badge'—a device utilizing the center shield of the *Pro Concordia Labor* flag—was invented by di Brazza to provide assistance in developing the 'inner resources' so that one can begin the work of practical, personal peace, and, ideally, develop into an instrument of peace. [https://www.proconcordialabor.com/Flag/]

An American Idyl by Countess di Brazza (Cora Slocomb), published by The Arena Publishing Company, Boston, MA, 1896, 244pp. The cover is purple cloth, stamped in gold and black; the spine is stamped in gold. The Countess was renowned for her fondness of the color purple.

The book is described as "an ethnographic, ethonobotanical and biological treatise on the Indians of Arizona and Northern Mexico, written in the form of a novel. A romance set in Southern Arizona between a scientist and a local Indian girl while exploring the flora and fauna of the region. The emphasis is on how the Pima Indian tribes lived in harmony with nature and utilized plants and animals in a caring and concerned, 'Idyllic' way."

AN AMERICAN IDYL

COUNTESS DI BRAZZÀ
(CORA SLOCOMB)

Appendix D

Clement Acton Griscom, Jr.
June 20, 1868 - December 30, 1918

Clement Acton Griscom, Jr. was born in Philadelphia, Pennsylvania into a family of great wealth and social standing. His father Clement Sr. (1841-1912) and his mother, Frances Canby Biddle (1840-1923), were both descendants of prominent Quaker families.

Griscom Sr. trained as a marine architect. He was one of the founders of the International Navigation Company which 'absorbed' the Red Star Line, acquired the Inman Line (renamed American Line) "and under Mr. Griscom's masterful management the International Navigation Company came to possess one of the biggest and finest fleets in the shipping trade." He then began to build palatial vessels, adding the *New York*, the *Paris,* the *St. Paul,* and the *St. Louis* to the fleet. He continued as President until 1904 when he resigned to become Chairman of the Board of Directors of the International Mercantile Marine Company, which he founded with J.P. Morgan, until his death on November 10th, 1912. He was also a Director of United States Steel Corporation, Pennsylvania Railroad Company, and a number of financial institutions, as well as a member of prestigious clubs. [*New York Times*, **Nov. 11, 1912**] Griscom Sr. was very well respected in life and business.

Clement Jr. was born June 20th, 1868, brother Rodman Ellison Griscom was born in 1870 (d.1944); brother Lloyd Carpenter Griscom was born in1872 (d.1959); his sister, Frances Canby Griscom, was born in 1879 (d.1973).

Clement Acton Griscom Jr. and Genevieve Sprigg Ludlow (July 28, 1868-September 2, 1958) married on September 18th, 1889 in Grace Church in Manhattan. Genevieve was the daughter of Brigadier General William Ludlow (1843-1901) and Genevieve Sprigg (1846-1926). They had three children: Ludlow (1890-1959), Acton (1891-1961) and Joyce (1893-1897).

Successful American described itself as "A Monthly Illustrated Magazine for the Home Circle and the Business Office". Their December 1902 issue [6:6, pp.733-734] summarized his professional career as follows:

> Clement Jr was educated in schools in Geneva, Switzerland, Frankfort-on-Main, Germany, and University of Pennsylvania, and graduated fourth in his class from the Wharton School of Political Economy (University of Pennsylvania) in 1887. During his University career he was prominent in athletics, being in both the University crew and football eleven, as well as representing his College in putting the shot and throwing the hammer. [He graduated at 18 years of age.]
>
> Immediately upon graduation he started work in the steamship business, entering the office of Peter Wright & Sons (General Agents of the International Navigation Company) as office boy. From there he was promoted to a position on the docks as delivery clerk and worked his way up step by step, through all the departments of the business, moving in succession from Philadelphia to New York to Chicago and back again to New York.
>
> In 1892 Mr. Griscom was made Supervisor of the International Navigation Company, and in 1894 was promoted to Manager. This Company owns the fleet of the "American Line," numbering four of the most palatial vessels afloat; controls the "Red Star Line" (a Belgian Company), which has recently been absorbed into the International Mercantile Marine Co., otherwise known as the shipping combination.
>
> Mr. Griscom is a born executive and organizer, working with great rapidity and sureness. His ability to accomplish much in a brief time is one of his salient characteristics, and has drawn the attention of the entire shipping world to his methods. The success of the weekly twin-screw service of the American line, involving as it does, the turning of the ships in something under three days is due largely to his genius.
>
> He is a man of unusual personal force and initiative. This combined with a sound and clear judgment, together with a really

Appendix D - Clement Acton Griscom, Jr.

remarkable memory, has made him at the age of thirty-four a distinct power in the business world. His success is directly attributed to his unremitting devotion to his business and the conscientiousness and untiring manner in which he has borne his great responsibilities, heavier than any one outside of the transportation business can easily appreciate. He is also a scholar and finds time to indulge his tastes, as a glance at the philosophical and scientific societies of which he is a member, would indicate.

In person Mr. Griscom is tall and athletic looking, standing six feet one inch in his stockings. His manner is a curious blending of outspoken frankness with a native courtesy and chivalry arising from a seemingly intuitive understanding and sympathy with those about him. It is perhaps the recognition of this understanding that is at the root of his great popularity with those in his employ, for all who come in contact with him, from the stevedores handling cargo on the piers to the various heads of departments under him, cannot fail to recognize that he is not only interested in them as employees of the Company, but in their personal welfare, and that they may not only expect from him justice but human sympathy.

Mr. Griscom is Manager not only of the International Navigation Company but of the International Mercantile Marine Company. He is also President of the James Reilly Repair and Supply Company, of New York, and Director of the Poland Mining Company, the Development Company of America; the Empire State Trust Company, New York; and Director and Member of Executive Committee Maritime Association. . . .

Clement Acton Griscom, Jr., belongs to the American Museum of Natural History, New York City, Society of Naval Architects and Marine Engineers, the Lawyers' Club, the Metropolitan Club, the Pennsylvania Society of New York, the Pennsylvania Society of Sons of the Revolution, the Chamber of Commerce, the Morris County Golf Club, the Merion Cricket Club, Philadelphia, The University Club, Philadelphia, the Society of Colonial Wars, the Department of Archaeology and Palaeontology of the University of Pennsylvania, the General Alumni Society of the University of

Pennsylvania, the Metropolitan Museum of Art, New York, the Somerset Hills Country Club, Morristown, New Jersey, the American Academy of Political and Social Science, Philadelphia, and the University of Pennsylvania Club, New York.

Like his father, Clement Jr. was well-liked and respected in the business world.

Theosophical Career

In late 1884, while Clement Jr. was in university, he first heard of Theosophy when the conversation one evening turned to a discussion of standards of conduct. He recognized the truth of it immediately, and pursued it with fervor. He read Sinnett's *Esoteric Buddhism* and *The Occult World* then *Isis Unveiled*, reading until the early morning hours. He went to New York to see W.Q. Judge sometime in 1885. His application for membership in the Theosophical Society indicates he joined March 21st, 1887. A profound friendship developed.

Griscom adopted 'watchwords' from Judge: *faith, courage, constancy*, which he evidenced throughout his life. Henry Bedinger Mitchell in his article "A Stone of the Foundation" **[*Theosophical Quarterly*, No.17, July 1919, pp.3-21]** surmises that it was because of the Theosophical Society and his friendship with Judge that Griscom moved to the vicinity of New York City. Clement married Genevieve Ludlow September 18th, 1889 in Manhattan, NY.

The "Twelfth Census of The United States" dated June 11th, 1900 indicates that the Mitchell and Griscom families lived next door to each other on Whitestone Avenue, NYC. Henry was twenty-five years old and Clement was a few days from his thirty-second birthday. Henry had first-hand knowledge of the time Judge spent at the Griscom home. He wrote:

> [W]hen Mr. Griscom moved to the vicinity of New York—and later into the city itself—his home became one of the most vital centres of the whole Theosophical movement. Mr. Judge came there as to a haven of rest; . . . It became his habit to take Sunday supper there, and to spend the evening. But often he would stay for weeks at a time, going into the city with Mr. Griscom in the

Appendix D - Clement Acton Griscom, Jr.

morning, but returning again in the afternoon. It was during such a visit as this that I first met Mr. Judge, . . . memory holds many pictures of him in this home where he loved to be. I can see him with the children on his knees, drawing pictures for them on one of those little pads of which he always seemed to have an unlimited number in his pockets. It was on them he would write the brief unexplained notes to the students whom he trusted; sometimes containing only a reference to a chapter or page of a book but which, when looked up, would throw a flood of light upon the untold subject of their recent meditations or upon some theme they had been discussing in his absence. I can see him unpacking barrels of china and arranging the books, when Mr. Griscom moved into town; or in one of his "wild Irish boy" moods, sitting on the floor and gravely trying to put his heel behind his head. But the picture that comes to my mind the most constantly is of his sitting with Mr. Griscom listening to the piano—in a silence so deep and still that it became part of the music—and to this day I cannot hear La Paloma, or certain of Mendelssohn's Songs without Words, without thinking of Mr. Judge in Mr. Griscom's home. [*TQ*, **July 1919, p.13**]

Griscom's name does not come up in an official capacity; having the same name as his father, he worked diligently in the background but did not permit it to become public. He was in constant correspondence with members to counteract the attacks upon Judge. The preliminary arrangements for the convention in Boston in April 1895 where 'the split' occurred were made at the Griscom home.

During the Crusade, with many of the prominent members away for nearly a year, a lot of responsibilities fell upon Griscom. He was extremely busy in his business life and this additional burden led to a health breakdown. His physician recommended a rest, and suggested an ocean voyage.

Uncertain about how to proceed following the untimely death of W.Q. Judge in March 1896, members got swept up by a series of pronouncements. In the first few days while coming to terms with their loss, an answer was said to have been found in Judge's notes which, when pieced together were taken to imply that he had a succession plan in place. Great enthusiasm at the American T.S. Convention in New York in April; the charade surrounding the new 'mahatma'; the strange ceremony at the Leonard/Wright wedding in May, and the revelation that the 'adept' was actually Katherine Tingley when a reporter followed her home; the 'school' in California; plans for the Crusade and big send-off on June 13th, — everyone seemed in a daze.

Within those short few months, a plan was also launched to develop a commune of sorts in southwestern California. With Griscom's health breaking down as a result of overwork and his physician's recommendation to take an ocean voyage, he decided to sail to Honolulu to meet the Crusaders on the final leg of the world tour. He combined this with the opportunity to search for a fitting piece of property, which had been determined to be on Point Loma, and to complete the purchase. He arrived in San Diego on January 9th and together with Edward Rambo, who arrived from San Francisco on the 15th, they proceeded to examine the properties on the point.

The *San Diego Union and Daily Bee* reported on January 27th, 1897:

> Mr. Rambo, acting on the instructions from Mr. Griscom, concluded the purchase of 120 acres on Point Loma, paying $12,000 therefor. The deeds were filed yesterday afternoon . . .

Griscom had left for San Francisco on January 24th, sailed for Honolulu on the 26th on the *Australia* and encountered storms which extended the time at sea; the ship pulled into port in Hawaii on February 2nd. The Crusaders arrived early on the morning of February 4th on the *S.S. Alameda*, having left Sydney, Australia seventeen days earlier. Griscom met them and then left with them for San Francisco that evening. [*The Honolulu Advertiser*, Feb. 5, 1897]

February 7th while at sea, Griscom wrote a glowing account of details and impressions he gathered from the crusaders. The subtitle of his article read "Work, Work, Work. — Stories of Narrow Escapes. The Courage and Endurance Shown by All." [*The Theosophical News*, 1:36, Boston, Feb. 22, 1897] He signed it "E. Hijo" one of his pseudonyms.

In this article he mentions the upcoming laying of the cornerstone ceremony which "promises to be very impressive judging from the plans." However, Griscom did not attend; he left shortly after arrival on the 11th. His brother, Rodman, was getting married in New York barely one week later, on February 17th. [*The Philadelphia Inquirer*, Feb. 18, 1897]

What he learned during the week on board ship with the crusaders, and the direction he observed the society taking under the dominance of Tingley's leadership led him to withdraw from active participation in the Society's councils and committees. He immediately became persona-non-grata. He was accused of disloyalty; workers at the Society's Headquarters who had been in the habit of spending weekends in his home were forbidden to come near him; slanderous accusations were written about him.

At the convention of the society at Chicago on February 18th, 1898,
> Mrs. Tingley's followers, overriding all protests, proclaimed a change in the name and constitution of the Society, and gave unrestricted power over the new body into her hands. She thus removed herself from The Theosophical Society; but she took with her nearly everything that had given it external manifestation: the majority of its members, its organization, headquarters, lists, records, press, magazines, and practically everything it owned. She left only its reality and its name. [*TQ*, **July 1919, p.15**]

The Theosophical Society in America had to rebuild from scratch; the entire administrative unit had been confiscated. Griscom took it upon himself to reconstruct it, which he could only do outside of his business responsibilities, which were demanding. Correspondence was an enormous task—he felt everyone who could be reached "was entitled to a clear statement of the actual facts and issues." He was convinced a magazine should become the official organ and means of communication with its members. [*TQ*, **July 1919, p.16**]

Henry Bedinger Mitchell explains:
> Mr. Judge's old magazine, *The Path*, had been first re-christened *Theosophy* and then *Universal Brotherhood*, under which title it was being carried on by Mrs. Tingley. But *The Theosophical Forum*, a little sixteen page monthly started by Mr. Judge in 1889 as a medium for questions and answers, had been discontinued in August 1897, and the only obstacle to reviving it was the labour and expense its publication and distribution would involve. These Mr. Griscom himself assumed. [*TQ*, **July 1919, p.16**]

The Theosophical Forum restarted with the Vol.3, No.5, February 1898 issue.

Judge had maintained personal copyrights as well as interest in the publishing business he had built, which became the personal property of individuals in his will. Griscom was determined to continue publishing and selling theosophical books. However with the dissolution of the W.Q. Judge Publishing Co. it became necessary to make other arrangements with different publishers, which proved unsatisfactory. Griscom put up the initial capital and with proceeds of sales, published other works. Business increased to the point where it needed to be formalized and The Quarterly Book Department was started.

In 1899 Griscom's health again broke down and he did not resume editorship of *The Theosophical Forum* after resuming full time work in January 1901. In 1903 the *Theosophical Quarterly* was started not "to compete with but to supplement *The Theosophical Forum*." In 1905 the two publications were amalgamated. [*TQ*, July 1919, p.18] Within its pages is contained important theosophical history.

Griscom wrote under a number of pseudonyms: G. Hijo, John Blake, Menteknis, The Pilgrim, as well as using one or more of his initials. [*TQ*, July 1919, p.19]

Public meetings were eventually discontinued but members met regularly informally in homes, and other groups were formed until it eventually became too many meetings/too many nights. Griscom fitted the studio building in the rear of his house to serve as a permanent centre and meeting place for the New York Branch. Eventually Griscom and others "laboured to create a living centre of true religion." [*TQ*, July 1919, p.21] Jesus was his ideal and his Quaker roots and Theosophy guided his entire life.

As painful as being spurned by his close theosophical friends had been when he withdrew from active involvement in the society following Tingley's dominating leadership, an exceptionally painful incident in the lives of Clement and Genevieve was the loss of their daughter, Joyce Olive, who died December 2nd, 1897, a few months short of her fifth birthday. Despite having been warned to stay away from the stove in her bedroom, it is assumed that Joyce opened its door, the flames shot out and her clothing caught fire. The nanny had left the room for a few minutes while Joyce was asleep. She heard her scream and ran back to find the little girl engulfed in flames. It was disheartening in 1900 when cruel comments surrounding this unfortunate incident appeared in a theosophical publication. Portions of a letter by Dr. J.D. Buck are quoted in the article "Inside Facts Concerning The Dream City of Esotero." He had written a response to a man's ambivalence about the real situation at Point Loma: "Read in *The Crusader* . . . the gloating over the burning alive of Griscom's little girl." [*The San Francisco Call*, **Aug. 5, 1900**] Basil Crump was the editor of *The Crusader*.

On December 30th, 1918 Clement Acton Griscom Jr. died of pneumonia at his home, 37 Fifth Avenue, Flushing, Queens County, New York. He was fifty years old. His ashes are interred in Woodlawn Cemetery, Bronx, NYC.

The April 1919 issue of *Theosophical Quarterly* devoted pages 312-326 to "Reminiscences" about Clement. Charles Johnston described the similar difficulties faced first by Blavatsky, then Judge and then by Griscom. Their tireless efforts were to ensure the original program as outlined by the Mahatmas was available to all sincere seekers. Their conviction and devotion never wavered. Johnston closed with:

> There remains but one thing that should be said: Through the long and arduous years of his great and fruitful labours, Clement Griscom always had, close at hand, the purest, highest and divinest inspiration; he always had the wisdom of the heart to accept and follow it. [p.326]

Genevieve survived Clement by forty years and passed away on September 2nd, 1958 in Bronx, NY. She wrote under the pseudonym Cavé. A series of articles titled "Fragments" appeared in issues of *Theosophical Quarterly* and then compiled into three little books titled *Fragments*. Volume I was published in 1908, II in 1916, and III in 1925. Her articles also appeared in *Theosophy*, *The Beacon* and *The Pacific Theosophist*. Her ashes are also interred in Woodlawn Cemetery, Bronx, NYC.

Appendix E

Documented Horror Cases
From the Early Days at the Homestead.

The hearing of the Cuban "Lotus Buds" case drew much attention nationwide. The case was brought to light by the New York Society for the Prevention of Cruelty to Children which requested an investigation to determine whether or not the eleven children brought from Cuba to New York on November 1st, 1902, should be allowed to enter the country. They were in the care of Dr. Gertrude van Pelt, destined for Point Loma and being held at Ellis Island. Protests had also been received in New York by cable from citizens, churches and newspapers in Cuba.

Immigration Commissioner W. Williams indicated:
> [T]he department is in possession of information which warrants it in instituting a very thorough investigation into the case. He said the Society for the Prevention of Cruelty to Children had asked that the children be withheld from the custody of Mrs. Tingley pending an investigation, and that the request would be complied with. It is probable that after a preliminary examination the matter will be turned over to the Board of Inquiry of the Immigration Department, and that a thorough investigation will follow. [*New York Herald*, Nov. 1, 1902]

Vernon M. Davis, president of the Society for the Prevention of Cruelty to Children claimed that "[t]he society fears that they may be subjected to an environment which would endanger their health and morals. . . ." [*New York Herald*, Nov. 1, 1902]

Mr. Davis explained that his reasons for requesting an inquiry were:
> [T]o determine whether the society [Tingley's] was capable of caring for the children, both in a financial way and in regard to their future welfare. Mr. Davis insinuated that everything was not as it should be in Mrs. Tingley's organization, and that the society which he represented had prevented her from forming similar

settlements of children here when she was a resident of this city. [*New York Herald*, **Nov. 2, 1902**]

He further indicated that the investigation by the Society for the Prevention of Cruelty to Children "would extend to the Pacific coast, until the light was let in on some of the 'mysteries' of Mrs. Tingley's institution." [*New York Herald*, **Nov. 2, 1902**]

Then on November 3rd, 1902
> The Board of Inquiry had given a preliminary decision of three to one against admitting them .... The case may be appealed to the General Commissioner of Immigration, Frank P. Sargent, and the Treasury Department constitutes the court of last resort to which aliens may appeal. [*New York Herald*, **Nov. 4, 1902**]

On November 4th, 1902, it was reported that
> Commissioner Williams did not accept the decision, but ordered a rehearing, moved thereto by the many communications he received for and against the admission of the children.

Members from Point Loma had been interviewed during the Inquiry.
> Vernon M. Davis, president of the Society for the Prevention of Cruelty to Children said yesterday that he thought the opinion of the California officials was biased, and suggested that the [re]hearing be held tomorrow, at which time he hopes to submit further proof. Elbridge T. Gerry, the former president and founder of the society, will be present as a witness. [*New York Herald*, **Nov. 4, 1902**]

The rehearing began on November 5th, 1902.
> During the proceedings Commodore Gerry was attacked, but he was serene, believing that the cause of public morality had been aided in the matter. He thanked the HERALD for helping his society and said that the Point Loma home may be the next object of an investigation. [*New York Herald*, **Nov. 8, 1902**]

Upon hearing that Elbridge Gerry had received damaging evidence, especially Edward Parker's letter from Tingley's first husband, it was reported that she sent a telegram to A.G. Spalding on November 6th to drop the Lotus Buds case proceedings and to leave it in the hands of the Cubans. At this point she was willing to let the children be sent back to Santiago, Cuba where she was planning to set up a home. Tingley realized that she could not win if the hearing were to focus on her, so she instead chose to redirect attention toward the United States Government in Washington D.C. and convince authorities that she could afford to support the children. One of the reasons she had asked Albert Spalding to help was that she expected his reputation, fame and wealth to have a great impact on these hearings.

Albert Spalding married Elizabeth Mayer in June 1900. Albert did not know very much about Tingley's personal history—he had only known her for a few years. Elizabeth had been in charge of the Lotus Circle at the Aryan Branch since 1893. Tingley's professed interest in children drew Elizabeth to follow her. Elizabeth was a music and drama educator; Tingley greatly benefitted from her expertise, especially at Lomaland.

In her November 6th telegram to Spalding, Tingley conveyed to him that he had done all he could. Newspapers reported that "no further effort will he made by Mr. A. G. Spalding to obtain admission to this country for the eleven Cuban children." [*New York Herald*, **Nov. 9, 1902**] Tingley was in California preoccupied with the Los Angeles Times-Mirror case and could not leave to go to New York City. Spalding's response on November 8th acknowledged receipt of Tingley's instructions and "[t]herefore I will do nothing more about them and will consider myself formally discharged as acting agent of the Raja Yoga School at Point Loma." [*New York Herald*, **Nov. 9, 1902**]

On November 7th, 1902, the Board of Special Inquiry at Ellis Island once again barred the children from entering the United States.

On November 9th, the New York *Herald* wrote,
> Defeated in her purpose to place the eleven Cuban children as "Lotos Buds" in her Raja Yoga School, at Point Loma, Cal., Mrs. Katherine C.[A.] Tingley's institution on the Pacific slope may yet be the subject of a rigid investigation by the Society for the Prevention of Cruelty to Children which has its headquarters in San Francisco. Through the testimony given before the Board of [I]nquiry which determined to restore the children to their parents

in Santiago many side lights were thrown on occultism as preached and practised by Mrs. Tingley and her followers.

Much more information is in the possession of Mr. Elbridge T. Gerry, as counsel, and Judge-elect Vernon M. Davis, president of the Society for the Prevention of Cruelty to Children in this city, than was placed on the records during the hearings that thwarted Mrs. Tingley's purpose to make the eleven little ones members of the peculiar cult known as the Universal Brotherhood and Theosophical Society. [*New York Herald*, Nov. 9, 1902]

Tingley did not want to be investigated by the Society for the Prevention of Cruelty to Children. In order to avert that she contacted the Mayor of Santiago and the Commissioner General of Immigration Frank P. Sargent at Washington D.C.

On November 3rd a number of dispatches had been sent to Commissioner Sargent emphasizing Tingley's financial stability, among them Emil Neresheimer's letter as acting Treasurer of the Raja Yoga School:

> I refer you to National Bank of Commerce, New York; National Park Bank, New York, and First National Bank, San Diego. Albert Spalding, of Spalding & Bros., resident at Albemarle Hotel, New York, is my agent, and I have authorized him to receive the children; I will assume the responsibility at the highest moral training of these children. [*New York Herald*, Nov. 9, 1892]

In addition, Neresheimer had sent a dispatch to Leslie M. Shaw, Secretary of the Treasury, reiterating that he would "assume the responsibility of the highest moral training for these children." These dispatches were followed by others protesting against detention and deportation. [*New York Herald*, Nov. 9, 1902]

The following day, November 4th, it had been reported that A. G. Spalding had contacted Señor Gonzalo de Quesada, the Cuban Minister at Washington, and asked him:

> to interfere in behalf of the eleven Cuban children. A. G. Spalding has represented to Minister Quesada that there was ample means to care for the children, which guaranteed beyond all question that they would not become charges of the United States. An appeal for the landing of the children will be brought to the office of the

Commissioner of Immigration in the Treasury Department. [*New York Herald*, **Nov. 4, 1902**]

Meanwhile, the offices of the San Francisco Society for the Prevention of Cruelty to Children was receiving a lot of information "which is treated as confidential by Superintendent Jenkins of the society, is said to concern Mrs. Tingley herself rather than the institution . . . it is arriving by every mail and is now beginning to come from a distance" adding that "the society will never consent to the admittance at this port of any 'Lotos Buds' bound for the home of the 'Purple Mother'." [*New York Herald*, **Nov. 11, 1902**] It was also reported that "Both President Davis and Mr. Gerry are appalled at the revelations that are being made to them, and determined to leave no stone unturned . . . ." Numerous affidavits had been received outlining experiences there. [*New York Herald*, **Nov. 13, 1902**]

On November 14th, 1902, the *New York Herald* reported that:
> Katherine A. Tingley's Universal Brotherhood is to be the subject of investigation by the United States Government. This announcement was made last night by Secretary of the Treasury Leslie M. Shaw. The investigation will be conducted independently of any action taken by the New York and California Societies for the Prevention of Cruelty to Children. . . .
>
> Elbridge T. Gerry, counsel, and Vernon M. Davis, president of the New York Society for the Prevention of Cruelty to Children, were surprised last night when informed by a HERALD reporter that Mrs. Tingley had carried the case to the Secretary of the Treasury. Acting as a stay against the deportation of the children, as the appeal does, until Secretary Shaw announces his decision and upholds or reverses the decision of the Board of Inquiry, there promises to be a very interesting hearing before the Secretary. . . .
>
> Mr. Davis, Mr. Gerry and E. Fellows Jenkins, superintendent of the society, were in consultation for more than an hour last night formulating plans for the work that is to be carried on in California. They thoroughly discussed the evidence they have received, and in addition to this arranged for the gathering of additional material. **[p.4]**

This decision proved to benefit Katherine Tingley greatly. Now the attacks were divided. All she had to do was to manage the situation, which she did with great success; the investigation was now focused on the physical location at Point Loma. Frank P. Sargent, the Commissioner-General of Immigration, "notified Secretary Shaw that he has already begun his personal investigation of the school." [*The Baltimore Sun,* Nov. 18, 1902] The following day:

> Immigration Commissioner Williams received a letter from the treasury department at Washington today, ordering that the case of the eleven Cuban children, detained on Ellis island be reopened. The department makes this order in response to the request of Mrs. Tingley, who says that she has a quantity of evidence to introduce, which she claims will utterly refute the charges which were made against her character at the former hearing. Mr. Williams cannot say yet when the new hearing will take place. [*San Diego Union,* **Nov. 19, 1902;** *New York Tribune,* **Nov. 19, 1902**]

Under headline "New Evidence Ready For Tingley Hearing", the *New York Herald* wrote:

> Though surprised by the action of the Secretary of the Treasury in reopening the hearing in the case of the "Lotus Buds" sent from Cuba to Mrs. Katherine Tingley's school of the Universal Brotherhood, at Point Loma, the officers of the Society for the Prevention of Cruelty to Children have much new evidence to offer. They had by no means exhausted their ammunition during the previous hearing before the board of inquiry, which ordered the deportation of the Cuban children.
>
> Commissioner of Immigration Frank P. Sargent, will leave San Francisco today for San Diego to begin his investigations at Point Loma. He will be accompanied by M. J. White, secretary of the San Francisco Society for the Prevention of Cruelty to Children, who will work in harmony with Mr. Sargent under the direction of the Board of Directors of the San Francisco society. The new hearing in this city [New York] will begin next week. [*New York Herald,* **Nov. 20, 1902**]

On November 18th *The Baltimore Sun* wrote:

The case will not be re-opened in New York, but all proceedings will be conducted in Washington. It was officially reopened when Mrs. Tingley made her appeal to the department and the new investigation began.

On November 23rd the morning edition of the *San Diego Union* published that the mayor of Santiago de Cuba and the proprietor of El Cubano Libre, "one of the largest and most influential daily newspapers in all Cuba. . . came to America for the express purpose of presenting to the Washington government the sentiment and feeling of their countrymen in the matter of the detention of the Cuban children at New York." Their train from New Orleans was delayed so Commissioner Sargent delayed his return to Washington.

> This gave ample time for the meeting and conference between the commissioner general and the two distinguished Cuban representatives, which took place at the Hotel Brewster last evening immediately after the arrival of the train. . . .
>
> By special request of Katherine Tingley, they came to San Diego before going to Washington, and last evening, in conference with Mrs. Tingley at the Hotel Brewster, the leader of the Universal Brotherhood and founder of the Raja Yoga schools, made it clear to the Cuban representatives that the United States officials were in no way to blame for the detention of the Cuban children, but that the entire blame must rest upon the New York Gerry Society for the Prevention of Cruelty to Children. . . . **[*San Diego Union*, Nov. 23, 1902]**

Further to Commissioner Sargent's visit to Point Loma, the *Los Angeles Times* reported that on November 21st:

> Immigration Commissioner Frank Sargent arrived here [San Diego] at 12:45 o'clock today and proceeded at once to Point Loma, where the Raja Yoga school is to be made the subject of inquiry. Sargent was accompanied by Congressman-elect Daniels, who went with him to Point Loma. At the depot here Sargent was met by Mayor Frary who introduced himself and spoke a few words to the commissioner. Frary stated to a reporter that he had been requested by some one at Point Loma to meet Sargent. . . .

The commissioner, Representative-elect Daniels and others of the party will spend the night on the point. **[Nov. 22, 1902]**

The *Sun* (New York) reported that
> [Commissioner Sargent] spent Friday [21st] afternoon and night at Point Loma and says that Mrs. Tingley gave him the fullest opportunity for investigation. . . .
>
> Secretary White of the San Francisco Children's Aid Society [Society for the Prevention of Cruelty to Children] had arranged to make a joint investigation with Sargent, but the Commissioner started earlier than he announced and when White arrived Mrs. Tingley gave orders not to admit him. ***[The Sun* (NY), Nov. 24, 1902]**

The *New York Herald*, with a headline from San Diego, mentioned Commissioner Sargent's visit and covered the incident involving M.J. White.
> Commissioner of Immigration Sargent, sent here to investigate the Tingley Raja Yoga school at Point Loma, returned to this city to-day, having spent yesterday afternoon and last night at the theosophical headquarters. . . .
>
> Mr. White reached this city last evening and was surprised to learn that Mr. Sargent had preceded him, and had begun the investigation. He also said he was surprised that Mr. Sargent had accepted favors from Mrs. Tingley. . . .
>
> Mr. White returned from his trip to Point Loma this afternoon. He said he had gone to the Egyptian gate and presented his card to the guard stationed there, stating his business and requesting permission to enter. He was informed that no further investigation was to be permitted at the school, and that he could not be admitted. **[Nov. 23, 1902]**

The rest of the story behind the exclusion of White came out in various newspapers a few days later.
> The Point Loma Theosophical authorities have served an injunction against M.J. White of San Francisco, agent of the

California Society for the Prevention of Cruelty to Children. This writ was prepared during the night by secretary Pierce and Attorney Wadham, the latter a director in the new local society alleged to have been formed to prevent cruelty to children, and it was signed by Superior Judge Torrance [the Superior Court judge in the ongoing Tingley vs Times-Mirror case] and served on Mr. White between 3 and 4 o'clock this morning at his hotel where he was asleep. The writ is issued at the prayer of the School for the Revival of the Lost Mysteries of Antiquity of Point Loma, and is operative to restrain the New York Society for Prevention of Cruelty to Children, the California society of similar scope and M.J. White, from entering the Raja Yoga school at Point Loma.

When Mr. White was interviewed he said he was amused by the proceedings and that he had no intention of again requesting permission to inspect the school. He said that the Point Loma people claimed to have been warned that he intended to come here to do injury to their school, but that nothing was further from his intentions or instructions. He said he would have been glad to inspect the school and report favorably if such a report would be warranted and that the only suspicion that he could have about the place is the determined opposition to his entrance. He will file an answer to the injunction. [*The Fresno Morning Republican*, Nov. 25, 1902; *Los Angeles Times*, Nov. 25, 1902; *San Francisco Chronicle*, Nov. 25, 1902; *San Francisco Call*, Nov. 25, 1902]

The circumstances surrounding the proposed joint investigation were rather strange. Why did Commissioner of Immigration Sargent proceed on his own? Why was M. J. White, secretary of the San Francisco Society for the Prevention of Cruelty to Children prevented from investigating? If Sargent did accept favors, what were they? Sargent claimed he had gone there expecting to pay his own expenses; did he in fact get compensated? If there were no concerns—that all was of the highest morality and honesty—why prevent an investigation? *Was* there something to hide?

While the Cuban children were being detained at Ellis Island the *New York Herald* wrote:

It is realized here that Mrs. Tingley, with the assistance of Frank Pierce and E. August Neresheimer, will do all she can to prevent the accomplishment of the society's efforts and prevent if possible any investigation of the strange doings of the brotherhood in the "Temple of Isis," the "Homes-stead" or on the "Holy Hill." **[Nov. 13, 1902]**

Important letters and affidavits were being received by Vernon M. Davis and Elbridge T. Gerry. One of these letters, published in the *New York Herald* was prefaced with the following:

> Dr. Mary E. Green, who lives in . . . Charlotte, Mich., rescued her grandchildren from the Raja Yoga school only by habeas corpus proceedings brought by her in the Supreme Court of California. Dr. Green believes that her daughter, Mrs. John J. Bohn, still an inmate of the brotherhood grounds, is "either crazed or hypnotized by this woman" (Mrs. Tingley). Dr. Green is anxious to give her testimony in a court of law. **[Nov. 13, 1902]**

Her letter to Mr. Gerry, follows:

> "After sending a despatch relative to the Cuban children I later learned they were to be returned to Cuba.
>
> "I sincerely wish it were in your power to take away the children now at Point Loma, under the harmful influence of this Katherine Tingley. She has several Cuban children there, and thousands of circulars are sent out soliciting money for their education, and hundreds of thousands of dollars are sent to Point Loma, which she uses to live in the most sumptuous manner. My daughter, Mrs. John J. Bohn, was either crazed or hypnotized by this woman and she took her two little boys there. Then Mrs. Tingley refused Mr. Bohn admittance, as everything there is secret and well guarded in enclosed grounds. The Supreme Court of California issued a writ of habeas corpus to take the children, the case was tried in Los Angeles and the children were removed from Point Loma and given to the father.
>
> "According to the statement of these boys, children all sleep in tents, about twenty boys and girls in a tent, on a bunk. Every night a girl about fourteen years old comes and ties their hands together,

then fastens them about their necks. No child is allowed to talk loud and only to whisper necessary things.

"All children are made to stand up when visitors come and say, 'We like our Lotos Mother and are glad to be here.' Children have meat only once a week; for noonday lunch they are given a cracker and an apple, the biggest boys getting two crackers. Thus are the children cared for.

"My grandchildren were there six weeks; they never saw their mother except as she marched by with a white robe on at sunrise, holding up her hand—as they are sun worshippers.

"Katherine Tingley is high priestess and all followers bow down and worship her. Surely I wish the government could take away the Cuban children—then her source of revenue would be gone. I spent some time in California, where the general impression and belief is that Point Loma is an immoral place; yet when people once get there they are powerless to get out; the grounds are fenced, all gates guarded and the greatest secrecy prevails. The temple of Isis is a most mysterious place.

"From what I know and have seen of this woman she lives like a queen; in fact, compares herself to Queen Victoria."

Mr. Gerry telegraphed to Dr. Green for further particulars when he received her first letter and yesterday this further detailed communication was received from Dr. Green:—

"My daughter, Mrs. Grace Green Bohn, was an unusually gifted bright girl and most happily married. She has pursued her art studies at both Cincinnati and Chicago, later becoming a teacher at the Chicago Art School. She also was graduated from kindergarten and was an exceptionally fine musician and was quite well known as a writer, when Katherine Tingley came to Chicago and she fell under the influence of this woman, who at once planned to have her go to Point Loma. She was married to John J. Bohn and was most happy with her husband and two little boys. Mrs. Tingley had Mrs. Bohn do a great amount of writing and sending out circulars setting forth the work Mrs. Tingley was doing and soliciting money for Cuban children and to aid in educating them. At one time Mrs. Bohn sent out two thousand of these circulars. Photographs have been sent out showing Cuban children. Twenty of these were sent here to Charlotte and an offer of $10 if they could be exhibited in a grocery window. I told the proprietor of the grocery store if they did not remove the pictures I would expose Katherine Tingley. The pictures were removed the same day.

"There have been articles printed here in the papers begging for money and praising Mrs. Tingley for what she was doing. As I said before, the Cuban children only serve to make Mrs. Tingley rich.

"While the children were rescued the mother still remains there under the spell of Katherine Tingley, who has been instrumental in having my daughter bring suit for divorce against her husband and naming her own mother as co-respondent—three such suits have been discharged from the Chicago courts, another has been begun in California.

"I enclose a drawing made by my little grandchild, Ralph Bohn, showing the tent where twenty children lived and slept, and the bunk on which Ralph and Donald slept. Ralph is seven years old. Boys and girls live together in this tent, but every night a girl fourteen years old comes and ties their hands together and fastens them about their necks. The children ate in another tent. Such is the place that my dear little grandchildren were taken to after living in a home of refinement and luxury. The children were half starved when rescued, while my daughter, their once devoted mother, did not bathe them or eat with them or put them to bed, but was marching about with a white robe on, barefooted, at sunrise worshiping the sun. Such is the story of her two little boys who were made to call Katherine Tingley 'Lotos Mother,' and to stand up and say to all visitors, 'we love our Lotus Mother and are glad to be here'." [*New York Herald*, **Nov. 13, 1902**]

Much more could be written about this case but it would require a couple of chapters to explain all the facts and details. It is truly a sad story with many strange twists.

Another serious incident involved Vespera Montalla Freeman, who was rescued from Point Loma by her older sister, Irene DeSilva Willis.

By 1878 Miss Irene Willis owned a famous music store in Hannibal, Missouri where she sold

> [a] beautiful assortment of first-class Pianos, Organs and Guitars. . . supplied teachers and agents largely throughout Missouri, Iowa, Nebraska and Texas. . . [and carried] a full stock of School and Miscellaneous Books, Chromos, Engravings and Pictures of every description. [*Hannibal Daily Courier*, **Jan. 15, 1878**]

She was described as a music dealer in the Tingley vs Times-Mirror case where "she was not permitted to relate the circumstances" under which she found her dying sister at Point Loma. [*Los Angeles Times*, **Jan. 1, 1903**] Judge Torrance declared "I will not permit you to show what appeared to be her condition." Mr. Daney, one of the lawyers for Times-Mirror asked Judge Torrance

> If we can show that this lady's sister was practically starved to death in that institution, have we not a right to claim, and justly claim, that this is a place of horror? We do not rely on that alone, there are other instances; there is other evidence . . . .

Torrance insisted they provide proof it was a place of horror, without allowing them to present any evidence to do so!

The November 13th, 1902 article in the *New York Herald* continued:

> Tales of cruelty on the part of Mrs. Tingley have also been heard the result of her complete domination of those who remain or are kept within the Brotherhood's grounds. The Society for the Prevention of Cruelty to Children has much evidence of this nature in its keeping. A letter that Superintendent B. Fellows Jenkins received yesterday [Nov. 12th] from Irene Willis, of Hannibal, Mo., said:—

> "My private opinion of Mrs. Tingley is that she is a woman who has a strange power over weak minds.

"My sister fell into her power. I found her, my sister, Mrs. [Vespera] Freeman, neglected, starved, dying, relegated when so broken and abused that she could no longer assist Mrs. Tingley to a wild place among the chaparral, which they call the 'Colony,' deprived of food fit to be eaten, even by the strongest, coarsest people, and forbidden to buy other food, lest it reflect upon the institution. No one was allowed to assist or comfort her. Willis Freeman, her son of sixteen, was kept at work ten hours a day, then kept on guard two hours every night—a young, growing lad, who had never handled a gun or firearms of any description—two hours in the middle of the night, on half rations and less of this miserable food, bread made of beans and peanuts ground together, and not allowed to buy a fresh egg or bottle of milk for his dying mother, although there was plenty of both for sale by the residents of Point Loma, just outside the Colony gates.

"The 'students' so called, of this abominable place are all hypnotized. They form rings and circles and gaze with a stupid somnolence into this woman's face, kiss her hands, her garments, call her Queen of the World, swear to worship her through this life and all lives hereafter. I know this is hard to believe, but it is true.

"Mrs. Tingley is fearfully afraid of assassination from without, and every male member of the society or inhabitant therein, from ten years to seventy, has to take turns watching, guarding and protecting her life night and day. The only education given the children or for which she seems to care is military drill. She is apparently trying to raise up an army for her bodily protection.

"Many of the children are badly treated always, I believe, if they show the least resistance to her authority or if they do not succumb at once to her domination.

"One little girl has been isolated from all beings except a demented, one-eyed grass widow, who acts as her jailer. She has been thus isolated for two years, while her wealthy father and mother and sisters (younger) board at a fabulous expense with Kate Tingley and approve of this incarceration of their pretty little daughter over at the 'colony.' " [*New York Herald*, Nov. 13, 1902]

Vespera Freeman was the younger sister of Irene Willis, both born in Illinois. Irene was born in 1842 and Vespera in 1848. Vespera Willis married H. Alfred Freeman in 1871, in Hannibal, Missouri. They had two sons Ned [Edward] in June 1872 and George Willis Freeman born June 1884. The Freemans lived in Jamaica, New York, when they joined the Aryan Branch of the Theosophical Society while W.Q. Judge was President. Vespera joined on January 14th, 1893 and Alfred joined six months later on June 6th. Alfred was a traveling salesman. He died in Charlotte, North Carolina, on July 14th, 1900.

After Alfred's death, Vespera and George must have considered Point Loma a place where they could be taken care of and study theosophy. What they discovered was that it became a place of horror. Since they had handed everything to Tingley they quickly realized that they had no resources if they wanted to leave.

Irene Willis and George Freeman both came from out of State to testify at the Tingley vs Times-Mirror case. When questioned on the witness stand George stated:

> My name is George Willis Freeman. I reside at Auburn Park, Chicago, Illinois. I was an inmate of the Point Loma colony from October, 1900, until April, 1901. Before I went to the colony I lived in Jamaica, Greater New York. I arrived at the colony on the 14th of October. My mother was with me. Her name was Mrs. Vespera Montalla Freeman. **[KT vs Times-Mirror, 2045-2046, p.512]**

And that was practically the only response Judge Torrance allowed him.

After her stay in a San Diego hospital George brought his mother to Chicago where his older brother was now residing. Ned was married on March 1st, 1902, and their mother, Vespera, died on March 9th.

An article in the *New York Times* summed up the overall outcome of the hearings and investigations that consumed so much time and involved so many people.

> Having obtained what he regards as convincing proof that children in the Point Loma school are not starved or otherwise maltreated as to their bodies, the Commissioner of Immigration has reported

to the Treasury Department that the school is all right; having obtained this report, the Treasury Department has reversed the decision of the New York Immigration Board, and, our local followers of a pseudo-philosophy falsely supposed to be Oriental having neatly stolen a march on the Society for the Prevention of Cruelty to Children, the eleven unfortunate "Lotus Buds" from Cuba are now on their way to California and the entirely unconvenanted mercies of the Tingley woman and her dupes. . . . The Tingleyites were cleared of charges nobody has made against them, while the reasons presented for holding them improper guardians for helpless children were to all appearances ignored. To speak well within bounds, the machinery of Government has worked in this case after a fashion to confuse the mind and mitigate our National pride. . . . **[Dec. 9, 1902]**

JUDGE SPARES MRS. TINGLEY.

Evidence Offered by the Defence in Her Libel Suit Is Barred Out.

SAN DIEGO, Cal., Jan. 2.—In the Tingley libel suit to-day Miss Irene Willis of Hannibal, Mo., who came out here to remove her dying sister from Point Loma, was not allowed to tell anything concerning the illness which proved fatal to her sister a few months after she was taken from the institution. Another witness, Edward W. Parker, who looked up Mrs. Tingley's record at Newburyport, Mass., was not permitted to testify. Emil A. Neroshumer, chairman of Mrs. Tingley's cabinet, was called by the defence and an effort made to show by him that Mrs. Tingley's distress of mind, alleged to be due to the newspaper article, may have been caused by quarrels in the cabinet. Judge Torrance ruled out all this testimony.

The constant barring out of testimony he has gathered has greatly disgusted Gen. Harrison Gray Otis, editor of the Los Angeles *Times*, and he has taken no pains to conceal his feelings. Whatever the verdict, the case will be taken to the Supreme Court.

Mrs. Tingley was called early in the afternoon session and entered a general denial of most of the things that have been said about her home at Point Loma.

[*The Sun* (New York), January 3, 1903]

Several individuals who were concerned about the Cuban children and who provided letters and affidavits at those hearings, also testified at the Tingley vs Times-Mirror court case in Los Angeles where Judge Torrance did not permit their testimony. An article from *The Sun*, included on the previous page, exemplifies his persistent rulings in support of the plaintiff, Tingley.

Several newspaper articles appeared at the time. The following, from the *Los Angeles Times*, Jan. 1, 1903, and is the most comprehensive and is included in full here.

[The "libelous article" referred to is the article that appeared in the *Los Angeles Times* on October 28th, 1901, titled "Outrages at Point Loma", and upon which the Tingley vs Times-Mirror case was based.]

Witness In Tears, Juror's Eyes Wet.

Pathetic Scene in Tingley-Times Trial While Sister of Dead Inmate of Point Loma Institution is on the Stand—Evidence Kept Out.
[By Direct Wire To *The Times.*]

San Diego. Dec. 31.—[Exclusive Dispatch.] A dog will lick the hand that has chastised him. Even "Spot," the sacred dog of Point Loma, might fawn upon his purple mistress after she had subjected him to discipline. There are slaves who love their masters in spite of harsh treatment and the crack of the lash over their shoulders. According to the testimony adduced today in Mrs. Katherine A. Tingley's libel suit against the Times-Mirror Company, the vassals of the "Purple Mother" regard the exaction of blind obedience and rigorous servitude as a kindness.

At least one witness, who testified to having passed through a period of bondage at Point Loma, admitted that she wrote a letter of thanks and gratitude and a pledge of love and fealty at the expiration of her term of slavery.

The witness who did this was Miss Matilda Kratzer, who testified yesterday that she was inveigled to Point Loma under the pretense that she was to receive a musical education there, but instead was put to the hardest kind of household drudgery, in spite of her tender age—she was barely 15 at the time—and she received in exchange for five and one half months of incessant toil only her board and lodging and five or six music lessons.

Yet the girl performed her labors in good spirit and uncomplainingly because she had espoused the cause of Theosophy and believed it was incumbent upon her, as a true Theosophist, to perform menial tasks taking up all of her time, for far longer hours than a tender, growing girl should work. For the general good of the Brotherhood, with such an unselfish purpose, pretty Tillie Kratzer worked herself almost to a frazzle for more than five weary months, and finally in separating from her oppressor, expressed gratitude and pledged undying fealty and love. The cause of her deliverance from the house of bondage, according to the testimony, was the fact the Mrs. Tingley banished the girl's mother from the Point Loma homestead because Mrs. Kratzer had rebelled against Tingley rule, and insisted upon being a law unto herself. When Mrs. Kratzer rebelled and left the domain of the "Purple She," who is more autocratic even than Rider Haggard's "She, who must be obeyed," her two young daughters elected to leave the "spookery" also, with tears in their eyes, not because of parting with Mrs. Tingley, but because they had no home to go to and knew not what would become of them.

Miss Kratzer is a delicate, refined, intelligent sort of girl, and gave her testimony in a manner that showed she was entirely free from bias or feeling against Mrs. Tingley on account of the treatment she had received at Point Loma. Rigid cross-examination failed to minimize her statements about the slavery she was subjected to, but plaintiff's counsel tried to make a great deal of a letter which they sprung on the witness, which she acknowledged she wrote to Mrs. Tingley just before leaving Point Loma, and in which gratitude was expressed for alleged kindness shown, and assurance of love and esteem was given.

However important this letter may seem to the plaintiff, it does not break the force of Miss Kratzer's testimony concerning the hard task imposed upon a delicate, refined girl, who was supposed to be attending the School for the Revival of Lost Mysteries of Antiquity for the purpose of obtaining an education.

Miss Kratzer's cross-examination consumed more than half of the morning session of the court on the trial of the Tingley libel suit today. The next witness called was Willis Freeman, a young man who came here all the way from Chicago to testify what a place of horror Point Loma was to his mother, who was rescued from the colony in a dying condition, and who died a few months later, competent witnesses are willing to testify, as a result of improper care and nourishment while an inmate of the institution at Point Loma. Young Freeman was at Point Loma with his mother, and feels very bitter over the treatment she received, but he was not allowed to testify anything about the circumstances of her illness or death. Judge Torrance ruling that such evidence was not admissible, because there was no mention of Mrs. Freeman's case in the alleged libelous article or in the pleadings.

The same ruling was made in regard to the proferred testimony of Miss Irene Willis, sister of the late Mrs. Freeman, and who rescued her from Point Loma when she was at the point of death. Miss Willis was so overcome at the mention of her unfortunate sister's name that she gave way to tears while on the witness stand. So sincere was her evident grief that one of the jurors was seen to furtively brush tears from his own eyes, although Miss Willis was not allowed to tell her pathetic story.

The remarks of Judge Torrance from the bench were the sensation of the day. He hauled defendant's counsel over the coals by telling them they were presenting their case back end forward. The court dwelt upon the allegation in the alleged libelous article in The Times that Point Loma was a "place of horror, surrounded by armed guards." The court said that before he would admit any more testimony regarding "armed guards," the defense would have to show that it was a "place of horror." In a long argumentative opinion, His Honor declared that so far the defense had practically not justified one iota of the alleged libelous publication.

The court's remarks were emphatically excepted to by defendant's counsel, but when counsel, in accordance with the suggestion of the court, abandoned for the time being the idea of furnishing proof about armed guards, and tried to introduce evidence that Point Loma was in a sense a place of horror, the court again blocked the way, by sustaining objections made by plaintiff's counsel.

So firmly met was every attempt to furnish proof of the alleged "horror," that it seemed that counsel for the defense was "up against" a stone wall.

Authorities were quoted in vain in support of defendant's contention that the evidence was competent. The court said he could not see it that way.

A large part of the day was spent in arguments of technical points, both by the court and counsel, the judge having much to say in support of the position he had taken. Finally an adjournment was taken till 10 o'clock Friday morning, when the defense will try a new tack to get in its evidence.

Following are the day's proceedings in detail:

Morning Session.

When the trial was resumed this morning, Miss Matilda Kratzer, the delicate girl who went to Point Loma to be educated, but who had to put in almost her entire time during the five and one-half months she was there in household drudgery, was taken in hand by Attorney Frederic Kellogg for cross-examination, for the purpose of breaking the force of the damaging testimony she gave yesterday against the plaintiff in the libel suit. Miss Kratzer was kept on the witness stand for an hour and a half, and emphasized the evidence she gave yesterday, in many particulars, although the plaintiff did gain a few crumbs of comfort from the fact that Miss Kratzer admitted that she wrote a letter to Mrs. Tingley, showing gratitude for kind treatment of herself, mother and sister, notwithstanding that that "kindness" consisted chiefly of being permitted to toil and slave for the Universal Brotherhood without any compensation except board and lodging and a few music lessons.

Miss Kratzer said in answer to questions put to her by Attorney Kellogg, that she didn't understand prior to going to Point Loma that she was to work all the time while there and receive no education. She and her mother expected to do some work for their keep, but it was understood that she was also to enjoy great educational advantages. Instead of that she had to rise early in the morning and work till late at night, having practically no time whatever for recreation or to practice on the piano. Once in a while she got time to read a little on Sunday afternoons. She had no time to walk around the grounds for pleasure, or to sit on the veranda watching the waves break on the shore of Point Loma. She had no time for social chats with friends or other members of the institution. She never had an hour nor even a half-hour for such diversions, except once she was a member of a picnic party on the beach on a Sunday afternoon, and she got very little recreation then.

The floors of the halls of the homestead were polished, and she had to sweep and mop with water every day the floors of the four halls of the second story. That task generally kept her busy for two hours. In the morning she waited on the table till about 8 o'clock. Then she cleaned the halls, after which she assisted the housekeeper with such work as she had in hand, till about 11 o'clock, when she had to get the tables ready for dinner and then wait on the tables till about 1 o'clock p.m. She also had to sweep the big dining-room and do chamber work in the afternoon, taking care of several rooms; had to wait on tables again at supper time, and help her mother in the kitchen till 9 o'clock at night. Sometimes she rose as early as 4 o'clock and worked till 10 or 11 o'clock at night—a long, hard day for a slender girl barely 15 years of age.

There were a few other girls who helped to wait on the table and do housework, and sometimes a Chinaman was also employed, but that did not give her any more time to take the music lessons that had been promised her. She was positive that she received only five or six lessons in all the time she was there. She was to have half an hour's practice on the piano every afternoon, the housekeeper to designate the time, but she never could be spared from her work; the best she could do was to snatch fifteen minutes' practice in the morning, which she sometimes did.

She made a memorandum of the number of music lessons she was given and fixed it in her memory because she thought she would some day have to testify in court. It was in the suit of her mother for wages earned and never paid her, as kitchen drudge at Point Loma, that she expected to be called as a witness. She did not know that she was going to be called as a witness in Mrs. Tingley's libel suit until about two weeks ago. She told her mother she did not want to go into court to testify because it would cause bad feelings on the part of people she knew. Her mother told her she saw no way out of it, and so she was giving her testimony without any ill-feeling toward Mrs. Tingley. She had no feeling of enmity for Mrs. Tingley. Her duties at Point Loma were disagreeable because she had to work so hard, but she did not complain, because at the time she believed it her duty, as a true Theosophist, to do whatever was required of her by the management of the Point Loma homestead.

Answering further questions as to opportunities for recreation while she was at the homestead, she said she had attended only two meetings of the Daughters of the Rising Sun, one meeting of the Sons of the Rising Sun, and taken part in one Greek play. The meetings were sort of social sessions; there were music and addresses and the Sons and Daughters of the Rising Sun wore Greek costumes made of a sort of cheesecloth. She did not know positively that the Daughters wore anything under their sleeveless, low-cut cheesecloth robes other than a slip. No shoes or stockings were worn, only sandals. Some of the men had sheets draped around them because they had no regular Greek costumes. The honored guests sat in chairs at these meetings, but the rest squatted on the floor on mats, probably because there were not enough chairs to go around, but she wasn't sure about that.

Just before leaving the Point Mrs. Tingley called her and her sister to her room and had a talk with them. Mrs. Tingley said that witness and her sister could return to Point Loma at any time, but their mother had tried to lay down the law for the Universal Brotherhood and could not return to the institution unless she signed an agreement to obey.

Miss Kratzer admitted that she cried at this interview with Mrs. Tingley, but it was not on account of regret at going away, but solely on account of the uncertainty of what would become of them, as they were not going to return to Los Angeles, and had no friends to go to in San Diego. They had no home, but had no desire to remain longer at the Point Loma homestead.

With a note of triumph in his voice Kellogg waved a piece of paper which he handed up to Miss Kratzer and asked if she recognized the writing upon it. She said it was a note she had written to Mrs. Tingley just prior to leaving Point Loma. She told in it how she had always done her work with good spirit and would always try to lead a noble life and remain a true Theosophist. In addition she expressed thanks for kindness received. Miss Kratzer explained this epistle by saying it was written after talking the matter over with her mother and sister, it being their conclusion that it would be better to leave with the good will of Mrs. Tingley than at the risk of having engendered her ill feeling.

Waited on the "Purp."

During the examination of the witness Mr. Kellogg incidentally referred to a little Cuban girl, Carmen, as being a "maid" to Mrs. Tingley. He tried to correct himself by getting Miss Kratzer to say that Carmen was not Mrs. Tingley's body servant.

He asked witness what were Carmen's duties, and the girl naively replied: "She took care of Spot part of the time," which made it appear that Carmen was lady in waiting not to the "Purple Mother," but to the "purp."

Former Guard Testifies.

Willis Freeman of Auburn Park, Chicago, was the next witness. He was an inmate of the colony at Point Loma, from October 14, 1900, to April, 1901. He went there with his mother, Mrs. Vespera Freeman, from Jamaica, N.Y.

Witness described the buildings of the colony and his duties while there. He lived in a tent and his mother in a cottage, with Miss Genevra Munson, assistant superintendent of the colony. At various times young Freeman stood guard, had charge of a herd of cows, scrubbed floors, cleaned and filled lamps, set the tables, picked fruit and made himself generally useful. He also pasted slips of paper on collection boxes sent out for money, known as "purple pence."

The witness was questioned closely as to his guard duty, how many guards there were, whether they were armed, etc. Plaintiff objected to examination along this line, and counsel engaged in a spirited discussion. The court took a hand and finally delivered a vigorous opinion, sustaining plaintiff's objections. "Nothing is gained," said the court, "by sitting here day after day listening to evidence which does not tend to prove the truth of the alleged libelous article. The principal headline of this article is 'Outrages at Point Loma,' in quotation marks." The court then quoted the definition of "outrages," according to the Standard dictionary, and continued: "We can shut our eyes to the true inference of this article. It says armed men were kept there as guards. It is perfectly immaterial whether armed guards were there or not. They have a right to have guards there to protect property and persons residing there. To prove that this is true in the sense it was published you must prove that armed men guarded this place of horror. You must first introduce evidence that it was a place of horror."

After the court had unburdened his mind of the statements quoted and a great deal more, Mr. Shortridge, for the defense, impressively objected to the court's ruling and the remarks of the court, on the ground that they were argumentative to the prejudice of the case of defendant.

"I admit that my remarks were intended to be argumentative," retorted the judge, and court then adjourned for the noon recess.

Sheets and White Stockings.

At the afternoon session the examination of young Freeman was resumed. The first question asked was: "State whether you know if any armed guards were maintained there."

Plaintiff's counsel objected and the court said: "This question is in direct opposition to the ruling of the court that before you introduce any more evidence about armed guards you must show that it was a place of horror."

Witness was permitted to describe some of the ceremonies he had observed, such as the greeting of sunrise, morning meditations, etc. In lieu of a Greek costume he sometimes wore two sheets draped around him, over his ordinary clothes, except the coat and shoes. He wore white stockings over his socks, and some of the men wore sandals.

At one ceremony in the "Aryan temple," they marched in two by two, in costume, and lay down on mats on the floor, where they remained to listen to a symposium consisting of philosophic discussion by students.

On New Year's Eve there was a celebration at which an enormous bonfire was lighted and the "colonists" were around all night in white robes.

Witness was not allowed to describe the food given him while a member of the colony.

In reply to one question witness said his mother, as long as she could, took her meals at the common table. On motion of plaintiff, this answer was stricken out, and on further objections by plaintiff's counsel, witness was not allowed to answer a single question regarding his mother's sad fate. The questions"Why did you go to Point Loma,[?]" "What was your mother's condition when she went there?" "What was her condition when she left the colony?" and many similar ones, were all stricken out, unanswered.

Died Last March.

Witness did succeed in answering the question "Where is your mother now?" Before plaintiff's counsel got in an objection, he said "She died last March," [March 9, 1902 at the age of 55 years] but the answer was immediately stricken out. Somehow or other, the illness and death of Mrs. Freeman seemed to worry plaintiff's counsel, and the court could not see that it tended to prove that Point Loma was a place of horror.

Seeing that it was futile to attempt to use the witness for the purposes intended, Freeman was excused without further questioning or cross-examination.

A recess of fifteen minutes was taken to allow defendant's counsel to talk with Kate Hansen to ascertain her availability as a witness for the defense. Plaintiff's counsel objected strenuously to the interview, but it was held in the presence of court. The little girl was not called as a witness, however.

Hadn't Enough To Eat.

Two girls from Pasadena, one 13 and the other 15 years of age, who had been at Point Loma two months, were called and testified to queer ceremonies they had witnessed. One was at a corner-stone laying, when a lot of people took hold of a rope called the "cable of brotherly love." When Mrs. Tingley or some one struck a triangle they raised the rope above their heads, at the same time closing their eyes, and when the triangle was struck again the rope was lowered and eyes were opened. This performance was repeated several times. Both girls testified that they did not get enough to eat while at Point Loma. The fare was good, what there was of it, but they wanted more and were denied it. There was no great variety of viands, and they did not get any meat, except fish occasionally.

The girls were not allowed to state whether the letters received from their mother had been opened before reaching them. Neither were they permitted to tell why they left Point Loma. The reason was that the children were homesick and their mother was not willing to relinquish maternal control of them for four years, as proposed. The mother of the girls was not a Theosophist and had no conception of the character of the place when she was persuaded to let her daughters go there for a visit at the solicitation of a Theosophist friend.

Witness In Mourning.

The last witness of the day was Miss Irene Willis of Hannibal, MO. Miss Willis was dressed in mourning for her sister, Mrs. Freeman, whom she rescued from Point Loma in a dying condition. The circumstances, which Miss Willis was not permitted to relate, were that she came to San Diego from the East when she heard her sister was very ill, and not properly cared for, at Point Loma. Upon arriving here she hired a carriage and went to Point Loma, where she was denied admittance to see her sister, but she persisted until she arrived at the colony, where she met a boy who proved to be her nephew, whom she had not seen since he was a baby. The boy piloted her to his mother's tent.

Death of Mrs. Freeman.

Mrs. Freeman was very feeble and was at once removed to San Diego by Miss Willis, who procured medical assistance for her. The doctor said the woman's condition was due to improper nourishment, that she was literally starving, and this was ultimately the cause of her death. The doctor recommended absolute quiet for the patient, but Dr. Wood and Mr. Neresheimer came to San Diego within a day or two, and, according to the statement of Miss Willis, forced their way to Mrs. Freeman's bedside, in spite of the protests of Miss Willis, and remonstrated with the sick woman for leaving Point Loma without Mrs. Tingley's consent, saying that doing so in her condition would injure the reputation of the institution.

All questions asked Miss Willis touching her sister's illness and rescue were ruled out by the court on objections by plaintiff's counsel. She was not allowed to answer any of the following:
"State the circumstances under which you came here."

"Did you go to Point Loma, and for what purpose?"
"Where did you find your sister?"
No objection was made to question:
"What was your sister's name?"

Tears and Emotion.

It was some minutes before she could answer, as tears came into her eyes and her voice was choked with emotion. The scene was the most dramatic that has occurred since the trial began. The sympathy of at least one juror went out to the bereaved witness, for tears welled from his eyes as he beheld the witness's sorrow.

Testimony Kept Out.

The name of her dead sister was about all of her testimony that got into the evidence, for the court and counsel took up the rest of the session in wrangling over the admissibility of the evidence.

Mr. Daney, who was conducting the examination, stated that it was purposed to show by the testimony of this witness that Point Loma was a place of horror, as charged by the defendant. The court replied:

"I have stated several times that you must set up particular facts and circumstances to justify the general libelous character of the publication. That's the conclusion I have reached. I am perfectly willing to hear counsel if they have any authorities to show that I am wrong. I am willing to be convinced.

"I don't say it by way of criticism that counsel is attempting to prove things by beginning at the wrong end. The fact that she found her sister there sick doesn't prove anything; it doesn't show that this is a place of horror. I think the objection is well taken.

"I don't desire to be considered arbitrary in this matter, but think it is my duty to exercise some control as to the order in which evidence should be introduced."

Mr. Daney and Mr. Shortridge both protested that they were endeavoring to present the case in logical order and should be given some latitude to prove the charges. Mr. Shortridge quoted numerous authorities in behalf of defendant's contention, but the court still wasn't convinced, and came back with a long reply, containing more pointed remarks affecting the position of the defense.

Mr. Shortridge retorted: "I submit it isn't for the court to construe this article; it is not the court's function to say this article is libelous; that is the function of the jury, under proper instructions of the court, of course."

"Objection sustained," said the court, as a clincher.

"We except to the ruling of the court and to all the remarks of the court as to the weight of the testimony introduced and now before the jury," said Mr. Daney.

Mr. Daney then, in rapid order, asked a dozen or more questions about Mrs. Freeman's illness and stay at Point Loma. All were ruled out as incompetent, irrelevant and immaterial, and the court at last said he wanted to hear no more questions in regard to Miss Willis's sister.

It being close to 5 o'clock by this time, an adjournment was taken over New Year's Day to Friday morning.

The fussy "Purple Mother" again sat close to Scottison of the Los Angeles "Hurled" [Herald] during a large portion of the day and exercised her hypnotic power in dictating and directing his report.

Los Angeles Times, **Thursday January 1, 1903, p.13**

See also:
Los Angeles Herald, Jan. 1, 1903, **Times Defense is Shattered: Testimony About Guards Ruled Out**.

San Diego Union and Daily Bee, Jan. 1, 1903, **It Was A Hard Day For The Los Angeles Times: Decisions Without Number Against Defendant In The Tingley-Times Libel Case**.

Appendix F

Richard Dean Arden Wade (Ingalese)
April 15, 1863 - October 2, 1934

Richard Dean Arden Wade was born in Savannah, Georgia, attended Columbia College Law School in New York in 1885, served as a justice of the peace in Omaha, Nebraska in 1889, then went to Chicago where he practiced as an Attorney. He married (Mrs.) Isabella Robins (1855-1934) in 1896; they moved to California in 1904 where he was licensed to practice in the Supreme Court in the State of California in May 1907. Richard and Isabella died only months apart in 1934 in Los Angeles, CA.

Somewhere along the way, Richard Wade changed his surname to Richard Ingalese under which name he published fifty books of a theosophical nature.

Wade perhaps initially met W.Q. Judge during his university years at Columbia. It is very likely that he did meet him in Chicago in January 1895 at which time Judge wrote that his "Chicago trip was all right and useful".

Judge had eventually agreed that the American Section T.S. should dissociate from Adyar, politically. At the convention in Boston, April 28th, 1895, 191 votes were in favor of seceding and 10 votes against. The resolution was thereby passed to establish the Theosophical Society in America. **[1895 *Report of Proceedings*, pp.37-38]**. One of the negative votes was from the Chicago Branch. Since many of the members had favored secession and did not agree with the 'no' vote on behalf of their branch, they formed a new one, chartered under T.S. in America, called the Loyalty Branch, on May 29th, 1895. Wade was elected president.

Following Katherine Tingley's takeover of T.S. in America, Wade, loyal student of theosophy and lecturer, could not accept the direction the society was going. Dissension was likely the reason why Tingley moved the site of the Convention (held April 26-27, 1896) from Chicago to New York mere days before the event.

Shortly after the unusual wedding ceremony of Claude Falls Wright and Leoline Leonard on May 3rd, 1896, where Tingley appeared as the 'veiled mahatma', Wade declared he could not serve under her leadership and resigned from the Loyalty Branch. This created another huge rift in Chicago.

In autumn 1895 Col. Olcott appointed Alexander Fullerton, one of the dissenting voters against Judge and the establishing of the Theosophical Society in America, as General Secretary of the revamped American Section T.S. [see *TJC*, Part I, p.243]

Immediately following the sketch of the "Boston Girl's Marriage" (see Chapter 2) the following short biography about Miss Leonard was published, giving historical context on how the Brotherhood suppers originated. Katherine Tingley immediately took full advantage of this concept and made it her own.

It Was a Ghastly Affair Under Theosophy Rites.

The theosophical marriage of May Katherine Leoline Leonard of Boston to Mr. Claude Falls Wright of New York, which was performed Sunday night, was according to the ancient Egyptian rites. That there might be no legal question to the validity of the nuptial bonds, a civil contract was also entered into before Alderman Robinson of New York city. The work of both these young people is well known, but particularly so here in Boston, where Miss Leonard has been actively engaged for some time past. She came to Boston to the convention which was held for the Theosophical Society on April 29, 1895.

The minds of the leaders impelled her to stay, and she forthwith became one of the leaders of the New England branch of the fraternity. Besides the work of lecturer for the society in this section of the land she has organized several societies throughout Massachusetts and Connecticut. The work which has made her more beloved by the poor of this city is a series of "brotherhood suppers." She would organize a branch of workers and give a supper on Sunday nights. It would be an informal lunch to which all thinking men were invited. After supper the lecturer, generally Miss Leonard, but frequently some brother theosophist, would introduce a subject, one of which, however, would not be above the intelligence of the audience, and after this an open discussion would follow. In this discussion every opinion, so long as it was sincere, was respected.

She was secretary of the Beacon branch of the society, and it was through this branch that the suppers were managed. She was president of the League of Theosophical Workers No. 3, which is the head of the society and which directs the energies.

In person she is singularly attractive. Her figure is slight and she is light complexioned with blonde hair and fair blue eyes. She was born in January, 1872 [actually January 28, 1871], and was converted to theosophy in 1891. Since this latter date she has devoted her life to the work and has been remarkably successful. Her mother is Mrs. Anna Byford Leonard, a prominent Chicago artist and the first woman living who was appointed supervisor of the sanitary condition of the schools. Her grandfather is Dr. William H. Byford, one of the best-known Western physicians. She has a private fortune and has undertaken the work at her own expense.

She has been connected with Mr. Wright for some time, and a number of signs and indications patent to those whose eyes are open to the astral light and influence convinced them both that their work would be furthered if their destinies were united. Each will keep up his and her work, but their efforts will be concentrated, and as they will travel together, the audience will be favored with two lecturers instead of one. [*Boston Post*, **May 5, 1896**]

Wade eloquently expressed his reasons, as so many other members might have, for disconnecting with the wave of "antics and trickery." He had joined the T.S. under W.Q. Judge's leadership but could not see himself supporting the nonsense of the leading participants in the current Theosophical movement. Wade's words reverberated throughout the United States and some variations of his resignation were published in many newspapers. The *Chicago Tribune* version is included here. Wade may have been the first to openly resign but hundreds more followed.

R.D. Wade Drops Out of Theosophy

Ex-President of the Chicago Branch Does Not Like the Existing Methods of Management.

There is trouble among the Theosophists in Chicago. R.D. Wade, who has been President of the local branch of the society, formally severed his connection with the organization yesterday.

"My reasons for resigning," said Mr. Wade, "are that I cannot accept the antics of a 'veiled prophet' as the inspiring presence of a wise adept, nor can I believe any circumstances would induce or compel a mahatma to hide his face behind a cotton sheet. I believe credulity is taking the place of reason in the society, and that the new occult leader must be suffering from like degeneracy, since he is, we are told, being handled with care in order to save hin from the thought waves of the world.

"The sugar plum called an 'occult college' is being held out to the faithful who will donate the requisite cash to pay for the establishment of the same, and then support its founders and teachers. This is applying commercial principles with a vengeance to occultism, and seems to be somewhat more like an adept factory than the establishment 'of a nucleus of universal brotherhood.'

"But, the order being brought from the metaphysical to the physical planes, Chicago has offset the victory of New York in capturing the 'Great Unknown' by securing the contract for wiring the Western Occult Kindergarten for electric lights.

"The object of inculcating credulity and selfishness is now, and is always, for the purposes of benefitting a certain few. Who can that few be in this case? Are they the 'crusaders' who wish a foreign tour at the society's expense ostensibly for the purpose of collecting material for a 'School for the Revival of the Lost Mysticism of Antiquity?'

"Perhaps the New York headquarters can give enlightenment, but to me the whole thing savors too much of the plan 'drop a dollar in the slot and get a degree of occultism.'

"I desire that this action of mine shall in no way be considered a renunciation of the philosophy which was once known as Theosophy, but it is simply because I can no longer in good conscience give my support to what I consider an unworthy vehicle." *[Chicago Tribune*, **May 19, 1896]**

Appendix G

Letter by Dr. Hyman Lischner

The following is a transcript of Dr. Hyman Lischner's letter of May 28th, 1931. It accompanied his 38-page document, dated May 8th, 1931 and titled *Some Correspondence Between Dr. G. de Purucker, Dr. J.H. Fussell and Hyman Lischner, M.D.*, which can be found under 'publications' on Edmonton Theosophical Society's website: theosophycanada.com

---

[6717 Whitley Terrace
Hollywood, Calif.]

To a Fellow Theosophist:

May 28, 1931

"The possibility of achievement for the individual lies not in following and pledging loyalty to any personal Leader, but by uncompromising devotion to the Idea,—to principle."

The realization of the truth to the above thought as summed up by the Editor, A.T. Barker in his introduction to "The Mahatma Letters to A.P. Sinnett" had not yet broken through the psychology of personal worship and dependence on the "Leader". I was going through a period of unhappiness and disappointment—I was beginning to feel as if my props were being removed from under me as inconsistencies in the every day life of the "Leader" and some of her immediate associates (as compared with the ideals they professed) forced themselves upon my conscience and resisted all my efforts at "explaining them away". One day, some three years ago, in response to a request for some information regarding H.P.B.'s personal character, Mr. E. August Neresheimer (prominent American Theosophist, a student of H.P.B., a co-worker of W.Q.J., and whom the latter called his "staunch friend and good adviser") placed the "Mahatma Letters", "Letters of H.P. Blavatsky", and later "The Real H.P. Blavatsky" by William Kingsland, into my hands.

I had reached a point where Madam Tingley's ban on these books did not prevent me from reading them, for which I am most thankful. These books have helped me immeasurably in my effort to free myself from a sectarian religious psychology which had gradually enveloped my being, in my association with the Point Loma Institution. Nothing like it before has given me such love and insight into that frank, robust yet tender character of what I might call "the Everyday H.P.B.". These books filled a need in my heart just at the right time. My nature was just beginning to timidly rebel against what I was gradually becoming aware of as priestly authority parading under the guise of "successorship", ceremonialism, emotionalism, "lying for the good of the Cause", and other doctrines and pretensions, "passed on" to the "devoted" and "privileged", by word of mouth and by various means of suggestion that were radically and shockingly different and contrary to public and published professions—all in the name of Theosophy and H.P.B.

I realize that unless the one who claims to be a "conscious Agent" presents, for instance, revelations as new and original to the times as those offered in "Isis Unveiled" or the "Secret Doctrine", there is great difficulty in recognizing fully the true nature of the claimant merely through his public utterances, pronouncement of policies or repetition of teachings seemingly in keeping with the teachings that have already been given out through H.P.B and the Masters.

A sense of duty to the Theosophical Movement and to H.P.B. prompts me to take the liberty of sending you a copy of some correspondence that has passed between Dr. de Purucker, Dr. Fussell and myself. Whether you look upon G. de P. as a "Spiritual Leader and Teacher" or not at this time, I feel sure that in any case you will read this rather lengthy correspondence with impartiality and give it your careful and logical attention. It may offer you a glimpse into the claims of successorship and equal status with H.P.B. as you will note in Dr. de Purucker's letter to me.

It is only fair to state that Katherine Tingley was ill for a number of years previous to her death, particularly after her cerebral apoplexy [stroke] in 1925. I was her physician and therefore had the opportunity of frequent and intimate contact with her, with members of her household and with her "cabinet", including Dr. de Purucker.

With few exceptions most of the members, young and old, including former students of H.P.B. and W.Q.J. who had opportunities of *close* personal contact with Katherine Tingley, left her organization sooner or later. Though I had the opportunity of observing this for over thirty years, it did not strike me to inquire as to the real significance of this fact. It was always attributed to "disloyalty" and a demonstration of some phase of the "lower nature" in those who went away, and I took it at that valuation. It did not occur to me to ascertain for *myself* the actual causes and reasons for the disaffection of really splendid men and women and young people. Finally, I began to see things in a different light, because circumstances became such that I was *forced* to see below the appearance of things. Each must gain his realization through his *own assumption* of responsibility.

The enclosed correspondence is made public in order that you and others may have one more evidence of the menace to the Cause of Theosophy and to all trustful Theosophists in accepting claims to "successorship" and spiritual authority by whomsoever made.

Yours cordially

Hyman Lischner.

Appendix H

Life in a Borrowed Body

The following article was originally published as part of *The Judge Case: A Conspiracy Which Ruined the Theosophical Cause*, Part 2, Appendix J, pp.487-493. It was deemed appropriate to include it here in order to reacquaint readers with details of the unusual life circumstance of William Q. Judge.

There are two classes of exalted beings which have been identified in early Theosophical literature. The first are the Mahâtmas, sometimes referred to as Adepts.[1] The second are the Nirmânakâyas. The former are alive in a physical body while the latter have overcome the need for a physical form. Both are considered White Adepts of the Great Lodge or Brothers of Light. These Adepts of occultism[2] have expanded their consciousness, over lifetimes, to embrace the Universe in proportion to their individual progress. Adepts signify proficiency, while Mahâtmas and Nirmânakâyas are Adepts who have attained what mortal men call impossible — that is, transcending time and space.

In 1851, at age twenty, while visiting in London, H.P. Blavatsky recognized a tall Hindu man in the street with some Indian princes. She immediately recognized him as the same person she had seen in the Astral. Her first impulse was to rush towards him but was given a sign not to. The following day she went for a walk in Hyde Park to contemplate this wondrous incident when she was approached by this man. He introduced himself to her and told her "he required her cooperation in a work which he was about to

---

[1] A Mahâtma is an Adept of the highest order.

[2] Occultism is defined as the science of the occult — or the science of the secrets of Nature — that being physical and psychic, mental and spiritual. An occultist is one who studies the various branches of occult science.

undertake".[3] He, "Morya", a Mahâtma, told her that she would have to undergo training in Tibet to prepare for this important task.

In 1858, at the age of seven, William Q. Judge, in Dublin, Ireland, at the time, was struck with a serious illness. "The physician declared the small sufferer to be dying, then dead; but in the outburst of grief which followed the announcement, it was discovered that the child had revived, and that all was well with him. During convalescence the boy showed aptitude and knowledge never before displayed, exhibiting wonderment and questioning among his elders as to when and how he had learned all these new things. He seemed the same, and yet not the same; had to be studied anew by his family, and while no one knew that he had ever learned to read, from his recovery in his eighth year we find him devouring the contents of all books he could obtain, relating to Mesmerism, Phrenology, Character-Reading, Religion, Magic, Rosicrucianism, and deeply absorbed in the Book of Revelation, trying to discover its real meaning."[4]

What happened to the lad at the age of seven remained a mystery for many years. Part of this mystery only came to light through the writings of his good friend and co-worker Mrs. Julia Campbell Ver-Planck.[5] He had approached her with the idea that she should write an occult novel about his experiences. Judge had agreed to furnish the material. It was obvious that the book was to be a study of ideas involving the spiritual soul's journey through the cycle of rebirths. It would also include the assembling of Skandhas ("bundles" or finite groups of attributes) and personal anecdotes or incidents in order to better explain this difficult topic.

---

[3]**Reminiscences of H.P.B.**, pp.56-57 and also in **BCW**, Vol. 1, pp.xxxviii-xxxix.

[4]**Letters That Have Helped Me** - J.N., Volume II, p.111, by Jasper Niemand. Also in **Cdn. Theosophist**, Vol. 13, March 1932, pp.20-21. Originally published in the **Irish Theosophist**, Vol. 4, February 1896, p.91.

[5]Mrs. J. Campbell Ver-Planck was a member of the staff at the New York headquarters. She wrote many articles for **The Path** and much of the correspondence with T.S. enquirers. The letters in **Letters That Have Helped Me** were written by Judge and received at her Pennsylvania home where she lived with her parents. She stated: "They were written for me . . . and for the use of others later on . . . at the express wish of H.P. Blavatsky." [**The Path**, Vol. 9, April 1894, p.16.] She became better known to theosophists as Julia Keightley after marrying Dr. Archibald Keightley in 1891, or by her *non-de-plume* "Jasper Niemand".

From time to time Judge would send his friend suggestions written on scraps of paper while waiting for his tram or for his next engagement in Court. Mrs. Ver-Planck appears to have had difficulties assembling all that was needed and would ask Judge for clarification on certain ideas. One such incident involved a different aspect of reincarnation, one which included the use of a borrowed body.

Blavatsky claimed about Judge "that he had been a part of herself and of the Great Lodge 'for aeons past' . . . and that he was one of those tried Egos who have reincarnated several times immediately after death; assisted to do so, and without devachanic rest, in order to continue his Lodge work".[6]

Judge describes his personal tale as follows:

> I must tell you first what happened to me in this present life since it is in this one that I am relating to you about many other lives of mine.
>
> I was a simple student of our high Philosophy for many lives on earth in various countries, and then at last developed in myself a desire for action. So I died once more as so often before and was again reborn in the family of a Rajah, and in time came to sit on his throne after his death.[7]
>
> Two years after that sad event one day an old wandering Brahmin came to me and asked if I was ready to follow my vows of long lives before, and go to do some work for my old master in a foreign land.[8] Thinking this meant a journey only I said I was.

---

[6]**Irish Theosophist**, Vol. 4, March 1896, p.115.

[7]Rajah or Râjâ is a Prince or King in India. Judge's close associates would often refer to him as the Rajah. — Compiler.

[8]In a letter to Olcott, dated March 4th, 1880, Judge wrote: "I have lived at one time in India 19 years . . . so you see I am not so much younger than you. . . ." [**The Theosophist**, Vol. 52, March 1931, p.459.] Olcott was born, August 2nd, 1832 and Judge was born April 13th, 1851. Adding 19 years to Judge's age would make him the same age as Olcott.— Compiler.

"Yes," said he, "but it is not only a journey. It will cause you to be here and there all days and years. To-day here, to-night there."

"Well," I replied, "I will do even that, for my vows had no conditions and master orders."

I knew of the order, for the old Brahmin gave me the sign marked on my forehead. He had taken my hand, and covering it with his waist-cloth, traced the sign in my palm under the cloth so that it stood out in lines of light before my eyes.

He went away with no other word, as you know they so often do, leaving me in my palace. I fell asleep in the heat, with only faithful Gopal beside me. I dreamed and thought I was at the bedside of a mere child, a boy, in a foreign land unfamiliar to me, only that the people looked like what I knew of the Europeans. The boy was lying as if dying, and relatives were all about the bed.

A strange and irresistible feeling drew me nearer to the child, and for a moment I felt in this dream as if I were about to lose consciousness. With a start I awoke in my own palace — on the mat where I had fallen asleep, with no one but Gopal near and no noise but the howling of jackals near the edge of the compound.

"Gopal," I said, "how long have I slept?"

"Five hours, master, since an old Brahmin went away, and the night is nearly gone, master."

I was about to ask him something else when again sleepiness fell upon my sense[s], and once more I dreamed of the small dying foreign child.

The scene had changed a little, other people had come in, there was a doctor there, and the boy looked to me, dreaming so vividly, as if dead. The people were weeping, and his mother knelt by the bedside. The doctor laid his head on the child's breast a moment. As for myself I was drawn again nearer to the body and thought surely the people were strange not to notice me at all. They acted as if no stranger were there, and I looked at my clothes and saw they were eastern and bizarre to them. A magnetic line seemed to pull me to the form of the child.

And now beside me I saw the old Brahmin standing. He smiled.

"This is the child," he said, "and here must you fulfil a part of your vows. Quick now! There is no time to lose, the child is almost dead. These people think him already a corpse. You see the doctor has told them the fatal words, 'he is dead'!".

Yes, they were weeping. But the old Brahmin put his hands on my head, and submitting to his touch, I felt myself in my dream falling asleep. A dream in a dream. But I woke in my dream, but not on my mat with Gopal near me. I was that boy I thought. I looked out through his eyes, and near me I heard, as if his soul had slipped off to the ether with a sigh of relief. The doctor turned once more and I opened my eyes — his eyes — on him.

The physician started and turned pale. To another I heard him whisper "automatic nerve action." He drew near, and the intelligence in that eye startled him to paleness. He did not see the old Brahmin making passes over this body I was in and from which I felt great waves of heat and life rolling over me — or the boy.

And yet this all now seemed real as if my identity was merged in the boy.

I was that boy and still confused, vague dreams seemed to flit through my brain of some other plane where I thought I was again, and had a faithful servant named Gopal; but that must be dream, this the reality. For did I not see my mother and father, the old doctor and the nurse so long in our house with the children? Yes; of course this is the reality.

And then I feebly smiled, whereon the doctor said:

"Most marvellous. He has revived. He may live."

He was feeling the slow moving pulse and noting that breathing began and that vitality seemed once more to return to the child, but he did not see the old Brahmin in his illusionary body sending air currents of life over the body of this boy, who dreamed he had been a Rajah with a faithful servant named Gopal. Then in the dream sleep seemed to fall upon me. A sensation of falling, falling came to my brain, and with a start I awoke in my palace on my own mat. Turning to see if my servant was there I saw him standing as if full of sorrow or fear for me.

"Gopal, how long have I slept again?"

"It is just morning, master, and I feared you had gone to Yama's dominions and left your own Gopal behind." [9]

No, I was not sleeping. This was reality, these my own dominions. So this day passed as all days had except that the dream of the small boy in a foreign land came to my mind all day until the night when I felt more drowsy than usual. Once more I slept and dreamed.

The same place and the same house, only now it was morning there. What a strange dream I thought I had had; as the doctor came in with my mother and bent over me, I heard him say softly:

"Yes, he will recover. The night sleep has done good. Take him, when he can go, to the country, where he may see and walk on the grass."

As he spoke behind him I saw the form of a foreign looking man with a turban on. He looked like the pictures of Brahmins I saw in the books before I fell sick. Then I grew very vague and told my mother: "I had had two dreams for two nights, the same in each. I dreamed I was a king and had one faithful servant for whom I was sorry as I liked him very much, and it was only a dream, and both were gone."

---

[9] In the **Vedas** Yama represents the god of the dead, the Lord of Death and Judge of men. — Compiler.

My mother soothed me, and said: "Yes, yes, my dear."

And so that day went as days go with sick boys, and early in the evening I fell fast asleep as a boy in a foreign land, in my dream, but did no more dream of being a king, and as before I seemed to fall until I woke again on my mat in my own palace with Gopal sitting near. Before I could rise the old Brahmin, who had gone away, came in and I sent Gopal off.

"Rama," said he, "as boy you will not dream of being Rajah but now you must know that every night as sleeping king you are waking boy in foreign land. Do well your duty and fail not. It will be some years, but Time's never-stopping car rolls on. Remember my words," and then he passed through the open door.[10]

So I knew those dreams about a sick foreign boy were not mere dreams but that they were recollections, and I condemned each night to animate that small child just risen from the grave, as his relations thought, but I knew that his mind for many years would not know itself, but would ever feel strange in its surroundings, for, indeed, that boy would be myself inside and him without, his friends not seeing that he had fled away and another taken his place. Each night I, as sleeping Rajah who had listened to the words of sages, would be an ignorant foreign boy, until through lapse of years and effort unremittingly continued I learned how to live two lives at once. Yet horrible at first seemed the thought that although my life in that foreign land as a growing youth would be undisturbed by vague dreams of independent power as Rajah, I would always, when I woke on my mat, have a clear remembrance of what at first seemed only dreams of being a king, with vivid knowledge that while my faithful servant watched my sleeping form I would be masquerading in a borrowed body, unruly as the wind. Thus as a boy I might be happy, but as a king miserable maybe. And then after I should become accustomed to this double life, perhaps my foreign mind and habits would so dominate the

---

[10]In **The Theosophical Glossary**, Rama or Râma-Chandra is described as the hero of the Râmâyana, the famous epic poem collated with the Mâhâbhârata. [Theosophy Company edition, 1973, p.275.]

body of the boy that existence there would grow full of pain from the struggle with an environment wholly at war with the thinker within.

But a vow once made is to be fulfilled, and Father Time eats up all things and ever the centuries.[11]

Judge lived his entire life adjusting to the difficulties of having two consciousnesses. He once explained:

> The whole thing comes from the particular fact of a person living in a house he did not build, and having two astrals at work.[12]

Clement A. Griscom, a close friend of Judge, described the difficulties he had adjusting to having two souls;

> It was the good fortune of a few of us to know something of the real Ego who used the body known as Wm. Q. Judge. He once spent some hours describing to my wife and me the experience the Ego had in assuming control of the instrument it was to use for so many years. The process was not a quick nor an easy one and indeed was never absolutely perfected, for to Mr. Judge's dying day, the physical tendencies and heredity of the body he used would crop up and interfere with the full expression of the inner man's thoughts and feelings. An occasional abruptness and coldness of manner was attributable to this lack of co-ordination. Of course Mr. Judge was perfectly aware of this and it would trouble him for fear his real friends would be deceived as to his real feelings. He was always in absolute control of his thoughts and actions, but his body would sometimes slightly modify their expression.[13]

Claude Falls Wright wrote:

---

[11] **Letters That Have Helped Me** - J.N., Volume II, pp.105-110. Also in The Theosophy Company, 1946 edition, pp.257-260, but slightly altered.

[12] **Letters That Have Helped Me**, p.174.

[13] **Theosophy (The Path)**, Vol. 11, May 1896, p.52. "The Greatest of The Exiles" was written by G. Hijo, a pseudonym for Clement A. Griscom.

In the early part of his last life I do not think he was completely conscious twenty-four hours a day, but several years ago he arrived at the stage where he never afterwards lost his consciousness for a moment. Sleep with him merely meant to float out of his body in full possession of all his faculties, and that was also the manner in which he "died" — left his body for good.[14]

Some forty years after the event, Cyrus Field Willard broke his silence and wrote about his experience at the Convention of 1891 in Boston.[15] He wrote:

I can tell, *now*, what I know, and saw with my own eyes, about this "borrowed body" and which was also seen and verified by at least ten other persons, who openly so stated at a meeting held in the headquarters of the Boston branch, shortly after Judge's death in 1896. And I think Brother Smythe can vouch for my reputation for veracity.[16]

It was at the Boston convention of 1891, where I served on a committee with Annie Besant, on her first visit to America, and was predisposed in her favour by her work for the Bryant & May match-girls.

---

[14]**The Lamp**, Vol. 2, April 1896, p.132, taken from the **New York Journal** of March 23rd, 1896. Claude Falls Wright was one of Blavatsky's secretaries, in London, during her last three years. After her death in 1891 he came to America and worked closely with Judge at the New York headquarters.

[15]Cyrus F. Willard was a trained and experienced newspaper man from Boston who joined the T.S. on November 23rd, 1889. Willard knew Judge well and would go visit him in his hotel room when Judge visited Boston, to talk and question him on some practical work for Universal Brotherhood. "Our conversation ranged over many subjects and often he would tell me things in which I had no interest, but which he evidently thought I should know for later developments." [**Cdn Theosophist**, Vol. 13, May 1932, p.69.]

[16]Albert E.S. Smythe, Editor of **The Canadian Theosophist** (and its predecessor **The Lamp**), was present at that Boston convention, on April 26th and 27th, 1891. Judge, as General Secretary of the T.S,, read a resolution that had been adopted by the Toronto T.S. at a regular meeting on April 23rd, 1891. The Toronto T.S. was chartered on February 25th, 1891. It was the last charter issued by Blavatsky before she died. [**Report Of Proceedings**, 1891.]

Word was sent to all members of the E.S.T. [Eastern School of Theosophy] which I had joined under H.P.B. in 1889, to be present at an E.S. meeting in the large double parlours of the Parker House. When I got in, it was early and from newspaper habit I walked down to the front row of seats and sat less than 10 feet away from Judge and Annie. As she has seen fit to publish the E.S. instructions, it will not therefore be without justification that I relate what occurred, in order to give Judge his due.

The rooms soon filled up with about 200 persons, and I noticed leaning up against the pedestal behind which Judge stood as presiding officer, so all could see and exposed for the first time, pictures of the two Masters, blessed be their name, for the knowledge they have given us. As he started to call the meeting to order, he leaned toward her, who stood on his right hand, and I heard him say to her in a low voice, "Sound the Word with the triple intonation." She replied in the same low voice, "I don't dare to," or, "I don't care to", but I think it was the first. I heard him say in a firm tone, "Then I will." He had been twirling his gavel in his hand but laid it down, stepped to his right, pushing her aside, and stepped to the side of the pedestal, facing his audience, with her behind him, and said:

"I am about to sound the Word, with the triple intonation, but before I do so, I have a statement to make which I do not care to have you speak to me about later, nor do I wish you to discuss among yourselves. I am not what I seem; I am a Hindu".

Then he sounded the Word with the triple intonation.

Before my eyes, I saw the man's face turn brown and a clean-shaven Hindu face of a young man was there, and you know he wore a beard. I am no psychic nor have ever pretended to be one or to "see things", as I joined the T.S. to form a nucleus of Universal Brotherhood. This change was not one seen by me only, and we did not discuss the import of his significant statement, until after his death when a meeting was held in the Boston headquarters to determine our future action. Then I mentioned it in a speech and his statement, and fully ten persons from different parts of the hall spoke up and said, "I saw it too." "I saw and heard what he said", etc. That would seem proof enough about the borrowed body. . . .

But why did he say he was a Hindu, when the Judge body was born in Ireland? I believe from what I saw that Judge was a Hindu, the Rajah, and never was moved by the charges against him. That is, the indwelling Ego in the Judge body was a Hindu, and that I saw him once. . . .

I have only come out of my long silence in order to do justice to Wm. Q. Judge, who was one of the sweetest, dearest companions and friends any man could have.[17]

The Tibetan technical term for the process described above is *Tulpa*.[18] There are many degrees of this condition and much of it is kept secret. If we are to accept Judge's own description of events, conditions became favorable at the age of seven such that another living being, a chela of the Masters, could be amalgamated with the consciousness of the young Irish lad. The reason for such a process is to mesh one's consciousness with that of another for a specific purpose. These conditions vary from a fully conscious to an unconscious incarnation. The reasons vary as well, but mainly it is to take advantage of certain situations in order to teach men.

Judge had many difficulties adjusting to the dual consciousness but when he went to India in 1884, the Mahatmas further seemingly complicated his condition. Blavatsky described what happened to Judge while he was in India. She wrote: "With you, it is the Nirmânakaya not the 'astral' that blended with your astral."[19] Now Judge had the guiding influence of a Nirmânikaya to contend with as well. The difficulties adjusting to all of

---

[17]**Cdn Theosophist**, Vol. 13, May 1932, pp.65-67.

[18]"Tulpa is the voluntary incarnation of an Adept into a living body, whether of an adult, child or new-born babe. [Tulpa is the magical process; Tulku is the result, although they are often used interchangeably.]" [**BCW**, Vol. 14, p.401.]

[19]**Theos. Forum** (P.L.), Vol. 3, August 1932, p.253, and **WQJ T. Pioneer**, p.19.

these entities eased somewhat by 1886 and Judge was able to align and focus his energies into great potency for the CAUSE.

Judge had described to his close friend and co-worker, in December 1894, what he was expecting to happen next. C.A. Griscom, wrote that "the Judge body was due by its Karma to die the next year and that it would have to be tided over this period by extraordinary means. He then expected this process to be entirely successful, and that he would be able to use that body for many years."[20] His friend may or may not have comprehended the whole significance of this. Judge may not have been implying that his actual physical body would have to die, but rather that a process would have to be undergone by which the kamic impulses tied to karmic conditions (that is, to his [Irish] natal body), would be relinquished in deference to the kamic impulses of the Rajah.

This process would have accelerated and facilitated the work that needed to be done for the Movement. Dr. Basu, in his astrological analysis, indicates this very clearly. Unfortunately, because of the negative influences over many of the members in the Theosophical Movement and their inability to overcome these influences, the Mahatmas decided to withdraw their support and leave the Society to its karma.

The three Founders of the Theosophical Society were each chosen by the Mahatmas for a specific task: H.P. Blavatsky to introduce Theosophy to the West, H.S. Olcott for his organizational skills, and W.Q. Judge to teach the morals and ethics of Theosophy, the "Heart" doctrine, to the western mind. Judge, a true Theosophist,[21] could have been saved from the poisonous effects on his body[22] — he could have survived — but he was "withdrawn" in 1896, as was Blavatsky five years earlier, in 1891.

— Compiler

---

[20]**Theosophy (The Path)**, Vol. 11, May 1896, p.52.

[21] A true Theosophist is one who follows his inner guiding principle and who works for the benefit of humanity, without the curse of separateness.

[22] See "What Killed W.Q. Judge?", **Fohat**, Vol. 7, Summer 2003 (Part I), pp. 29-34, and Fall 2003 (Part II), pp.60-64, 69-70, where it is suggested that Judge died from iatrogenic causes as a result of being prescribed potassium cyanide following a diagnosis of pulmonary tuberculosis.

Works Cited

Adyar Library and Research Centre
The Theosophical Society, Adyar, Chennai, India.

Albuquerque Journal
Albuquerque, NM. Published 1880 to present (under various names).

Arlington National Cemetery
Arlington National Cemetery.net/Ludlow

The Aryan Path
Edited by Sophia Wadia, Bombay, India. Published by Theosophy Co. Ltd., 1930 to 1979.

The Atlanta Constitution
Atlanta, GA. Published 1868 to present (now as Atlanta Journal-Constitution).

The Baltimore Sun
Baltimore, MD. Published 1837 to present.

The Barre Daily Times
Barre, VT. Published 1897 to 1959.

Biographical Notes
Robert Crosbie: Biographical Notes, compiled by Wayne Kell, 1998.

Birmingham Age-Herald
Birmingham, AL. Birmingham Iron Age (founded 1874) merged with The Daily Herald (founded 1887) in 1888. Published 1888 to 1950.

The Birmingham News
Birmingham, AL. Published 1888 to 2012.

BCW
H.P. Blavatsky Collected Writings, compiled by Boris de Zirkoff, Wheaton, IL: Theosophical Publishing House, Vol.1, 1966 to Vol. 15, 1991, including Index.

Boston Daily Globe
Boston, MA. Published 1872 to 1960.

The Boston Post
Boston, MA. Published 1831 to 1956.

Brooklyn Daily Eagle
Brooklyn, NY. Published 1841 to 1955. [see Brooklyn Eagle]

Brooklyn Eagle
Originally joint named The Brooklyn Eagle and Kings County Democrat, later The Brooklyn Daily Eagle then Brooklyn Eagle. Published in Brooklyn, NYC, 1841 to 1955.

Brooklyn Times Union
Brooklyn, New York City; launched in 1848 as the Williamsburgh Daily Times, renamed Brooklyn Daily Times in 1855 after the unification of Brooklyn and Williamsburgh, and eventually became the Brooklyn Times Union. 1848 to 1937.

California Utopia
California Utopia: Point Loma: 1897-1942 by Emmett A. Greenwalt. San Diego, CA: Point Loma Publications, Inc., 1978, 244 pp. First published as The Point Loma Community in California: 1897-1942, 1955.

The Canadian Theosophist (CT)
The Canadian Theosophist, edited by Albert E.S. Smythe until 1947, published 1920 to present.

Chicago Daily Tribune
Chicago, IL. Published 1872 to 1963.

Chicago Tribune
Chicago, IL. Published 1847 to present.

The Commercial Appeal
Memphis, TN. Published 1841 to present.

Cypress Hills Cemetery
Correspondence with Cypress Hills Cemetery, Nov. 2022.

Democrat and Chronicle
  Rochester, NY. Published 1833 to present.

Dictionary of American Biography
  Allen Johnson and Dumas Malone. Published by Charles Scribner's Sons, New York, 1936.

District Court Record for Weld County.
  19th Judicial District, Greeley, CO.

Eclectic Theosophist
  Edited by W. Emmett Small, Helen Todd. Published by Point Loma Publications, Inc., 1971 to 1991.

Eirenicon
  Quarterly published by Peace Lodge of The Theosophical Society, Cheshire, England. Likely edited by T.H. Redfern. Ran circa early 1940s to Jan. 1966, No.152.

The Encyclopedia of Arkansas History and Culture
  https://onlinebooks.library.upenn.edu/webbin/book/lookupid?key=olbp74947

The Evening Journal
  Wilmington, DE. Published 1888 to 1932.

The Evening Star
  Washington, DC. Published 1852 to 1981.

The Evening Tribune
  San Diego, CA. Published 1895 to 1939.

The Evening World
  New York, NY. Published 1887 to 1931.

Fohat
  Quarterly published by Edmonton Theosophical Society, Edmonton, AB, Spring 1997 to Winter 2008.

The Fort Collins Express
Fort Collins, CO. Published 1916 to 1923.

Fort Wayne Daily
Fort Wayne Daily News, Fort Wayne, IN. Published 1874 to 1???.

The Franklin Democrat
Brookville/Franklin, IN. Published 1859 to 1895.

The Fresno Morning Republican
Fresno, CA. Published 1876 to 1932.

The Future of the Theosophical Publishing Co.
by Julia Keightley (Jasper Niemand). New York, 1898. 35 pp.

The Gods Await
By Katherine Tingley. Pasadena, CA: Theosophical University Press, 1926 (Second and Revised edition 1992), 150 pp.

The Grail
London. Edited by Herbert Coryn, Basil Crump. Published Mar. to Sep. 1897, 20 pp.

The Hanford Sentinel
Hanford, Tulare County, CA. Published 1886 to 1893.

Hannibal Daily Courier
Hannibal, MO. Published 1832 to present; now as Hannibal Courier-Post.

Harper Encyclopedia of Military Biography
by T.N. Dupuy, C. Johnson, D. Bongard; Harper Collins Pub., 1992. 834 pp.

The Honolulu Advertiser
Honolulu, HI. Published 1856 to 2010, under various names, now Honolulu Star-Advertiser.

The Hutchinson News
Hutchinson, KS. Published 1872 to present.

Independence Daily Reporter
Independence, KS. Published 1882 to 1923.

Indianapolis Journal
Indianapolis, IN. Published 1825 to 1904.

The Inter Ocean
Chicago, Illinois. Published 1872 to 1902.

The Internationalist
Formerly the Irish Theosophist, edited by H.A. Coryn and G.W. Russell. Published Oct. 1897 to Mar. 1898.

The Irish Theosophist
Edited by D.N. Dunlop, Dublin. Published Oct. 1895 to Sep. 1897.

The Journal of San Diego History
San Diego, CA. Published intermittently since 1955.

The Judge Case: A Conspiracy Which Ruined the Theosophical Cause
by Ernest E. Pelletier. Published by Edmonton Theosophical Society, 2004. Part 1, 472 pp.; Part 2, 511 pp.

The Lamp
Edited by Albert E.S. Smythe. Toronto, ON. Published 1894 to 1899.

Letters That Have Helped Me
Compilation published by The Theosophy Company, Los Angeles, CA and New York, NY:, 1946, 300 pp.

The Lewiston Daily Sun
Lewiston, ME. Published 1893 to 1926.

The Link
"Issued by the O[uter] H[ead] of the School." May 1908 to Feb. 1913.

Los Angeles Express
Los Angeles, CA. Published 1871 to 1931.

Los Angeles Herald
Los Angeles, CA. Founded in 1873, merged with the Los Angeles Express in 1931 and became the Los Angeles Herald-Express.

Los Angeles Times
Los Angeles Daily Times, Los Angeles, CA, 1881. Renamed **Times-Mirror Company** in 1882, then Los Angeles Times to present.

The Lotus Circle
by Shawn F. Higgins. Published July 5, 2023, 32 pp.
https://www.patheos.com/blogs/marginalia/2023/07/the-lotus-circle/

Lucifer
Founded by H.P. Blavatsky. London, Published 1887 to 1897.

Massachusetts Death Records
Ancestry. Massachusetts Vital Records, 1620-1988.

The Montgomery Advertiser
Montgomery, AL. Published 1829 (as The Planter's Gazette) and as Montgomery Advertiser since 1833 to present.

Muskogee Times-Democrat
Muskogee, OK. Published 1906 to 1971.

Mysteries and Romances of the World's Greatest Occultists
By "Cheiro" (Count Louis Hamon). Published by Herbert Jenkins Limited, London. 1935. 315 pp.

Neutrality of the T.S. An Enquiry
The Neutrality of the Theosophical Society: An Enquiry Into Certain Charges Against The Vice-President, Held in London, July, 1894. London: The Central Council of the Theosophical Society, 1894, 16 pp. Reprinted in *Lucifer*, Vol. 14, Aug. 1894, pp.449-464.

The New Century
New York, NY. Published 1897 to 1899.

New York Herald
>New York, NY. Published 1834 to 1924.

New York Journal
>New York, NY. Published 1882 to 1937 (various titles).

New York Press
>New York, NY. Published 1896 to 1916.

New York Times
>New York, NY. Published 1851 to present.

New York Tribune
>New York Tribune (published 1841-1842), then New York Daily Tribune (published 1842-1866), then New York Tribune (published 1866-1922).

Omaha Daily Bee
>Omaha, Nebraska. Published 1871 to 1922, then variations of the name until 1937.

O.E. Library Critic
>The O.E. [Oriental Esoteric] Library Critic. Edited by Dr. H.N. Stokes. Washington, DC. Published 1911 to 1942.

Pall Mall Gazette
>London, UK. Published 1865 to 1923.

The Morning Journal-Courier
>New Haven, CT. Published 1848 to 1987; as New Haven Register since 1987.

The Path
>Published and Edited by William Q. Judge, New York, NY. 1886 to 1896.

The Philadelphia Inquirer
>Philadelphia, PA. Published 1829 to present.

The Pittsburgh Press
>Pittsburgh, PA. Published 1884 to 1992.

The Record
    National City, CA. Published as National City Record 1882 to 1898, then as The Record (National City)1898 to 19??

Record of the Times
    Wilkes-Barre, PA. Published 1866 to 1901.

Reminiscences
    Some Reminiscences of William Q. Judge by Emil August Neresheimer, sworn before a Notary Public in Los Angeles, CA, February 25, 1932, 14 pp.

Report of Proceedings T.S. in America
    Ninth Annual Convention, American Section T.S. and First Convention, Theosophical Society in America. Held at Boston, Mass., April 28-29, 1895. Report of Proceedings. Published by Theosophical Society in America, 1895, 62 pp.

Report of Proceedings T.S. in America
    Second Annual Convention of The Theosophical Society in America, Held at New York City, April 26-27, 1896. Report of Proceedings, 48 pp.

Richmond Times
    Richmond, VA. Published under this name in 1890 and became Richmond Times-Dispatch in 1903 to present.

San Bernardino County Sun
    San Bernardino, CA. Published 1894 to present.

San Diego Union
    The San Diego Union, San Diego, CA. Published 1868 to present. (San Diego Union-Tribune since 1992 merger of The San Diego Union and the San Diego Evening Tribune.)

San Diego Union and Daily Bee
    San Diego, CA. Published 1889 to 1922. (Union and Bee merged in 1889.)

San Francisco Call
    San Francisco, CA. Published 1856 to 1965 (with various mergers and name changes).

San Francisco Chronicle
San Francisco, CA. Published 1865 to present.

San Francisco Examiner
San Francisco, CA. Published 1863 to present.

The Search Light
New York and Point Loma, 1898-1911. Published by the Defence Committee, Clark Thurston, Chairman.

The Slocombs of America and Their Alliances
History of the Slocums, Slocumbs and Slocombs of America: Genealogical and Biographical, from 1637 to 1908, Vol. 2, by Charles Elihu Slocum, MD, PhD, LLD. Published by the Author, Defiance, Ohio, 1908, 549 pp.

South Bend Tribune
South Bend, IN. Published 1872 to present.

The Splendor of the Soul
By Katherine Tingley. Theosophical University Press, electronic version: https://www.theosociety.org/pasadena/splendor/spl-1.htm

St. Paul Daily Globe
St. Paul, MN. Published 1878 to 1905 (with various name changes).

St. Vincent Health System, Mission and History
UALR Center for Arkansas History and Culture.

Successful American
"A Monthly Illustrated Magazine for the Home Circle and the Business Office". Published by The Writers' Press Association, New York, NY, 1896 (?) to ??

The Times-Picayune
New Orleans, LA. Published 1837 to present; as The Times Picayune/The New Orleans Advocate since 2019.

The Sun (NY)
The Sun (New York City). Published 1833 to 1950.

Sunrise
> ***Sunrise: Theosophic Perspectives***. Published by Theosophical University Press, 1951 to 2007.

Tacoma Daily Ledger
> Tacoma, WA. Published 1883 to 1937.

Theosophical Forum (New Series)
> The Theosophical Forum New Series, published by The Theosophical Society in America, New York, NY, 1895 to 1905.

Theosophical Forum (Point Loma)
> The Theosophical Forum. Published by The Theosophical Society, Point Loma, CA, 1929 to 1951.

The Theosophical Glossary
> by H.P. Blavatsky. Published by Theosophy Company, Los Angeles, CA, 1973, 389 pp.

The Theosophical Movement 1875-1925
> ***The Theosophical Movement: 1875-1925: A History and A Survey***. New York, E.P. Dutton & Co., 1925, 705 pp.

The Theosophical News
> "A Weekly Report of Activities." Boston, MA. Published June 1896 to September 1897.

The Theosophical Path
> Point Loma, CA. Published 1911 to 1945.

Theosophical Quarterly **(TQ)**
> The Theosophical Quarterly. Founded by Clement A. Griscom. Published by The Theosophical Society in New York, 1903 to 1938.

The Theosophist
> Adyar, Chennai, India. Published 1879 to present.

Theosophy
>Theosophy, formerly The Path. New York: Theosophical Publishing Company. Continued as Theosophy, Vol. 11, Apr. 1896 to Vol. 12, Oct. 1897 [republished by Edmonton TS]. (Then changed to Universal Brotherhood, Vol. 12, Nov. 1897 to Vol. 14, Dec. 1899.)

Tingley vs Times-Mirror
>*Supreme Court of the State of California, Transcript on Appeal, Katherine Tingley vs Times-Mirror Company*; Filed August 13th, 1904, 928 pp.

To a Fellow Theosophist
>Letter by Dr. Hyman Lischner, May 28, 1931.

The Topeka State Journal
>Topeka, KS. Published 1892 to 1980.

Trenton Evening Times
>Trenton, NJ. Published 1891 to 1922.

Universal Brotherhood Path
>Formerly The Path (1886-1896) then Theosophy (1896-1897), then Universal Brotherhood (1897-1899) then Universal Brotherhood Path (1900-1903).

Vanity Fair
>British monthly magazine published 1868 to 1914.

Vital Records of Newbury, Mass.
>To the end of the year 1849, Volume 1—Births, Published by The Essex Institute, Salem, Mass., 1911.

The Washington Herald
>Washington, DC. Published 1906 to present.

The Washington Post
>Washington, DC. Published 1877 to present.

The Weekly Courier
>Fort Collins, CO. Published ?? to 1923.

The Wilkes-Barr Semi-Weekly Record
  Wilkes-Barr, PA. Published weekly/semi-weekly, and The Record of the Times. 1876 to 1972.

Will and Probate Records for George W. Parent and Petition in N.Y. Surrogate's Court.
  County of New York, In the Matter of the Estate of George W. Parent, dec'd, filed December 21, 1888.

WQJ: Theosophical Pioneer
  William Quan Judge 1851– 1896: The Life of a Theosophical Pioneer
  by Sven Eek and Boris de Zirkoff, compilers. Published by The Theosophical Publishing House, Wheaton, IL, 1969, 96 pp.

Who's Who on the Pacific Coast
  Edited by Franklin Harper, Los Angeles, published by Harper Publishing Co., 1913, 642 pp.

The World
  New York, NY. Published 1860 to 1931.

www.ingramcontent.com/pod-product-compliance
Lightning Source LLC
Chambersburg PA
CBHW060501090426
42735CB00011B/2066